BLACKSTONE'S GUIDE TO

The Terrorism Act 2006

BLACKSTONE'S GUIDE TO

The Terrorism
Act 2006

Alun Jones QC, Rupert Bowers, and
Hugo D Lodge

OXFORD
UNIVERSITY PRESS

OXFORD
UNIVERSITY PRESS

Great Clarendon Street, Oxford OX2 6DP

Oxford University Press is a department of the University of Oxford.
It furthers the University's objective of excellence in research, scholarship,
and education by publishing worldwide in

Oxford New York

Auckland Cape Town Dar es Salaam Hong Kong Karachi
Kuala Lumpur Madrid Melbourne Mexico City Nairobi
New Delhi Shanghai Taipei Toronto
With offices in
Argentina Austria Brazil Chile Czech Republic France Greece
Guatemala Hungary Italy Japan South Korea Poland Portugal
Singapore Switzerland Thailand Turkey Ukraine Vietnam

Oxford is a registered trade mark of Oxford University Press
in the UK and in certain other countries

Published in the United States
by Oxford University Press Inc., New York

© Alun Jones QC, Rupert Bowers, and Hugo Lodge 2006

The moral rights of the author have been asserted

Database right Oxford University Press (maker)

Reprinted 2009

ISBN 978-0-19-920843-2

Printed in the United Kingdom by
Lightning Source UK Ltd., Milton Keynes

Preface

The Terrorism Act 2006 is a hurried piece of legislation. Many of its provisions are a direct consequence of the London bombings in July 2005. The new offences it creates are complex and in parts obscure. They appear to add little to the range of existing criminal offences available in UK law for terrorist cases. The Act now permits the detention of suspected terrorists without charge for 28 days. It is a measure of the change to the British way of life produced by terrorism, or the fear of terrorism, that the reduction from the 90-day period first proposed by the Government and senior police officers was regarded in the House of Commons as a mark of good sense and restraint.

The 2006 Act also demonstrates the piecemeal but rapid fortification of the powers of law enforcement agencies over individuals and property, characteristic of so much recent legislation.

The authors are grateful to all their colleagues at Great James Street Chambers, in particular to Neil Baki and Abigail Bache, for their research and assistance in the preparation of this book.

The authors wish to thank the Council of Europe for their permission to reproduce the European Convention for the Prevention of Terrorism (May 2005, CETS 196—Prevention of Terrorism, 16.V.2005) (© Council of Europe, <http://conventions.coe.int>).

Great James Street Chambers
37 Great James Street
London WC1N 3HB

Contents—Summary

Contents

Table of Cases

References are to paragraph numbers.

Table of Legislation

References are to paragraph numbers.
*Paragraph references in **bold** indicate that the text is reproduced in full.*

Commencement Provisions

Commencement provisions for the Terrorism Act are set out in s 39. That section came into force on 30 March 2006, when the Act received Royal Assent.

On the same date, the Terrorism Act 2006 (Commencement No. 1 Order) (SI 2006/1013) was made. It appears at Appendix 4. As at 15 May 2006, no other commencement orders have been made. Almost all of the provisions of the Act have been brought into force apart from the detention provisions, ss 23–25 inclusive.

1

INTRODUCTION

A. THE SCOPE OF THE BOOK

1. The Terrorism Act 2006 and the Terrorism Act 2000

This book is a guide to the Terrorism Act 2006 ('the 2006 Act').[1] One purpose of **1.01** the 2006 Act was to create offences to penalize conduct which was thought to fall outside existing statutes and the common law. The 2006 Act also supplements and amends the Terrorism Act 2000 ('the 2000 Act')[2] in important respects, particularly by extending the period for which terrorist suspects might be detained for questioning by the police without charge, and by enlarging police powers of search and seizure. Accordingly, the relevant parts of the 2000 Act are considered in the following chapters, together with those few sections of the Anti-terrorism, Crime and Security Act 2001 ('the 2001 Act') which the 2006 Act amends. Most of the provisions of the 2001 Act and the Prevention of Terrorism Act 2005 ('the 2005 Act') are beyond the scope of this book.[3]

2. The Criminal Law Background

Until the late twentieth century, UK law responded to terrorism through the **1.02** use of its ordinary criminal law, sometimes creating new offences, such as the Explosive Substances Act 1883, introduced after Fenian and anarchist bombings in London.[4] Such crimes are still frequently indicted, together with murder,

---

[1] Appendix 2.
[2] Relevant extracts, as amended by subsequent statutes including the 2006 Act, are Appendix 1.
[3] For a thorough review of the 2000 Act and the 2001 Act, see Clive Walker, *Blackstone's Guide to the Anti-Terrorism Legislation* (OUP, 2002).
[4] See further Ben Brandon, 'Terrorism, Human Rights and the Rule of Law; 120 Years of the UK's Legal Response to Terrorism' [2004] Crim LR 969.

manslaughter, and crimes defined in the Offences against the Person Act 1861. The offences of making threats to kill, contrary to s 16 of the 1861 Act, and the common law offences of incitement to murder and conspiracy, contrary to s 1 of the Criminal Justice Act 1977, have frequent application in the trials for terrorist crimes.

1.03   The enlargement of extra-territorial jurisdiction introduced by Part 1 of the Criminal Justice Act 1993, brought into force in 1999, now makes it possible for the UK courts to try an agreement to commit any offence abroad if any act pursuant to the conspiracy took place in the United Kingdom. The radical extent of this change in transnational allegations of crime is not always fully understood. In September 2005, the Central Criminal Court in Madrid convicted a person resident in Spain of conspiring to cause the deaths of all the victims of the Al Qaeda attack on the United States in September 2001. The co-conspirators were the suicide pilots and their companions on the hijacked planes, and also two persons resident in the United Kingdom, said to have joined the conspiracy by telephone calls from England.

1.04   If this allegation were supported by evidence in England, the entire 11 September 2001 conspiracy would be triable in England by virtue of the 1993 Act; curiously, not as 2,700 murders, but as conspiracy to murder. It is anomalous that no mechanism exists under English law at present for deciding where a crime which has been committed in more than one jurisdiction should be tried.

1.05   In the case of 'international crimes', a more systematic approach has been established for many years. After the Second World War, the international community developed the concept of crimes which are so serious as to amount to an attack on the international order, not just an individual state. A succession of international Conventions under the auspices of the United Nations has created a body of international crimes, and procedures for dealing with them, which have been enacted into national laws. Some of them constitute crimes listed in Sch 1 to the 2006 Act, discussed in subsequent chapters.

1.06   These Conventions characteristically provide that a state in which a person accused of such a crime is found has an obligation either to extradite that person to a state which wishes to try him or her, or to prosecute him or her itself (*aut judicare, aut dedere*), wherever the crime was committed, and whatever the nationality of perpetrator and victim. Again, these Conventions are silent as to whether, and in what conditions, extradition should be preferred to trial in the state where the suspect is found.

3. Legislative History

1.07   By 2000, therefore, a UK prosecutor already had at his or her disposal a range of offences, some national crimes, originally territorially-based, but now with extended jurisdictional reach; and international crimes of universal jurisdiction.

1.08   Before 2000, there was only one statutory regime applicable to mainland Britain which regulated procedures by which terrorist suspects were brought before the courts. The Prevention of Terrorism (Temporary Provisions) Act 1974, provided for the extension of time during which police might hold an arrested terrorist suspect before charge to a maximum of seven days. The Bill's passage through Parliament was completed in two days following the IRA attacks on Birmingham in November 1974 which killed 22 people and wounded many others.

As might be expected paradoxically from its title, the provisions of the Act **1.09** became permanent, and it was renewed annually with occasional modifications. Until the coming into force in 1986 of the careful framework of rules and protections introduced by the Police and Criminal Evidence Act 1984, prolonged and unregulated private interrogations were common features of UK police investigations. The sad history of miscarriages of justice which has been revealed in the decades since 1974 suggests a pattern. Those people who confessed to IRA terrorist crimes in police custody were generally innocent: those who, in response to advanced training, maintained silence by invoking the privilege against self-incrimination were guilty.

In 1995, Lord Lloyd of Berwick conducted a review of the legislation **1.10** relating to terrorism. He concluded that though the threat of terrorism centred on Northern Ireland could be expected to diminish, the global terrorist threat was likely to intensify. He also recommended that any new UK legislation would have to be compatible with the European Convention on Human Rights.

The 2000 Act embodies many of the recommendations of Lord Lloyd. It **1.11** performed three functions relevant to an analysis of the 2006 Act. First, it added a number of offences to fill perceived gaps in the range of existing provisions punishing terrorist conduct (see Appendix 1). Secondly, it developed the practice of proscribing terrorist organizations, introduced by the 1974 Act. Thirdly, it provided new regimes for the detention of suspects without charge, and search and seizure.

Though the scheme of the 2001 Act is not considered in detail here, its **1.12** purpose was to ensure that the UK Government, following the 2001 attacks on New York and Washington, had the necessary powers to counter the perceived threat from terrorism. The measures were intended to stifle terrorist funding, ensure that Government departments and agencies collected and shared information required to counter the threat, and to simplify relevant immigration procedures. Schedule 3 permitted the Secretary of State to detain a non-British national pending the making of a deportation order against him, provisions now repealed and replaced by the new regime of control orders, set out in the 2005 Act, considered below. Other purposes of the 2001 Act were to ensure the security of the nuclear and aviation industries, to improve the security of dangerous substances that may be targeted or used by terrorists, to extend police powers, and to ensure that the United Kingdom could meet its European obligations relating to police and judicial co-operation and its international obligations to counter bribery and corruption.

1.13   Part 1 of, and Schs 1 and 2 to, the 2001 Act contained provisions to prevent terrorists from gaining access to their money. They complemented the scheme now set out in the Proceeds of Crime Act 2002, and were designed to ensure that investigative and freezing powers were available wherever funds could be used to finance terrorism. The 2001 Act also introduced monitoring orders enabling police officers to require financial institutions to provide information on customers' accounts for the previous 90 days. The 2001 Act gave law enforcement agencies the power to seize terrorist cash anywhere in the United Kingdom, and the power to freeze assets at the start of an investigation.

1.14   Part 10 of the 2001 Act contained powers which gave the police the authority to search for identifying marks, to take fingerprints of suspects solely for the purpose of identifying them, and to photograph suspects and where necessary to demand the removal of facial coverings or face paint in order to take a positive photograph. It also strengthened police powers to require the removal of face coverings worn for the purpose of concealing identity and to seize any such items.

1.15   The main purpose of the 2005 Act was to provide for the making of 'control orders' imposing obligations on individuals suspected of being involved in terrorism. It was enacted in the light of the decision of the House of Lords in *A (FC) v Secretary of State for the Home Department*.[5] A control order may impose any obligations 'necessary' for preventing or restricting an individual's further involvement in terrorism. The intention was that each order would be made particular to the risk posed by the individual concerned. Obligations that may be imposed include, for example, prohibitions on the possession or use of certain items, restrictions on movement to or within certain areas, restrictions on communications and associations, and requirements as to place of abode.

1.16   Breach of an obligation imposed by a control order, without reasonable excuse, is a criminal offence punishable, following conviction on indictment, with a prison sentence of up to 5 years, or a fine, or both; or, following summary conviction, to a prison sentence of up to 12 months (or 6 months in Scotland or Northern Ireland), or a fine, or both.

1.17   A person who was made subject to a non-derogating control order was one of 12 people who challenged such orders: see *Re MB*.[6] The judge characterized the procedures by which such orders were obtained as 'conspicuously unfair' and dismissed supposed safeguards as a 'thin veneer of legality',[7] and made a declaration of incompatibility with Art 6.1 of the ECHR under s 4 of the Human Rights Act 1998. The procedure was an example of 'executive decision-making untramelled by any prospect of effective judicial supervision'. Moreover, pur-

---

[5] [2004] UKHL 56.
[6] [2006] EWHC 1000 (Admin) 12 April 2006 (Sullivan J).
[7] At para [103].

ported non-derogating control orders were found to be so onerous as to amount to a breach of Art 5(1).[8]

B. THE 2006 ACT

The Terrorism Bill of 2005 was introduced as a direct reaction to the terrorist bombings and attempted bombings in London in July 2005. On 4 August 2005, the Prime Minister announced to the mass media various proposals to tighten anti-terrorist laws, some of which have been enacted. The following general observations apply to the 2006 Act as a whole and are developed in subsequent chapters. **1.18**

1. Extra-Territorial Jurisdiction

There are no geographical limits to most of the offences in the 2006 Act. The United Kingdom has taken universal jurisdiction: see s 17 of the 2006 Act. If a person, whatever his or her nationality, does an act anywhere in the world which, if done in the United Kingdom, would amount to any of the offences under this Act or the 2000 Act as described in s 17(2), he or she is guilty of an offence. The members of the 'public', by reference to whom guilt must be assessed in relation to s 1, for example, is to be construed in accordance with s 20(3) and refers to the public of any part of the United Kingdom or of a country or territory outside the United Kingdom (or any section of the public). **1.19**

On 16 May 2005, the members of the Council of Europe signed the Convention on the Prevention of Terrorism ('the 2005 Convention').[9] As described in Chapter 2, this instrument was one of the stimuli for the offence created by s 1 of the 2006 Act ('Encouragement of terrorism'). Nothing in the 2005 Convention or any other international instrument obliges the United Kingdom to take universal jurisdiction. The UN Conventions establishing international crimes, appearing in Sch 1 to the 2006 Act, usually require a state to prosecute or extradite a person found in its territory for a crime committed anywhere in the world. In contrast, Art 14 of the 2005 Convention obliges a Party to prosecute a person for an offence committed in its territory, or on board one of its ships, or against its own national. **1.20**

This last provision reflects the 'active personality principle' in force in most European states, by virtue of which those states prosecute their own nationals rather than extraditing them to the state where the criminal conduct was committed. (This principle has been modified by most members of the European Union pursuant to the European Framework Decision of 2002 in relation to the European Arrest Warrants, but only in relation to surrender within the European Union). **1.21**

---

[8] *Re JJ and others* (QBD) 28 June 2006 (Sullivan J).
[9] Appendix 3.

1.22   Article 14.2 of the 2005 Convention permits, but does not require, a state to establish its jurisdiction over extra-territorial conduct in defined and limited circumstances. Article 14.3 requires a state to prosecute an individual found in its territory if it does not extradite him or her to a Party to the Convention whose jurisdiction to prosecute is similar. Article 14.4 asserts that the Convention does not exclude any criminal jurisdiction exercised in accordance with national law.

1.23   Section 1 of the 2006 Act, for example, applies to the encouragement of terrorism within the meaning of the section if committed by a person living in Pakistan, publishing matter in relation to conflict in Kashmir; to a Palestinian living in the West Bank praising those who have died in actively resisting Israeli occupation; to an Iranian exile resident in Paris advocating armed struggle in Iran; or to an Irish-American in Connecticut calling upon modern Irishmen to emulate those executed after the Easter Rising in Dublin in 1916. Extradition, as contemplated by Art 19 of the 2005 Convention, will be available for such offences under the terms of the European Framework Decision of 2002, in accordance with procedures set out in the Extradition Act 2003.

1.24   It may be thought that the assumption of universal jurisdiction is not harmful, and amounts to little more than an anti-terrorist gesture; after all, the consent of the Director of Public Prosecutions is required for proceedings to be brought for offences under Part 1 of the Act by virtue of s 19(2) of the 2006 Act. Further, if it appears to him that the alleged offence 'has been committed for a purpose wholly or partly connected with the affairs of a country other than the United Kingdom', the consent of the Attorney-General is necessary.

1.25   However, the tendency of states in matters of international criminal law enforcement, as the UN Conventions make clear, is to develop reciprocal and similar principles relating to prosecution and extradition, and often to enact similarly-worded offences. It has been regarded as desirable to secure co-operation and consent for a departure from narrowly territorial approaches to the exercise of criminal jurisdiction. It may be doubted whether this consensus is enhanced by a spontaneous extension of jurisdiction into areas of political controversy which may seem to have little connection with any UK interest or dispute.

1.26   A practical example of the dangers of such unilateral action as is contained in the Act is evident in the current controversy over the ratification by the US Senate of the 2003 extradition treaty between the United Kingdom and the United States. There is serious opposition in the Senate to the proposed transfer of the power from the courts to the executive of the power to decline to extradite a person for some types of offences of a political character or motivation, as envisaged in the new treaty. The opposition comes from civil liberties groups and people sympathetic to Irish republicanism. Underlying the principles invoked by these opponents is an expressed belief that Irish or Northern Irish suspects, extradited to the United Kingdom, will not receive a fair trial. In the light of the weaker 'specialty' protection (that is, the rule that a person may not be tried after extradition for criminal conduct not underlying his or her extradition) now embodied in the new treaty, such groups will no doubt cite the provisions of the 2006 Act as an example of the dangers of unprotected extradition.

It will be argued, for good legal reason, that persons extradited from the United States to the United Kingdom are liable to prosecution for praising, for example, the actions or teachings of the participants in earlier Republican struggles, or more recent figures celebrated for violent resistance to the United Kingdom in Northern Ireland. Such concerns are unlikely to be allayed by the power of veto conferred on the Director of Public Prosecutions or Attorney-General by the 2006 Act.   **1.27**

The wide extension of jurisdiction also provokes questions as to how and in what circumstances the police should be obliged or entitled to investigate such crimes abroad. There are no conventions applicable to the United Kingdom for determining which state or territory should investigate or prosecute allegations of crimes which are triable in more than one jurisdiction.[10] The question arises, if a complaint is made to the police in the United Kingdom about the alleged commission outside the country of an offence under the 2006 Act, how the discretion of the Attorney-General will be exercised. It is the Attorney-General's position, as expressed in argument in the High Court in the extradition appeal under the Extradition Act 2003 of *Bermingham, Darby and Mulgrew v Government of the United States of America*,[11] that neither he nor the Director of Public Prosecutions nor the Director of the Serious Fraud Office (both of whom by statute he superintends) has a policy for determining this question.   **1.28**

Accordingly, it appears that any decision of the Attorney-General as to prosecution will be taken ad hoc, and be vulnerable to the allegation that he is motivated in any one case by political rather than legal considerations.   **1.29**

As is argued in later chapters, the criminal offences set out in the 2006 Act may prove popular only temporarily with prosecutors, since more familiar and established criminal offences are available to them. The unilateral extension of extra-territorial jurisdiction, and the current absence of a framework for determining how decisions to prosecute should be made in practice, is unlikely to improve the reputation of the UK criminal justice system, either at home or abroad.   **1.30**

2. The Prospect of Expert Evidence

One of the problems created by the 2006 Act is that many of its provisions require an assessment of what members of the public who may be abroad are   **1.31**

---

[10] However, the European Commission has published a detailed and reasoned Green Paper on Conflicts of Jurisdiction in December 2005, proposing solutions and criteria where two or more states have jurisdiction to prosecute the same offence.

[11] [2006] EWHC 200 (Admin) (23 February 2006).

likely to understand by statements and publications. Under the Obscene Publications Act 1959, to take one example, the courts have held that it is for a jury to decide whether articles are 'obscene', normally without the assistance of experts. (See, further, the discussion in Chapter 2.)

1.32   It is submitted that expert evidence is more clearly relevant to questions arising as to how 'some members of the public' are likely to understand statements or publications within the meaning of ss 1 and 2 of the 2006 Act, particularly when they may be abroad. In the Committee Stage of the Bill in the House of Lords, Lord Lloyd of Berwick (whose report formed an important part of the legislative history of the 2000 Act), observed:

So guilt will or may depend upon how a statement is likely to be understood in, for example, Palestine or Pakistan, because they are included under the term 'members of the public'. I do not know how a jury is supposed to form a view about that.[12]

1.33   Under the 1959 Act, the House of Lords held that, where publication was to take place abroad (apparently in the United States and Canada), magistrates in forfeiture proceedings were entitled to form an opinion, from their own knowledge and without evidence, that having regard to the likely readers an article was so clearly obscene as to be likely to deprave and corrupt: *Gold Star Publications Ltd v DPP*.[13]

1.34   A 'statement' within s 1, or a 'publication' within s 2 of the 2006 Act, may, however, be much more difficult to interpret than a piece of pornography. There may be little room for the calling of expert evidence in an allegation of incitement to kill,[14] or to cause explosions. An appeal to emulate the conduct or carry out the preachings of a religious leader who lived centuries ago in another culture is not only likely to permit prosecution and defence to call expert evidence, but it may in practice oblige them to do so.

1.35   The likelihood that trials will become protracted and complicated by the evidence of expert witnesses on both sides is another reason, in addition to the opacity of many of the new offences, why the new offences in the 2006 Act are unlikely to form an important practical tool in our criminal justice system.

3. Detention without Charge, Search, and Seizure

1.36   The draconian character of these new provisions is considered in detail in Chapters 7 and 8. If the new offences may be of limited utility to prosecuting lawyers, the powers to detain and interrogate will no doubt be employed to the full. It is argued in Chapter 7 that the new capacity to detain and interrogate for 28 days is a retrograde change, likely to re-introduce into criminal trials the

---

[12] *Hansard*, HL vol 676, col 486 (5 December 2005).
[13] (1981) 73 Cr App R 141.
[14] Though some limited defence evidence was held admissible to assess the context of observations in the trial of Abu Hamza at the CCC in January 2006 for incitement at common law.

controversies and evidential disputes surrounding confessions that so tarnished our criminal justice system in the years leading to the enactment of the Police and Criminal Evidence Act 1984.

The search and seizure provisions in the 2000 Act, and the investigatory powers contained in a variety of other modern statutes, are now extended incrementally by the 2006 Act. This Act is only the latest in a succession of hastily-drafted statutes, passed in recent years, which make serious erosions into individual and civic freedom. **1.37**

2

ENCOURAGEMENT, ETC
OF TERRORISM

A. SECTION 1—ENCOURAGEMENT OF TERRORISM

1. The Legal Background

It is important to trace the legislative history of this complicated and difficult **2.01** provision. In April 2005, the Labour Party manifesto for the general election contained this undeveloped statement:

> We will introduce new laws to help catch and convict those involved in helping to plan terrorist activity or who glorify or condone acts of terror.

On 16 May 2005, the members of the Council of Europe signed the Conven- **2.02** tion on the Prevention of Terrorism.[1] Article 5 embodied an agreement to create an offence of 'public provocation to commit a terrorist offence', meaning:

> the distribution, or otherwise making available, of a message to the public, with the intent to incite the commission of a terrorist offence, where such conduct, whether or not directly advocating terrorist offences, causes a danger that one or more such offences may be committed.

Article 5.2 required each Party to the Convention to adopt such measures **2.03** as may be necessary to establish such an offence in its domestic law 'when committed unlawfully and intentionally'.

On 5 August 2005, following the terrorist attacks in London of 7 July, and **2.04** other incidents on 21 July, the Prime Minister announced publicly, among other

---

[1] Appendix 3.

proposals, that a new offence of glorifying terrorism would be introduced in a new Bill.

2.05 On 14 September 2005, the UN Security Council passed Resolution 1624. Part of the preamble reads:

Condemning in the strongest terms the incitement of terrorist acts and *repudiating* attempts and the justification or glorification (*apologie*) of terrorist acts that may incite further terrorist acts.

2.06 The body of the Resolution, among other things:

1. *Calls upon* all states to adopt such measures as may be necessary and appropriate and in accordance with their obligations under international law to:
   (a) Prohibit by law incitement to commit a terrorist act or acts;
   (b) Prevent such conduct;
   (c) Deny safe haven to any persons with respect to whom there is credible and relevant evidence giving serious reasons for considering that they have been guilty of such conduct.

2.07 Section 1 of the Act is an amalgamation of two separate offences originally set out in the Terrorism Bill in October 2005. At first, the Bill contained an offence of 'encouraging terrorism' and another of 'glorifying' it. In response to substantial political and legal criticism, the proposal for a separate offence of 'glorification' of terrorism was omitted from the Bill at an early stage, but 'glorification' became embodied in s 1(3) as a means of defining 'indirect encouragement' within the meaning of s 1(1).

2.08 This legislative history may explain the odd structure of the section. The offence-creating provision is s 1(2): the section applies to statements within the meaning of s 1(1), as amplified by s 1(3):

This section applies to a statement that is likely to be understood by some or all of the members of the public to whom it is published as a direct or indirect encouragement[2] to them to the commission,[3] preparation or instigation of acts of terrorism or Convention offences.[4]

2. The Statements to Which the Section Applies

2.09 These statements are defined in s 1(1), as further explained in s 1(3):

This section applies to a statement that is likely to be understood by some or all of the members of the public to whom it is published as a direct or indirect encouragement

---

[2] Any further references to 'encouragement' in this chapter should be read so as to include a reference to 'other inducement'.

[3] Any further references to 'commit' in this chapter should be read so as to include a reference to 'prepare or instigate'.

[4] Any further reference to 'acts of terrorism' or 'terrorist acts' in this chapter should be read so as to include a reference to 'Convention offences' save when the term is used with reference to an offence under s 2 in B below.

or other inducement to them to the commission, preparation or instigation of acts of terrorism or Convention offences.

The provision was intended to cover offending speeches at meetings, sermons **2.10** at places of worship, chants and placards at demonstrations, as well as printed literature, broadcasts, and material posted on the internet. The circumstances and manner of publication to which a jury must have regard in considering whether a statement offends against this section will vary widely, and depend largely on the medium by which publication is made as well as to whom it is made.

By virtue of s 1(4) the question of how a statement is likely to be understood **2.11** and what members of the public could reasonably be expected to infer from it must be determined having regard both to the contents of the statement as a whole, and to the circumstances and manner of its publication.

It is not clear how a court of trial is to identify 'the members of the public to **2.12** whom it is published.' The larger the class of persons who may read or hear the statement, the more obvious are the problems. A statement published in a British book, newspaper, pamphlet, or magazine may be read, either in hard-copy or on the internet, by UK nationals, foreign visitors, and people abroad; there may be secondary publication by other media.[5] The larger, and more diverse, the 'members of the public' may be, the more difficult will be the eviden-tial problems of proving that some members of the public may be particularly susceptible to such statements so as to consider them as an inducement to the commission of acts of terrorism.

By virtue of s 1 of the Obscene Publications Act 1959, an article: **2.13**

shall be deemed obscene if its effect or (where the article comprises two or more distinct items) the effect of any one of the items is, if taken as a whole, such as to tend to deprave and corrupt persons who are likely, having regard to all relevant circumstances, to read, see or hear the matter contained or embodied in it.

In *R v Calder and Boyars Ltd*,[6] the Court of Appeal held that the jury should **2.14** decide, as a simple matter of fact, whether the effect of a book was to tend to deprave or corrupt 'a significant proportion' of those persons likely to read it: 'A book may tend to deprave or corrupt a significant but comparatively small number of its readers or a large number or indeed the majority of its readers. The tendency to deprave or corrupt may be strong or slight.'[7]

The reference in s 1(1) to 'some members of the public' arguably refers to a **2.15** lesser number than 'a significant' number; after all the 1959 Act refers simply to

---

[5] See the decision in *R v Perrin* [2002] EWCA Crim 747 where it was held that a webpage was published to anyone with ability to access it. The prosecution did not have to prove that anyone actually did, or would, see it.

[6] (1968) 52 Cr App R 706.

[7] ibid 716.

'persons who are likely . . . to read', not to 'some of the persons . . .'. It is foreseeable that the higher courts (should this cumbersome provision be chosen by a prosecutor and should a jury convict) may rule that 'some of the members' means some number more than one that is not de minimis. 'Some' members of the public, literally, could be as few as two people. In *DPP v Whyte*,[8] however, in a case which approved the 'significant proportion' test, Lord Pearson said that the statutory definition:

> refers to 'persons', which means some persons, though I think in a suitable case, if the number of persons likely to be affected is so small as to be negligible—really negligible— the de minimis principle might be applied. But if a seller of pornographic books has a large number of customers who are not likely to be corrupted by such books, he does not thereby acquire a licence to expose them for sale or sell such books to a small number of customers who are likely to be corrupted.

2.16   What constitutes a statement 'as a whole' is not clear. The definition of 'statement' in s 20(6) is limited ('a communication of any description, including a communication without words, consisting of sounds or images or both'). If some of the contents of a book, spread through various chapters, could be regarded as encouraging acts of terrorism, is it the entire book that qualifies as the statement, or are there various statements properly to be indicted in different counts? If a magazine is published containing various articles by different authors, is it the entire magazine that should be considered the 'statement'?[9] Similar problems obviously arise in relation to a documentary film, or a website. The prudent prosecutor will wish to avoid the risk of duplicity, and the selection of a narrow 'statement' is more likely to promote a fair trial.

2.17   The above cited authorities under the 1959 Act may be relevant, but the absence of a statutory definition in the 2006 Act is unsatisfactory. A more instructive definition of what would amount to a 'whole statement' in a particular set of circumstances is desirable.

2.18   It is curious that, unlike s 2, s 1 refers not to persons or individuals, but to 'members of the public' as the targets of the encouragement. For the offence to be proved, the 'statement [must be] likely to be understood by some or all of the members of the public to whom it is published' as an encouragement to them to commit acts of terrorism. It is not only unclear how it is to be discerned what proportion of the public would be sufficient to amount to 'some members', but also to what extent it must be 'likely' that they should be encouraged to commit acts of terrorism. Certainly, it would appear insufficient that the encouragement be directed at a single person since that person would only be an individual member of the public.[10]

---

[8] [1972] AC 849 (HL).

[9] See the decision in *R v Anderson* (1972) 56 Cr App R 123, considering an offence under the Obscene Publications Act 1959, in which it was held that it would be 'entirely wrong' for this approach to be taken in the case of a magazine.

[10] See para 2.42.

By virtue of s 1(5) it is irrelevant whether the encouragement in the statement   **2.19** relates to acts of terrorism or Convention offences generally, and whether any person is in fact encouraged or induced to conduct himself or herself in the way envisaged.

Expressions used in Part 1 of the 2006 Act have, by virtue of s 20, the same   **2.20** meaning as those in the 2000 Act. An 'act of terrorism' includes any action as defined by s 1(2), (3), or (5) of the 2000 Act for the purposes of terrorism as so defined by that Act. Accordingly, the offence of encouraging an act of terrorism in s 1 is committed if at least some members of the public to whom the statement is published are encouraged to resort to the use or threat of action[11] designed to influence the government,[12] an international governmental organization,[13] or to intimidate at least a section of the public or benefit a proscribed organization, and the use or threat is made for the purpose of advancing a political, religious, or ideological cause. It should be noted that this definition includes the government of any country; as a result s 1 covers the encouragement of acts of terrorism, as so defined, against undemocratic or even despotic regimes. Included in 'acts of terrorism', pursuant to the 2000 Act, is conduct that may not readily be viewed by many as 'terrorist', such as the disruption of an electronic system. An allegation of indirect encouragement may include the 'glorification' of acts in the past, future, or in general.

It is anomalous that, although there is no offence in law of 'committing acts   **2.21** of terrorism', it is now an offence to encourage such acts in statements. In the process of criminalization of terrorism offences, Parliament has previously and intentionally avoided the enactment of such an offence on the basis that the prosecution of persons for such an offence might create willing martyrs.

'Convention offences' are, by virtue of s 20 those listed in Sch 1 to the 2006   **2.22** Act, the familiar UN Conventions establishing international crimes.

3. Direct and Indirect Encouragement

The distinction between 'direct' and 'indirect' encouragement obviously reflects   **2.23** the provisions of Art 5 of the 2005 Council of Europe Convention on the Prevention of Terrorism,[14] as we have seen. It is an offence by virtue of s 1(2), subject to proof of the mental element in s 1(2)(b), to 'publish' a statement containing such encouragement.

'Publish' is to be construed in accordance with s 20(4) and refers to publishing   **2.24** the statement in any manner to the public, providing an electronic service

---

[11] As defined by s 1(2) of the 2000 Act.
[12] By virtue of s 17(1) this would include the government of another country.
[13] Section 34 of the 2006 Act amends s 1(1)(b) of the 2000 Act to insert the words 'or an international governmental organisation' after the word 'government'.
[14] Appendix 3.

whereby the public will have access to the statement, or using an electronic service provided by another to enable or facilitate public access to the statement. It may also apply where a person (unwittingly) publishes a statement on behalf of another.

(a) *Direct Encouragement*

2.25 A person will commit the offence of publishing a statement in which it is alleged there is a direct encouragement of terrorism if:

(a) he publishes, or causes another to publish the statement;

(b) he intends at that time members of the public to be directly encouraged or otherwise induced by the statement to commit, prepare or instigate acts of terrorism or Convention offences; or

(c) he is reckless as to whether members of the public will be so encouraged; and

(d) the statement is likely to be understood by some or all of the members of the public to whom it is published as a direct encouragement or other inducement to them to the commission, preparation or instigation of acts of terrorism or Convention offences.

2.26 For the offence to be established the 'statement [must be] likely to be understood by some or all of the members of the public to whom it is published' as a direct encouragement to them to commit acts of terrorism. The notion of 'direct encouragement' causes little difficulty.

2.27 The actus reus of publishing material intending direct encouragement to the commission of acts of terrorism or Convention offences is for all practical purposes indistinguishable from that required to prove an offence of incitement, except for the enlarged jurisdiction conferred by s 17. The 'glorification' provisions, considered below, apply only to indirect encouragement. Since, however, the maximum sentence for an offence is seven years' imprisonment, a prosecutor may no doubt choose to reflect such an allegation in the much more easily understood offence of incitement.

(b) *Indirect Encouragement—'Glorification of Terrorism'*

2.28 A person will commit the offence of publishing a statement in which it is alleged that there is indirect encouragement of terrorism under s 1 if:

(a) he publishes, or causes another to publish a statement;

(b) he intends at that time members of the public to be indirectly encouraged or otherwise induced by the statement to commit, prepare or instigate acts of terrorism or Convention offences; or

(c) he is reckless as to whether members of the public will be so encouraged; and

(d) the statement is likely to be understood by some or all of the members of the public to whom it is published as an indirect encouragement or other inducement to them to the commission, preparation or instigation of acts of terrorism or Convention offences.

The 'glorification' of terrorism offence was one of the most contentious clauses of the Bill in its passage through Parliament. Concern centred on how widely the offence has been drawn, the possible implications for freedom of expression, and whether the offence has reasonable legal certainty. The 2005 Convention did not refer to the concept of 'glorification'. **2.29**

The Third Report of the Joint Committee on Human Rights expressed concern that the glorification provisions would infringe Art 10 of the European Convention on Human Rights. The Government declined to implement an amendment by the House of Lords on 15 February 2006 that 'indirect encouragement' should comprise the making of a statement that the listener would infer that he or she should emulate it, winning the vote by 315 to 277. **2.30**

The Secretary of State stated in Parliament on 15 February 2006 that s 1(3) is intended to give an 'exemplary description' of what would amount to glorification of terrorism but is not intended to be exhaustive. Hence in s 1(3) statements that provide indirect encouragement 'include' those that glorify acts of terrorism, but are not limited to them. **2.31**

There is little difficulty in understanding the mischief at which this provision is aimed. It is encouragement which is rhetorically concealed ('Who will rid me of this turbulent priest?'). The question, however, is whether it is possible or desirable to fashion disapprobation of this mischief into a coherent legal test. A jury often has the responsibility, not merely of finding facts, but of determining and applying the standards of the community in which it lives: whether conduct is 'dishonest'; whether an article is 'obscene'; whether self-defence is 'reasonable'. Section 1(1), however, requires the jury to assess qualitatively the impact of statements not amounting to direct encouragement on members of a particular community which is not its own. **2.32**

A prosecutor will probably wish to allege that the jury may find that the statement, considered as required by s 1(4) 'as a whole', and in the circumstances and manner in which it is published, constitutes both direct and indirect encouragement. Yet the 'glorification' provision applies only to indirect encouragement. Section 1(3) deems certain statements, as a matter of fact, to be statements of the kind described factually in s 1(1), and introduces the word 'glorifies', as partially defined in s 20, as including 'any form of praise or celebration'. Accordingly, a judge will have to direct the jury in an 'indirect' case: **2.33**

(a) that they have to find whether, as a matter of fact, a statement amounts to indirect encouragement to some members of the public to whom it is published;

(b) that, irrespective of their own approach to this factual question, a statement which they find falls within subsection (3) necessarily amounts to a statement within subsection (1);

    (c) that statements falling within subsection (3) include every statement that glorifies the commission of acts to which the section refers but since subsection (3) only 'includes' such statements as indirectly encouraging, the jury should consider whether the statement indirectly encourages regardless of whether it glorifies;

    (d) that 'glorification' includes any form of 'praise or celebration' but, since the definition in s 20(2) is partial and only 'includes' such praise or celebration, the jury should consider whether glorification includes some other concept;

    (e) that those members of the public to whom the statement is published could reasonably be expected to infer that what is being glorified is being glorified as conduct that should be emulated by them in existing circumstances;

    (f) that, even if the jury does not find that the statement in question falls within subsection (3), it may still find that the statement falls within subsection (1).

2.34   Logically, the jury would be entitled to find that, but for s 1(3), the statement would not, as a matter of fact fall within s 1(1) as indirect encouragement; alternatively, that the statement does not fall within s 1(3), but nonetheless falls as indirect encouragement within s 1(1). If this section comes to be used, practical problems will be caused to a jury, and controversy will arise in the light of the decision in *R v Brown (K)*,[15] as to the extent of the matters on which members of a jury must agree, unanimously or by a sufficient majority, before they can return a conviction.

2.35   Problems are plainly foreseeable. Whilst in many cases the jury may well be considering general members of the public, the 'members of the public to whom the statement is published' may be finite in number and identifiable as individuals, within the mischief that the section was designed to tackle: meetings of small groups of individuals, or small cohesive congregations.

2.36   To illustrate the point outlined above an extreme example can be considered. X writes a short pamphlet expressing his views on the justification for acts of terrorism. He prints one copy of his pamphlet and hands it to his friend Y for his consideration. X and Y are overheard discussing the pamphlet by a policeman and X is arrested and the pamphlet seized.

2.37   In the prosecution of X for encouraging acts of terrorism, Y is therefore the only member of the public to whom the statement is published for the purposes of s 1(1).

2.38   If X were prosecuted for direct encouragement then to be guilty he would have to either intend or be reckless as to whether Y would understand any statement in the pamphlet as a direct encouragement to commit acts of terrorism. Whether Y was so encouraged is irrelevant.[16] However it must still be

---

[15] (1984) 75 Cr App R 115.
[16] See s 5(b).

proved that 'the statement . . . is likely to be understood by some or all of the members of the public to whom it is published' as a direct encouragement under s 1(1). As Y is the only person 'to whom the statement is published' it is relevant to consider whether he as an individual would be likely to understand the statement as a direct encouragement to commit an act of terrorism. If Y stated in evidence that he would never have been likely to understand the statement as a direct encouragement to commit an act of terrorism, and gave reasons for this, it is submitted that the offence would not be made out.[17] This would be so even if X intended that Y would be so encouraged.

2.39 In the absence of any statement within the pamphlet which could be construed as a direct encouragement X is prosecuted for indirect encouragement. On the above facts the understanding of Y would become irrelevant. Whilst Y remains the only member of the public to whom the statement is published under s 1(1), the prescriptive nature of s 1(3) has the effect of deeming Y to have such an understanding if the jury decides that the statement fulfils s 1(3)(a) and (b).

2.40 So, if on the trial of X for an offence of indirect encouragement the jury found that the statement was one which glorified the commission of acts of terrorism for the purposes of s 1(3)(a), it would go on to consider whether s 1(3)(b) was fulfilled: whether Y 'could reasonably be expected to infer that what is being glorified is being glorified as conduct that should be emulated by [him] in existing circumstances'. Section 1(4) sets out that what Y 'could reasonably be expected to infer [from the statement] must be determined having regard both:

(a) to the contents of the statement as a whole; and

(b) to the circumstances and manner of its publication.'

2.41 The jury is not required to have regard to what Y in fact understood from the statement. The combined effect of s 1(3) and (4) is to impose a test referable to the statement itself rather than to the actual understanding of the members of the public to whom the statement was published. Thus if the jury found that Y 'could reasonably be expected to infer' that what was 'being glorified was being glorified as conduct that should be emulated by [him] in existing circumstances' the fact that Y did not understand that to be the case is irrelevant. The question is not 'what did Y understand?' but rather 'what was Y likely to understand?'

2.42 However, it must be remembered that the mens rea for the offence is an intention that *members* of the public will be directly or indirectly encouraged or recklessness as to this consequence. So if X has an intention to encourage one person only, Y, an individual member of the public, he lacks the mens rea for the offence altogether. This is surprising since it means that the encouragement of individuals is not caught by s 1 of the Act, unless a strongly 'purposive'

---

[17] Assuming he was believed.

interpretation is applied to the section. Upon a natural construction, however, since s 2(6) specifically includes reference to 'one or more persons' for the purposes of the offence created by that subsection, the absence of a similar provision in s 1(1) should be taken to be deliberate.

2.43   Since the offence of indirect encouragement can be committed recklessly, a person publishing a statement, such as a newspaper proprietor, will have to consider not only what his target audience will understand from his words but how a jury might interpret them should he be prosecuted for indirect encouragement. In this regard it should be remembered that s 1(3) is not exhaustive; statements can amount to indirect encouragement which do not fall within s 1(3).

2.44   A further problem arises in this respect. It is unclear how the jury is to decide whether the statement 'is likely to be understood [as indirect encouragement] by some or all of the members of the public to whom it is published' unless it hears evidence from some of those persons, or expert evidence in relation to a particular group or culture to whom the statement is published.

2.45   For example, XY is renowned for committing acts of terrorism. Z publishes the statement, 'XY is a great man'. This appears not to form a basis for a prosecution for direct encouragement, since the statement does not urge anyone to do anything. Neither does the statement amount to glorification within s 1(3) because it does not praise or celebrate acts of terrorism. It is possible, however, that some people could understand the statement to be an indirect encouragement to commit acts of terrorism within s 1(1).

2.46   However, the identity of the persons to whom the statement was published would be important, and the jury would need evidence that the persons knew, at the very least, of the reputation of XY. If in this example the members of the public had heard of XY, and knew of his reputation, there would be evidence upon which it could be concluded that some of those persons would be likely to understand the statement as an encouragement to commit acts of terrorism. Proof is required of the state of mind of at least some of the persons to whom the statement is published.

4. Mens Rea

2.47   The mental element of the offence appears in s 2(b). A person is guilty of an offence if he publishes a statement to which the section applies and at that time intends members of the public to be directly or indirectly encouraged or otherwise induced by the statement to commit, prepare, or instigate acts of terrorism or Convention offences; or is reckless as to whether members of the public will be directly or indirectly encouraged or otherwise induced.

2.48   The decision in *R v G*[18] will apply; a person will commit the offence recklessly if he is aware that there is a risk that some members of the public will be directly

---

[18] [2004] 1 AC 1034.

encouraged to commit acts of terrorism, and nevertheless takes that risk where, in the circumstances known to him, it is unreasonable for him to take the risk of publication.

Whilst Art 5 of the 2005 Council of Europe Convention on the Prevention of **2.49** Terrorism was the part of the legislative history of the s 1 offence, Art 5 did not specify that such an offence could be committed recklessly.

5. Specific Defence

Section 1(6) enacts a specific defence in the case of an allegation of recklessly **2.50** publishing a statement, that the statement did not express the defendant's views, nor had his endorsement, and that it was clear in all the circumstances that that was the case. The inclusion of this specific defence is a concession to those who feared that this offence would undermine the right to freedom of expression under Art 10 of the European Convention on Human Rights.

There will be an evidential burden upon the defendant to raise the defence **2.51** and the Crown will then have to prove that it is not made out to the criminal standard. Therefore in a case of reckless publication the Crown will have to prove that the defendant was subjectively reckless at the time he published the statement as to whether the statement would encourage those members of the public to whom it was published to commit acts of terrorism. It would then be for the defence to assert that the statement neither expressed the defendant's views nor had his endorsement, and that that is clear from all the circumstances of the statement's publication.

It was decided in *Sheldrake v DPP; Attorney-General's Reference (No 4 of* **2.52** *2002)*,[19] that the specific defence set out in s 11(2) of the 2000 Act (membership of a proscribed organization) imposed only an evidential burden on the defendant, where he was required to 'prove' the defence, as opposed to a legal burden on the balance of probabilities. The same principle should apply to s 1(6). A different view appears to have been taken by a sponsoring Minister, Baroness Scotland, in Parliament in relation to defences under the 2006 Act.[20]

The defence will be of particular relevance to those who publish statements of **2.53** which they are not the authors, in other words those who produce the media that carry the statements to the public: newspapers, television companies, website providers, and publishers. It may also be available to others such as newscasters and those taking part in political debates. Anxiety was expressed in Parliament during the passage of the Bill that this provision might catch librarians distributing controversial political or religious histories. The fact that the offence may be committed recklessly, and by corporate bodies, will give those responsible for the publication of topical and controversial material reason to be cautious.

---

[19] [2005] 1 AC 264 (HL).
[20] *Hansard*, vol 676, col 709 (7 December 2005).

2.54   It may be difficult to argue, for example, that a newspaper that publishes a statement engaging s 1 neither expressed the newspaper's opinion nor had its endorsement. It must be noted that there is no defence of 'public good', as there is under s 4 of the Obscene Publications Act 1959, which provides that if the defendant shows that the article is justified 'in the interests of science, literature, art or learning, or of other objects of general concern', he should be acquitted.

2.55   As to the availability of the defence to a person who has failed to comply with a notice issued under s 3, and is therefore deemed to endorse the statement, the wording of the section is far from clear. A person who demonstrates that the statement neither in fact expressed his views nor had his endorsement will pass the test in s 1(6)(a). If so, the jury must then consider whether he also satisfies the test in s 1(6)(b). It is the effect of the words in brackets in s 1(6)(b) that is not clear. Paragraph 27 of the Explanatory Note to the Act suggests that the effect of these words is to make the defence unavailable to someone who has failed to comply with such a notice. It does indeed appear that the deeming provision in s 3 would have little practical effect were the defence to remain. However, any ambiguity as to the availability of the defence under this opaque provision should be construed in favour of the defendant, according to the canon of construction against doubtful penalization.

6. Certainty and Human Rights

2.56   Apart from its complexity, the most serious weaknesses of this new offence are its lack of certainty, and its tendency to undermine the right protected by Art 10 of the European Convention on Human Rights:

1. Everyone has the right to freedom of expression. This right shall include freedom to hold opinions and to receive and impart information and ideas without interference by public authority and regardless of frontiers. This Article shall not prevent States from requiring the licensing of broadcasting, television or cinema enterprises.

2. The exercise of these freedoms, since it carries with it duties and responsibilities, may be subject to such formalities, conditions, restrictions or penalties as are prescribed by law, and are necessary if a democratic society, in the interests of national security, territorial integrity or public safety, for the prevention of disorder or crime, for the protection of health or morals, for the protection of the reputation or rights of others, for preventing the disclosure of information received in confidence, or for maintaining the authority and impartiality of the judiciary.

2.57   In English criminal law, charges and counts have, since the nineteenth century, been liable to be held defective or void for uncertainty or duplicity, but almost always on the ground that a particular charge included an allegation of more than one type of offence specified in an enactment. It is likely that this danger will be avoided by careful drafting under the Indictment Rules 1971. The offence lies in publishing a statement to which the section applies; a count alleging that a person published a statement likely to be understood by some or all of the members of the public as a direct or indirect encouragement, etc would not be bad for duplicity; it is one offence.

On the other hand, offences which might be committed intentionally or reck- **2.58** lessly (under the Criminal Damage Act 1971, for example) are always indicted as separate, usually alternate, counts.

An offence alleged under this section may nonetheless contravene Art 7 of the **2.59** European Convention on Human Rights:

1. No one shall be held guilty of any criminal offence on account of any act or omission which did not constitute a criminal offence under national or international law at the time when it was committed. Nor shall a heavier penalty be imposed than the one that was applicable at the time the criminal offence was omitted.
2. This Article shall not prejudice the trial and punishment of any person for any act or omission which, at the time it was committed, was criminal according to the general principles of law recognised by civilised nations.

This Article requires that the criminal law should be sufficiently accessible and **2.60** precise to enable an individual to know in advance whether his conduct is criminal. See, for example, *Handyside v UK*,[21] a case in which the European Commission held in relation to an allegation under the Obscene Publications Act 1959 that Art 7 'includes the requirement that the offence should be clearly described by law': this requirement did not invalidate a general description set down in a statute, interpreted and applied by the courts.

Allegations of publishing a statement likely to be understood as *indirect* **2.61** encouragement, being *reckless as to the consequences*, are obviously vulnerable to a challenge based on s 6 of the Human Rights Act 1998: allegations of *intentionally* publishing a statement likely to be understood as *direct* encouragement, are unlikely to be judged uncertain under Art 7, but for the reason that they are, in effect, allegations of incitement to commit terrorist acts.

Article 7.2 cannot be invoked by a prosecutor. The offence in s 1 is much wider **2.62** than the provisions of Art 5 of the 2005 Convention, which in any event is confined to the European states party to it.

The Third Report of Session 2005–6 of the Joint Committee of the House of **2.63** Lords and House of Commons on Human Rights[22] recorded various expressions of concern that the glorification provisions would infringe Art 10 of the European Convention on Human Rights.

Those prosecutions likely to be vulnerable to attacks based on Art 10 will be **2.64** those for making statements likely to be understood as indirect encouragement, being reckless as to the consequences; particularly having regard to the absence of the 'public good' defence as found in the Obscene Publications Act 1959. The Third Report suggested that 'a "reasonable excuse" or "public interest" defence . . . should be included to make it less likely that the offence would

---

[21] (1974) YB 228, 290.
[22] HL paper 75-II, HC 561-II (5 December 2005).

be incompatible with article 10'. The Government has failed to heed this warning.[23]

7. Penalties

2.65 The offence is punishable on indictment with up to seven years' imprisonment or a fine, or both. In the Crown Court, the level of fine is unlimited. On summary conviction to a term of six months' imprisonment or a fine not exceeding the statutory maximum (£5,000), or both. When s 154(1) of the Criminal Justice Act 2003 comes into force increasing the sentencing power of Magistrates' Courts to 12 months' imprisonment, the maximum sentence on summary conviction will be increased to 12 months' imprisonment in England and Wales.

B. SECTION 2—DISSEMINATION OF TERRORIST PUBLICATIONS

2.66 We have noted that 'publishing a statement' includes by virtue of s 20(4)(a) 'his publishing it in any manner to the public'. As a result, many cases of disseminating terrorist publications will be caught by s 1, but by virtue of s 2(3)(b) the definition of a 'terrorist publication' is wider than that of 'statement'. Whilst the definition of a 'statement'[24] will include speeches given live, a 'publication' is defined by s 2(13) and:

means an article or record[25] of any description that contains any of the following, or any combination of them—
i. matter to be read;
ii. matter to be listened to;
iii. matter to be looked at or watched

The section applies to publications that do not encourage the commission of acts of terrorism but are understood to be useful in the commission or preparation of terrorist acts.

2.67 It is irrelevant whether the terrorist publication makes reference to any terrorist acts, either general or specific and it is similarly irrelevant whether any person is in fact encouraged to commit acts of terrorism or in fact makes use of the publication in the commission or preparation of such acts.[26]

---

[23] The same recommendation was made in relation to offences under s 2.

[24] See para 2.16.

[25] Section 20(8) states: 'In this Part references to what is contained in an article or record include references (a) to anything that is embodied or stored in or on it; and (b) to anything that may be reproduced from it using apparatus designed or adapted for the purpose.'

[26] See s 2(7) and (8).

1. The Conduct to Which the Section Applies

Section 2 will catch persons who may not be the authors of the terrorist publica- **2.68** tions. Section 2(2) refers to the 'conduct' of those who distribute, circulate, give, sell, or lend a terrorist publication; or those who offer to sell or lend terrorist publications. It applies to those who provide a service to others that enables them to obtain, read, listen to, look at, or acquire a terrorist publication. It also applies to those who transmit the contents of such a publication electronically or to someone who has such a publication in his possession with 'a view' to it being disseminated in any of the ways outlined above.

What amounts to being in possession of such a publication 'with a view' to it **2.69** becoming the subject of other conduct within s 2(2) is not clear. If a person merely possesses a terrorist publication no offence is committed under the Act.[27] The phrase 'with a view' in s 2(2)(f) is akin to conditional or provisional intent; perhaps to disseminate the terrorist publication at a propitious time. The phrase 'with a view' may connote something less than a conditional intent, perhaps a statement of mind in which use is merely a contemplated possibility.

The Third Report of the Joint House of Lords/House of Commons Commit- **2.70** tee on Human Rights expressed the view (Session 2005–6, 5 December 2005) that the:

offence of 'disseminating terrorist publications' is unlikely to be compatible with the right to freedom of expression in Article 10 ECHR in the absence of an explicit requirement that the dissemination of such publications amounts to an incitement to violence and is both intended and likely to do so.

No such explicit requirement has been included in the section.[28]

2. Definition of 'Terrorist Publication'

By virtue of s 2(3) a publication is a 'terrorist publication' if either (s 2(3)(a)) **2.71** matter contained in it is likely to be understood by some or all of the persons to whom it is, or may become available,[29] as a direct or indirect encouragement to them to commit acts of terrorism; or (s 2(3)(b)) matter contained in it is likely to be useful in the commission or preparation of acts of terrorism, and to be understood as such by some or all of those persons to whom it is or may become available, wholly or mainly for the purpose of being so useful to them. Many publications will obviously fall within both definitions.

Similar problems arise in relation to the meaning of 'some' persons as out- **2.72** lined in relation to s 1 above. As we have noted, whereas s 1(1) refers to members

---

[27] Although it is likely that he would commit an offence of 'possession for terrorist purposes' under s 57 of the 2000 Act.

[28] See *Erdogu v Turkey* (2002) 34 EHRR 50.

[29] As a consequence of the conduct outlined in para 2.67 above.

of the public to whom the statement is in fact published, s 2(3) refers to 'persons' to whom the publication 'may' become available.

2.73   The result achieved will be the same, as in both sections if either the publication or the proposed dissemination is wide and, at least in part, made to unidentified individuals, then the likely understanding of those individuals necessarily falls to be considered. The effect is that the same test is applied to a 'statement' under s 1(1) as is applied to a 'terrorist publication' under s 2(3)(a).

2.74   The second definition of 'terrorist publication' under s 2(3)(b) will have application to publications such as so-called 'terrorist handbooks' or other manuals that might assist in the commission or preparation of terrorist acts. The definition could also include confidential maps or plans of potential terrorist targets.

2.75   A publication will only fall within this second definition if the publication will be understood[30] as being 'wholly or mainly' (rather than incidentally) useful for the commission or preparation of acts of terrorism. As in the case of offences under s 1, it would be necessary for a jury to assess the possible understanding of persons who are not witnesses as to whether they would regard a publication as being mainly useful for the commission or preparation of acts of terrorism. It may be that, in fact, a certain publication may possess that quality but that in itself is insufficient; a publication will only become a 'terrorist publication' under s 2(3)(b) if:

(a) the jury find as a fact that there is matter in the publication that is likely to be useful;[31] and

(b) it will be understood to be useful, by the persons to whom it is or may be made available, as wholly or mainly for the purpose of being so useful.

2.76   By virtue of s 2(5) the question what is likely to be understood must be determined as at the time the publication is disseminated, and having regard to both the contents of the publication as a whole and to the circumstances in which that conduct occurs; not at the time of the trial.

2.77   The whole 'publication' may also be different to the 'statement' which would fall to be considered for an offence under s 1(2). The natural meaning of 'statement', poorly defined in s 20(6), is narrower than 'publication'. This produces an anomaly. A book is a publication, and under s 2 the jury have to consider it as a whole. Under s 1, the jury would consider a statement in the book, or more than one statement, as set out, no doubt, in different counts.

3. Indirect Encouragement

2.78 What amounts to matter that is likely to be understood as indirectly encouraging the commission of acts of terrorism is set out in s 2(4) and is in much the

---

[30] By some or all of the persons to whom it is or may become available.

[31] In the commission or preparation of acts of terrorism.

same terms as s 1(3), save that the subsection refers to 'a person' rather 'members of the public'. In other respects, the comments made above in relation to s 1 apply.

4. Mens Rea

A person disseminating terrorist publications must at the time he does so either **2.79** (s 2(1)(a)) intend that his conduct will be a direct or indirect encouragement to the commission of acts of terrorism; or (s 2(1)(b)) intend that an effect of his conduct will be the provision of assistance in the commission of such acts; or under s 2(1)(c) be reckless as to either of the above. It is of note however that whilst s 2(2)(f) purportedly deals with 'conduct' sufficient for the offence, the conduct so stated is 'possession [of the publication] with a view to its becoming the subject of conduct falling within any of paragraphs (a) to (e).' The 'conduct' therefore under s 2(2)(f) contains an element of mens rea in addition to that which would also be required under s 2(1).

The defendant need not intend that the only effect of his dissemination of the **2.80** publications is to encourage or assist; only that it is *an* effect. Whilst the *mens rea* required for an offence under s 2(1)(a) is consistent with the intention required for an offence under s 1(2), the intention required for an offence under s 2(1)(b) is consistent with the second definition of a 'terrorist publication' as a publication useful in the commission or preparation of acts of terrorism.

By virtue of s 2(6), it is sufficient for the defendant to intend that his conduct **2.81** shall be understood by one or more persons as either an encouragement to commit acts of terrorism or as a publication wholly or mainly useful in the commission or preparation of such acts. It is submitted that para 34 of the Explanatory Notes to the Act is unhelpful in explaining the effect of this subsection, and ignores the effect of s 2(2)(f).

If the offence is committed recklessly the defendant must be reckless in **2.82** accordance with the principle in *R v G*,[32] considered in relation to s 1, above.

5. Specific Defence

The combined effect of s 2(9) and (10) is to provide a defence if: **2.83**

(a) the publication in question is a terrorist publication as defined by s 2(3)(a);

(b) the defendant does not have the intention specified in s 2(1)(a); and he can show:
    i.   that the matter by reference to which the publication was a terrorist publication neither expressed his views nor had his endorsement; and
    ii. that it was clear in all the circumstances of the conduct that the matter did not express his views and did not have his endorsement.

---

[32] [2004] 1 AC 1034.

2.84 The defence does not apply to terrorist publications under s 2(3)(b); those that would be understood to be useful to the commission or preparation of terrorist acts. The defence may not be available if there has been a failure to comply with a s 3 notice, as discussed above.

2.85 The defence will be available even if the prosecution shows that an effect of the defendant's conduct will be the provision of assistance in the commission or preparation of acts of terrorism, provided that the terrorist publication is one which is likely to be understood by some or all of the persons to whom it is or may become available as a direct or indirect encouragement to commit acts of terrorism, rather than one that would be useful in the commission or preparation of such acts; and the defendant can show that the publication did not express his views or have his endorsement.

2.86 For example, X distributes a publication, believing it be an instruction manual for making explosives. He does so with the intention of assisting potential terrorists to make explosives. If the publication is merely propaganda on behalf of a terrorist organization, and is not in fact an instruction manual as the defendant believed, he will have a defence if he shows that the publication did not represent his views or did not have his endorsement. The publication may be in a language or code that the defendant did not fully understand, or he may have been acting on instructions from a third party. There may be a variety of reasons why he did not know the true content of the publication but still held an intention to assist terrorists.

2.87 A further difficulty lies in the fact that the defence is only available if the publication to which the conduct relates is a terrorist publication by virtue of s 2(3)(a). As argued above it is not only possible but quite likely that a publication would contain matter that would make it a 'terrorist publication' under both paragraphs of s 2(3); as a publication that was both an encouragement to commit acts of terrorism and practically useful in that respect. Since the contents of the publication as a whole must be considered in determining whether the publication is a 'terrorist publication' it is difficult to envisage how a defence could be available in relation to the parts of the publication that were caught by s 2(3)(a), but not to those caught by s 2(3)(b).

6. Penalties

2.88 A person is liable to the same penalties as under s 1.

7. Convention Offences

2.89 A s 2 offence cannot be committed in relation to any of the Convention offences contained in Sch 1. There appears to be no logical reason for this.

C. SECTION 3—APPLICATION OF SECTIONS 1 AND 2 TO INTERNET ACTIVITY, ETC

1. Application

Section 3 applies to s 1 in relation to statements that are published on the internet or by way of some other electronic service and to s 2 in relation to conduct that falls under s 2(2) involving the dissemination of terrorist publications using such systems. The section also deals with the giving of notices to those who use the internet and electronic services to publish or disseminate 'unlawfully terrorism related'[33] material on the internet or other electronic service.[34] **2.90**

2. Definition of 'Unlawfully Terrorism-Related'

A statement, article or record is 'unlawfully terrorism-related' if in the opinion of the constable giving the notice under s 3 it constitutes or contains: **2.91**

(a) something that is likely to be understood, by any one or more of the persons to whom it has or may become available, as a direct or indirect encouragement or other inducement to the commission, preparation or instigation of acts of terrorism or Convention offences; or
(b) information which—
  (i) is likely to be useful to any one or more of those persons in the commission or preparation of such acts; and
  (ii) is in a form or context in which it is likely to be understood by any one or more of those persons as being wholly or mainly for the purpose of being so useful.

The test set out above is an amalgamation of the tests arising under ss 1 and 2; the definition in s 3(8) of what is likely to be understood as indirect encouragement to commit acts of terrorism is in much the same terms as ss 1(3) and 2(4). **2.92**

An anomaly arises in relation to an offence under s 2, which, as noted above, cannot be committed with reference to any of the Convention offences in Sch 1. However, if the dissemination is by way of the internet or other electronic system, s 3(7) will apply, and a s 3 notice may be issued in relation to a statement, article, or record if it relates to Convention offences. The consequences of non-compliance with such a notice are unclear. The relevant person would be deemed by virtue of s 3(3)(c) to have endorsed the statement, article, or record, but may not in any event have committed an offence under s 2 if that statement, article, or record relates to Convention offences only and not to acts of terrorism. Whilst many Convention offences would fall within the broader definition **2.93**

---

[33] As defined by s 3(7).
[34] See s 3(1).

of 'acts of terrorism', they do not necessarily do so: cf the offences contained within Sch 1 and 'action' within s 1(2) of the 2000 Act.

3. Section 3 Notices

2.94   By virtue of s 3(3)(a), a constable may give a notice declaring that, in his opinion, the material to which the notice relates is unlawfully terrorism-related. The notice will then require[35] the 'relevant person' to whom the notice is given either to remove the terrorism-related material from public access or to modify it so that it will no longer be so related. The power is only available to police officers.

2.95   There is no requirement under s 3(3) for the constable to explain in what respect he has found any given statement, article, or record to be unlawfully terrorism-related; whilst, therefore, the relevant person is entitled to modify the material so that it is no longer unlawfully terrorism-related, he may have been given no guidance on how this might done. It seems that the constable need only make a declaration as to his opinion of the entire statement, article, or record without the need for giving reasons or making any explanation for holding that opinion.[36]

2.96   The notice must further explain that a failure to comply with the notice within two working days[37] will result in the statement, article, or record being regarded as having his endorsement, and must also explain the effect of initial compliance with the notice, but then making it available again at a later date in the same, or for all practical purposes the same, form; a 'repeat statement'. Paragraph 45 of the Explanatory Notes to the Act points out that:

[i]n such a situation it may be difficult to tell if the statement is the statement to which the notice relates or a new one. A mechanism is needed to ensure that a person is only liable for statements that he knows about . . .

It is of concern that the Explanatory Note points to a deficiency such as this in the legislation it exists to explain. All the more so as the intended effect of non-compliance with the notice is to remove the specific defences available under ss 1 and 2.

2.97   The intended sanction for non-compliance with the notice is that the statement or publication is regarded as having the relevant person's endorsement for the purposes of an offence under s 1 or s 2. The intended effect is that the specific defences to recklessness under those sections is unavailable but as already noted above, the wording in ss 1(6) and 2(9) is ambiguous.

---

[35] Section 3(3)(b).
[36] It is implicit in the giving of the notice that the constable would have found that subsection (7) had been satisfied in some respect.
[37] For the definition of 'working day' see s 3(9).

4. Repeat Statements

Section 3(4) makes it unnecessary to serve a further s 3 notice if there has been **2.98** initial compliance but subsequent publication. If there is publication after initial compliance, the notice is deemed to have been served already, and that there has been a failure to comply. In these circumstances the relevant person is to be regarded as endorsing the statement, article, or record (the 'repeat statement').

By virtue of s 3(5) and (6), s 3(4) will not have this effect if the defendant **2.99** shows that:

(a) he was unaware of the publication of the repeat statement or having become aware of it had taken every step that he reasonably could to secure that it either ceased to be available to the public or was modified so that it was not unlawfully terrorism-related; and

(b) before the time of publication he has taken every step he reasonably could to prevent the repeat statement becoming available to the public and to ascertain whether it has.

5. Challenge

There is no mechanism within the Act by which a s 3 notice can be challenged by **2.100** the relevant person if he considers it to be unjustified. Since the power will tend to limit freedom of expression under Art 10 of the European Convention on Human Rights, a claim for judicial review of the constable's decision to issue the notice could be made on the basis that the issuing of the notice was disproportionate in the circumstances and thus breached the affected person's Art 10 rights.

It is noteworthy that s 3 does not refer to a constable of any particular rank; **2.101** any police officer may use the power conferred.

D. GIVING OF NOTICES UNDER SECTION 3

1. Persons Who May Be Given a Notice under Section 3

A s 3 notice may be served upon an individual,[38] a body corporate,[39] a firm,[40] or **2.102** an unincorporated body or association.[41] There are different requirements of service as to who may take valid delivery of the notice, dealt with in each subsection. The reader is referred to the text of the Act.[42]

In general terms it will be sufficient if the notice is sent by recorded post to **2.103** either (in the case of an individual) his last known address or (in the case of

---

[38] Section 4(1). [39] Section 4(2). [40] Section 4(3).
[41] Section 4(4). [42] Appendix 2.

another body) to the 'appropriate person' as defined by s 4(6) at the registered or principal office.

2.104   For the purposes of complying with the notice within two working days as is required by s 3, time runs from either the time of delivery when delivery is effected by hand to the appropriate person or, when it is sent by recorded post, the recorded time of delivery.

3

PREPARATION OF TERRORIST ACTS AND TERRORIST TRAINING

A. SECTION 5—PREPARATION OF TERRORIST ACTS

1. Elements of the Offence

A person commits the offence if: **3.01**

(a) he intends to commit acts of terrorism; or

(b) he intends to assist another to commit such acts; and

(c) he engages in any conduct in preparation for giving effect to his intention.

'Acts of terrorism' are defined in s 20 as including anything constituting an **3.02** action taken for the purposes of terrorism within the meaning of the 2000 Act. Section 5(2) states that 'it is irrelevant . . . whether the intention and preparation relate to one or more particular acts of terrorism, acts of terrorism of a particular description or acts of terrorism generally'. The provision thus creates a broad offence. There was no substantial opposition to the creation of this new offence in Parliament.

The offence applies to preparatory acts not sufficiently proximate to the **3.03** commission of the full offence to amount to an attempted offence within the meaning of the Criminal Attempts Act 1981. If a person buys chemical ingredients for the purpose of making poison so that he can introduce it into the water supply, he may intend to commit the offence of murder, but will not be guilty of attempted murder unless his actions are more than merely preparatory to the commission of the choate offence. He certainly intends to do something that 'creates a serious risk to the health or safety of the public or a section of the public' under s 1(2)(d) of the 2000 Act and is liable to prosecution for an offence under s 5 of the 2006 Act as a result.

3.04 The real emphasis in s 5 is on the intention, rather than the conduct, of a defendant. There can surely be no room for an attempt to commit this offence, because every preparatory act would amount to the full offence. If a potential terrorist were to commit to his diary his intention, at some future time, of committing acts of terrorism by the use of home made explosives, the range of actions within the phrase 'any conduct in preparation' is almost unlimited. The action of putting on a coat for the purpose of leaving a house, intending to catch a bus to a library for the purpose of borrowing a chemistry text book to discover the identity of the appropriate chemicals would be sufficient; or withdrawing cash from a bank in order to buy chemicals.

3.05 Crimes requiring proof of pre-attempt conduct are still uncommon in English criminal law.[1] If no other criminal offence is available to try a terrorist suspect, the use of this offence would surely imply that the person was being tried principally for having criminal thoughts, the actus reus of any offence being non-specific and very easy to prove.

2. Penalty

3.06 The offence is punishable with imprisonment for life, in striking contrast to the maximum of seven years' imprisonment for offences contrary to ss 1 and 2.

B. SECTION 6—TRAINING FOR TERRORISM

1. Providing Instruction or Training

3.07 Under s 6(1) it is an offence to provide instruction or training in any of the named 'skills' in s 6(3). For the offence to be made out the defendant must have known at the time he provided the instruction or training that the person receiving it intended to use those skills either for or in connection with the commission or preparation of acts of terrorism or Convention offences, or for assisting others in that purpose.

---

[1] See and compare 'going equipped to steal' (s 25 of the Theft Act 1968); 'being knowingly concerned in, or the taking of steps with a view to, the fraudulent evasion of VAT' (s 72 of the Value Added Tax Act 1994); and the common law crime of 'doings acts tending and intended to pervert the course of justice'.

2. Receiving Instruction or Training

Under s 6(2) it is an offence to receive instruction or training in any of the **3.08** named skills in s 6(3) if at the time when the instruction or training is received the defendant intends to use those skills for or in connection with the commission or preparation of acts of terrorism or Convention offences, or for assisting others in that purpose.

There is scope for certain conduct to be caught by s 6 as well as by either **3.09** s 1 or s 2 if 'instruction' and 'training' are widely interpreted by the courts. Neither term is defined further by the Act. The publication and dissemination of a 'terrorist publication' for the purposes of an offence under s 2 would include, for example, an instruction manual on making explosives. A person disseminating such a publication may also be guilty of giving instruction or training in terrorist skills, because such a publication will inform the reader as to one of the named skills in s 6(3).

3. The Relevant Skills in Section 6(3)

Section 6(3) states that: **3.10**

The skills are—
(a) the making, handling or use of a noxious substance,[2] or of substances of a description of such substances;
(b) the use of any method or technique for doing anything else that is capable of being done for the purposes of terrorism, in connection with the commission or preparation of an act of terrorism or Convention offence or in connection with assisting the commission or preparation by another of such an act or offence; and
(c) the design or adaptation for the purposes of terrorism, or in connection with the commission or preparation of an act of terrorism or Convention offence, of any method or technique for doing anything.

These offences are similar to those under s 54 of the 2000 Act of providing or **3.11** receiving 'weapons training', save that the skills as defined in s 6(3) will cover a wider range of conduct,[3] encompassing any conduct that could be used in the commission or preparation of acts of terrorism. This could include usually legitimate skills—flying an aeroplane, for example—which would be caught by

---

[2] 'Noxious substance' is defined is s 6(7) and means—

(a) a dangerous substance within the meaning of Part 7 of the Anti-terrorism, Crime and Security Act 2001; or
(b) any other substance which is hazardous or noxious only in certain circumstances;
'substance' includes any natural or artificial substance (whatever its origin or method of production and whether in solid or liquid form or in the form of a gas or vapour) and any mixture of substances.

Section 58(4) and (5) of the 2001 Act define a 'dangerous substance' with reference to Sch 5 to that Act which lists a variety of pathogens and toxins.

[3] Section 54 of the 2000 Act deals only with instruction and training in the making or use of firearms, radioactive material, or weapons designed or adapted for the discharge of any radioactive material, explosives, or chemical, biological, or nuclear weapons.

the section if coupled with the necessary knowledge that the person receiving the training intends to use it to commit acts of terrorism. It is noteworthy that the offence requires knowledge of the intention of the person receiving the instruction or training; accordingly, proof of belief in, or suspicion of, such an intention would be insufficient. Contrary to the recommendation in the Third Report of the Joint Committee on Human Rights[4] no defence of 'reasonable excuse' or 'public interest' has been included.

3.12   By virtue of s 6(4) it is irrelevant for proof of either offence whether the instruction or training is provided to one or more persons or generally; whether the person receiving the training intends any specific act of terrorism; whether the person receiving the instruction or training intends to provide assistance to others; or whether he has in fact identified the person or persons to whom he will provide such assistance.

4. Penalties

3.13   The offence is triable either way and punishable with up to 10 years' imprisonment.

C. SECTION 7—POWERS OF FORFEITURE IN RESPECT OF OFFENCES UNDER SECTION 6

3.14   By virtue of s 7 a court before which someone is convicted of an offence under s 6 has power to order the forfeiture, retention, handling, destruction, and disposal of anything that the court considers to have been in the person's possession for purposes connected with the offence. These forfeiture provisions are again similar to those under s 54 of the 2000 Act.

3.15   Under s 7(2) an opportunity to be heard must be afforded to anyone who has an interest, or claims to be the owner of the thing, before any order is made. The court has power to vary its order at any time; accordingly, any order for forfeiture made without the knowledge of a person who has an interest in it may be varied when that person becomes aware of the order.

D. SECTION 8—ATTENDANCE AT A PLACE USED FOR TERRORIST TRAINING

1. Elements of the Offence

3.16   The offence is committed if:

(a) a person attends at any place;

---

[4] Paragraph 57.

(b) while the person is there instruction or training within the meaning of s 6(1) of the 2006 Act or s 54(1) of the 2000 Act is provided or made available there;

(c) that instruction or training is provided at least partly for purposes connected with the commission or preparation of acts of terrorism or Convention offences; and

(d) the person knows or believes that instruction or training is being provided there at least partly for purposes connected with such conduct; or

(e) a person attending at that place throughout the period of that person's attendance could not reasonably have failed to understand that instruction or training was being provided there at least partly for such purposes.

The offence may be committed in any jurisdiction; indeed, one of the main purposes of this offence was to catch those who attend so-called terrorist training camps abroad, particularly in countries such as Afghanistan and Pakistan. The offence is committed by simply attending at the 'place', although this is not further defined by the Act, and by s 8(3) it is irrelevant whether the person so attending actually receives any instruction or training, or intends to receive any instruction or training.   3.17

The *mens rea* of the offence is either knowledge or belief that that instruction or training is being provided, or alternatively an objective test as outlined above.[5]   3.18

2. Evidential Difficulties

There are likely to be significant evidential difficulties in proving an offence under this section. Since the offence is aimed at those who merely attend such training camps rather than those who actually receive instruction or training, and intend to use those skills in committing terrorist acts who could be prosecuted under s 6, it may be difficult to obtain evidence of knowledge or belief, or indeed any evidence upon which the objective test could be applied.   3.19

No defence is expressly provided under the section. It would therefore be irrelevant if a defendant were able to demonstrate that he was at the place for a purpose wholly unconnected with terrorism (delivering mail or groceries, for example) provided that it be proved that he knew or believed, or could not reasonably have failed to understand, that instruction or training was being given at the place. It follows that a person attending such a place for the purposes of legitimate journalism would similarly commit an offence.   3.20

If the training camp is abroad, serious evidential difficulties will arise. It is difficult to see how the evidence of activities at the training camp would be gathered. Political and diplomatic considerations would also play a part in this instance. The 'war on terror' arguably began after the bombing of the *U.S.S.*   3.21

---

[5] At para 3.16(e).

Cole in Aden harbour on 12 October 2000. Following the attacks on the World Trade Center and the Pentagon on 11 September 2001, President Bush asserted in an address to a joint session of Congress and the American people on 20 September 2001:

... we will pursue nations that provide aid or safe haven to terrorism. Every nation, in every region, now has a decision to make. Either you are with us, or you are with the terrorists. From this day forward, any nation that continues to harbor or support terrorism will be regarded by the United States as a hostile regime.

3.22   The United Kingdom together with the 'coalition of the willing', has supported US foreign policy in this respect. If the authorities in the United Kingdom knew of a terrorist camp in country X they would know either through proper diplomatic channels or by some covert method of intelligence. If the former, the government of X would similarly be aware of the training camp. If that government had done nothing to close the camp and prosecute those involved, it would be vulnerable to military action from the United States. If the intelligence was covert, and therefore unknown to the government of X, then it is difficult to see how this evidence would be presented in open court during the course of a criminal prosecution in the United Kingdom.

3.23   Gathering evidence from abroad to mount a prosecution in the United Kingdom would present obvious difficulties and dangers to those charged with the task of such an investigation. It is difficult to see how any meaningful and independent enquiries could be carried out by the defence into allegations of this type.

3.24   A further problem lies in procuring the attendance of the suspect in the United Kingdom to face trial. Unless the person were to return voluntarily, extradition by any conventional means would be improbable given the nature of the case. There are likely to be few prosecutions for offences under ss 6 and 8; the main motive for enacting these provisions appears to have been a desire to give the appearance of determination to combat the terrorist threat. It may well be, as the Joint Committee on Human Rights advised in their Third Report,[6] that criminalizing mere attendance at such a place is disproportionate in the absence of any requirement to prove an intention that the training be used for terrorist purposes.

3. Penalties

3.25   The offence is punishable with up to 10 years' imprisonment.

---

[6] Paragraph 59.

4

SECTIONS 9 TO 12—OFFENCES INVOLVING RADIOACTIVE DEVICES AND MATERIALS AND NUCLEAR FACILITIES AND SITES

A. Overview	4.01
B. Offences	4.05

A. OVERVIEW

Sections 9, 10, and 11 relate to offences involving radioactive material. These **4.01** offences build on those created by s 47 of the Anti-Terrorism, Crime and Security Act 2001 relating to nuclear weapons. Whereas the offences under that Act relate to offences involving nuclear weapons and other nuclear material per se, the offences in the 2006 Act are specifically terrorism-related. In addition the sections refer to 'radioactive device[s]' and 'radioactive material' as defined in s 9(4) and (5), and cover devices capable of dispersing 'nuclear material or any other radioactive substance' which have the capacity to cause serious bodily injury, serious damage to property, endanger life, or create a serious risk to the health or safety of the public.

Plainly it was considered that the 2001 Act provisions, despite the definition in **4.02** s 47(6),[1] were not broad enough and that further offences were needed to cover the use of other radiological material that might not explode but might be used as a contaminant or 'dirty bomb'.[2] The justification for these new offences was the need to ratify the UN Convention on the Suppression of Acts of Nuclear

---

[1] '(6) In this section "nuclear weapon"' includes a nuclear explosive device that is not intended for use as a weapon.

[2] For fuller consideration of this issue, see Clive Walker, *Blackstone's Guide to the Anti-Terrorism Legislation* (OUP, 2002), para 9.2.2.

Terrorism. Nevertheless, this group of offences will probably be seldom used, if at all.

4.03   Section 12 amends the Serious Organised Crime and Police Act 2005 so as to make it an offence to trespass on nuclear and protected sites. At the time of writing there have been two arrests; those of two veterans of the Greenham Common protests, arrested for allegedly walking a few feet across the sentry line at the US military base at Menwith Hill.

4.04   Sections 9 to 11 carry life imprisonment.

B. OFFENCES

1. Section 9—Making and Possession of Devices or Materials

4.05   A person commits an offence if:

(a) he makes or has in his possession a radioactive device, or

(b) he has in his possession radioactive material with the intention of using the device or material in the course of or in connection with the commission or preparation of an act of terrorism or for the purposes of terrorism, or of making it available to be used.

4.06   By virtue of s 9(2) it is irrelevant whether the person intends any specific act of terrorism.

2. Section 10—Misuse of Devices or Material and Misuse and Damage of Facilities

4.07   Section 10(1) creates a similar offence to s 9, save that the offence relates to the actual use of the radioactive device or material in the course of or in connection with the commission of an act of terrorism or for the purposes of terrorism.

4.08   An offence under s 10(2) is committed by a person if 'in the course of or in connection with the commission of an act of terrorism or for the purposes of terrorism', he uses or damages a nuclear facility in a manner which either:

(a) causes a release of radioactive material; or

(b) creates or increases a risk that such material will be released.

4.09   'Nuclear facility' is defined by s 10(4) and includes a nuclear reactor including one installed on a transportation device, such as a nuclear submarine, or a plant or conveyance used to process, store, or transport radioactive material.

3. Section 11—Terrorist Threats Relating to Devices, Materials, or Facilities

Under s 11(1) a person commits an offence if: **4.10**

(a) in the course of or in connection with the commission of an act of terrorism or for the purposes of terrorism he makes a demand:
  - (i) for the supply to himself or another of a radioactive device or of radioactive material;
  - (ii) for a nuclear facility[3] to be made available to himself or another; or
  - (iii) for access to such a facility to be given to himself or to another;

(b) he supports the demand with a threat that he or another will take action if the demand is not met; and

(c) the circumstances and manner of the threat are such that it is reasonable for the person to whom it is made to assume that there is a real risk that the threat will be carried out if the demand is not met.

The offence is similar to blackmail. It is interesting that the offence can be **4.11**
committed only in relation to acts of terrorism, not to Convention offences, and that it can be committed 'in the course of or in connection with' acts of terrorism rather than including preparation for acts of terrorism. This is curious: a person might wish to obtain such devices or materials, or gain access to nuclear facilities, for the purpose of carrying out acts of terrorism in the future. A person already in the process of committing the act is unlikely to make such a demand at that stage.

Under s 11(2) a person commits an offence if: **4.12**

(i) he makes a threat to use radioactive material, a radioactive device, or to use or damage a nuclear facility in a manner that releases radioactive material or creates or increases a risk that such material will be released;

(ii) the threat is made in the course of or in connection with the commission of an act of terrorism or for the purposes of terrorism; and

(iii) the circumstances and manner of the threat are such that it is reasonable for the person to whom it is made to assume that there is a real risk that the threat will be carried out, or would be carried out if demands made in association with the threat are not met.

It is apparent that there need not actually be any radioactive device **4.13**
or material in existence; the offence is completed by the making of the threat alone.

---

[3] See para 4.09.

4. Section 12—Trespassing, etc on Nuclear Sites

4.14 This section amends the Serious Organised Crime and Police Act 2005 so as to substitute the word 'protected' for 'designated' in relation to designated sites in ss 128(1), (4), and (7), and 129(1), (4), and (6).[4] The effect of this is to introduce the definition of a 'protected site' through s 12(3). This includes the definition of a designated site which survives in the original text of the Act in s 12(2), but adds within the definition of a protected site a 'nuclear site'. 'Nuclear site' is then defined in the new s 12(1B). This amendment makes it unnecessary for any nuclear site as so defined to be specifically designated by the Home Secretary and it will be an offence under s 128(1) to trespass on any such site.

4.15 It is a defence to prove that a person charged with this offence did not know, and had no reasonable cause to suspect, that the site was a protected site. This will again place an evidential burden on the defendant, for the reasons explained in Chapter 2. The offence is summary only.

---

[4] The corresponding offence in Scotland.

5

INCREASES OF PENALTIES AND INCIDENTAL PROVISIONS RELATING TO OFFENCES

A.	Increases in Penalties	5.01
B.	Incidental Provisions About Offences	5.04

A. INCREASES IN PENALTIES

1. Maximum Penalty for Possessing for Terrorist Purposes

By virtue of s 13 of the 2000 Act, the penalty under s 57(4)(a) of the 2000 Act 5.01 for an offence under s 57(1) is increased from 10 to 15 years for offences committed after the commencement of the section. Section 57(1) creates an offence of possessing an article in circumstances which give rise to reasonable suspicion that the person's possession is for a purpose connected with the commission, preparation, or instigation of an act of terrorism.

2. Maximum Penalty for Certain Offences Relating to Nuclear Material

Section 14 increases the penalty for offences under s 2 of the Nuclear Material 5.02 (Offences) Act 1983 from 14 years' imprisonment to life imprisonment for offences occurring after commencement. The offence involves the making of threats to commit various offences including murder by using nuclear material. This increase is in conformity with the penalties for similar offences involving radioactive material in the 2006 Act.

3. Maximum Penalty for Contravening a Notice Relating to Encrypted Information

Section 15 increases the penalties for offences of failing to comply with notices 5.03 requiring disclosure under s 53 of the Regulation of Investigatory Powers Act

2000. The penalty is increased from two to five years' imprisonment in a 'national security case' as inserted by s 15(2). A case is a 'national security case' if it has been specified in the notice that the disclosure is required in the interests of national security. The increase applies to offences committed after the commencement of the section.

B. INCIDENTAL PROVISIONS ABOUT OFFENCES

1. Preparatory Hearings in Terrorism Cases

5.04 Section 16 amends s 29 of the Criminal Procedure and Investigations Act 1996, making it mandatory to hold a preparatory hearing in any case in which at least one person is charged with a terrorism offence or with an offence that carries a maximum penalty of at least 10 years' imprisonment and it appears to the judge that the evidence on the indictment reveals a terrorist connection. In a case that the judge has determined involves an allegation of serious or complex fraud as well as terrorism offences, the judge should not make an order for a preparatory hearing under s 29 as amended, but under s 7 of the Criminal Justice Act 1987, the provision under which a judge may order a preparatory hearing in cases of serious or complex fraud.

5.05 The definition of 'terrorism offence' is inserted into s 29 by s 16(5). Section 16(8) sets out that conduct has a 'terrorist connection' if it is or takes place in the course of an act of terrorism or is for the purposes of terrorism.

2. Commission of Offences Abroad

5.06 The effect of s 17(1) is to permit the prosecution of a person in the United Kingdom for acts he has committed in another jurisdiction, provided those acts would constitute an offence in the United Kingdom under s 17(2) if committed here.[1] In addition, the effect of s 17(3) is that not only may the acts be committed outside the United Kingdom against a foreign government but the person committing those acts need not even be a British citizen or company incorporated in the United Kingdom. The sum of these provisions is to give jurisdiction to the United Kingdom to prosecute any person, regardless of nationality, for committing any of the offences in ss 1–6 and 8–11 if they occur anywhere in the world.

5.07 In addition, s 17(2) extends the jurisdiction in the same way for offences of membership of a proscribed organization under s 11, and weapons training under s 54 of the 2000 Act. Similarly, jurisdiction is extended for the corresponding inchoate offences. Section 17(5) amends s 3 of the Explosive Substances Act 1883. Previously offences in preparation for use of explosives with intent to

---

[1] Section 17(2)(a) refers to any offence under ss 1–6 of the 2006 Act and s 17(2)(b) to any offence under ss 8–11.

endanger life or property were indictable if there was an intent to endanger life in the United Kingdom or the Republic of Ireland. The word 'elsewhere' is now substituted for 'the Republic of Ireland'. If offences are committed outside the United Kingdom, by virtue of s 17(4) they may be tried in any part of the United Kingdom.

The implications of the extension of jurisdiction effected by s 17 are more generally discussed in Chapter 1. **5.08**

3. Liability of Company Directors, etc

Where a body corporate commits an offence under Part 1 of the Act and it is proved that the offence has been committed with the consent or connivance of a director, manager, secretary, or other similar officer of the body corporate, or someone purporting to act in such a capacity, that person is also guilty of that offence and shall be liable to be proceeded against. This is of course a provision to be found in statutes dealing with other crimes. **5.09**

The effect of s 18 is simply that if a company is indicted, various of its officials may also be indicted. The jury would have to determine the state of mind of the body corporate in any event, obviously by reference to the company officials as possible directing minds of the company (see, for example, *Tesco Supermarkets Ltd v Nattrass*[2]). It is apparent that once a company has been found guilty it is sufficient for a company official to be found guilty if he has consented to or connived at the criminal act of the company. **5.10**

4. Consents for Prosecutions

Consent for any prosecution under Part 1 must be given by the Director of Public Prosecution unless it appears to him that an offence 'has been committed for a purpose wholly or partly connected with the affairs of a country other than the United Kingdom' when his consent may only be given with the permission of the Attorney-General.[3] **5.11**

The provisions of s 19 are also discussed generally in Chapter 1. **5.12**

---

[2] [1972] AC 153.
[3] There are corresponding provisions for Northern Ireland.

6

PROSCRIPTION

A. OVERVIEW

The regime for 'banning' organizations is predominantly executive; the Home **6.01** Secretary adds to and amends a list of proscribed groups (Sch 2 to the 2000 Act). The 2006 Act gives him an even broader discretion than was previously available. He may order that an organization that does not appear on the list shall be treated as if it did so appear, if he believes it is in fact a proscribed organization acting under a different name. Any proscribed organization (or one treated as such) or person affected by proscription can apply to the Secretary of State for removal from the Schedule. If he refuses, there is limited recourse to the courts, first to the Proscribed Organisation Appeal Commission ('POAC'), then, in certain circumstances, the Court of Appeal.

Proscription is not a new concept, though it remains largely symbolic. Par- **6.02** ticipation in terrorist organizations was an offence in Britain under s 2 of the Prevention of Terrorism (Temporary Provisions) Act 1989, and its predecessors. The 2000 Act expanded the geographical ambit of proscription, no longer focusing solely on Irish (including Ulster) groups. Another significant extension in the 2000 Act was the wider interpretation of 'organization' to include more loose associations.

The Joint Committee on Human Rights received evidence from the British **6.03** Irish Rights Watch[1] 'Proscribing organisations and prosecuting their members

---

[1] HL Paper 75-II, Ev 97 (28 November 2005).

drives them underground and increases their allure for certain people. Membership is difficult to prove and prosecutions on such a basis are open to abuse.'

6.04   Section 21 of the 2006 Act widens the grounds for proscription. A group may be considered to promote or encourage terrorism under s 3(5)(c) if its activities include 'glorification' of terrorism. This is considered in detail below.

6.05   Certainly, this regime expresses the revulsion of a Western liberal democracy towards groups which espouse or encourage terrorism. It may do little else. Few people will be caught with membership cards or uniforms of proscribed groups. It will be more fruitful for the authorities to pursue those who commit (or encourage) terrorist acts and plots.

B. CRIMINAL OFFENCES

6.06   Three offences in relation to proscribed organizations survive from the 2000 Act, relating to membership, support, and uniforms.

1. Membership

6.07   It is an offence under s 11(1) of the 2000 Act to belong to, or profess to belong to, a proscribed organization. A person charged under s 11(1) has a defence under s 11(2) if he can prove that:

(a) the organization was not proscribed on the last (or only) occasion on which he became a member or began to profess to be a member, and

(b) that he has not taken part in the activities of the organization at any time while it was proscribed.

6.08   The penalty on conviction on indictment is a maximum of 10 years' imprisonment and/or a fine. On summary conviction, the maximum sentence is 12 months' imprisonment and/or a fine not exceeding the statutory maximum.

6.09   'Proscribed' means proscribed for the purposes of any of the following:

(a) the Northern Ireland (Emergency Provisions) Act 1996;

(b) the Terrorism Act 2000;

(c) the Northern Ireland (Emergency Provisions) Act 1991;

(d) the Prevention of Terrorism (Temporary Provisions) Act 1989;

(e) the Prevention of Terrorism (Temporary Provisions) Act 1984;

(f) the Northern Ireland (Emergency Provisions) Act 1978;

(g) the Prevention of Terrorism (Temporary Provisions) Act 1976;

(h) the Prevention of Terrorism (Temporary Provisions) Act 1974;

(i) the Northern Ireland (Emergency Provisions) Act 1973.

It appears that this is merely an evidential burden, not a legal one, imposed on **6.10** a defendant by s 11(2) of the Terrorism Act 2000: *Sheldrake v DPP; Attorney-General's Reference (No 4 of 2002).*[2] This subject is also discussed in Chapter 2.

It would be a clear disregard for the presumption of innocence if a defendant **6.11** charged under s 11(1) was required to establish a s 11(2) defence on the balance of probabilities. A s 11(2)(b) defence may be particularly difficult to prove because such organizations do not keep minutes and witnesses who attend such meetings would be almost impossible to find and they would be reluctant to testify.

If the burden were a legal one, there would be no discretion if the defendant **6.12** failed to prove the specified matters and the court would be obliged to convict. The Court in *Sheldrake* noted that the consequences on conviction were serious. In recognizing that security considerations must always carry weight, the Court did not absolve the state from its duty to ensure basic standards of fairness.

2. Support

An offence is committed, punishable under s 12(1) of the Terrorism Act 2000, if **6.13** a person:

(a) invites support for a proscribed organization; and

(b) the support is not, or is not restricted to, the provision of money or other property (within the meaning of s 15).

A person commits an offence under s 12(2) if he arranges, manages, or assists **6.14** in arranging or managing a meeting which he knows is:

(a) to support a proscribed organization;

(b) to further the activities of a proscribed organization; or

(c) to be addressed by a person who belongs or professes to belong to a proscribed organization.

A person also commits an offence under s 12(3) if he addresses a meeting and **6.15** the purpose of his address is to encourage support for a proscribed organization or to further its activities.

Where a person is charged with an offence under s 12(2)(c) in respect of a **6.16** private meeting it is a defence, under 12(4), for him to prove that he had no reasonable cause to believe that the address mentioned in s 12(2)(c) would support a proscribed organization or further its activities. Again, the defendant bears an evidential burden not a legal one: see s 118 of the 2000 Act.

For the purposes of s 12(2) to (4) above, 'meeting' means a meeting of three **6.17** or more persons, whether or not the public are admitted, and a meeting is private if the public are not admitted.

This offence carries the same penalties as s 11 of the 2000 Act above. **6.18**

---

[2] [2005] 1 AC 264 (HL).

3. Uniform

6.19 A person in a public place commits an offence under s 13(1) of the 2000 Act if he:

(a) wears an item of clothing; or

(b) wears, carries, or displays an article;

in such a way or in such circumstances as to arouse reasonable suspicion that he is a member or supporter of a proscribed organization.

6.20 Pursuant to s 13(3) this is a summary only matter and the penalties are: imprisonment for a term not exceeding six months [51 weeks], a fine not exceeding level 5 on the standard scale, or both.

6.21 In s 13(3)(a), '51 weeks' is substituted for 'six months', as from a day to be appointed, by the Criminal Justice Act 2003, s 281(4) and (5). The increase has no application to offences committed before the substitution takes effect: ibid, s 281(6).

C. GROUNDS FOR PROSCRIPTION

6.22 Section 21 of the 2006 Act widens the grounds for proscription, by amending s 3 of the 2000 Act. A group may be considered to promote or encourage terrorism under s 3(5C) of the 2000 Act, as now amended, if its activities include the unlawful glorification of terrorism or its activities are carried out in a manner that ensures that it is associated with statements containing unlawful glorification of terrorism. Glorification of conduct is unlawful if persons who may become aware of it could reasonably be expected to infer that the conduct is glorified as conduct that should be emulated in existing circumstances. 'Glorification' and 'statement' are both defined in s 3(5C), as now amended, in conformity with the definition in s 20(2), applicable to Part 1. 'Glorification' includes praise and celebration. 'Statement' includes a communication without words consisting of sounds, images, or both. These concepts are discussed in Chapter 2.

6.23 An organization is proscribed for the purposes of the 2000 Act if (under Part II, s 3) it is listed in Sch 2, or if it operates under the same name as an organization listed in that Schedule unless, in this latter case, its entry is the subject of a note in that Schedule.

6.24 The Secretary of State may (pursuant to s 3(3) of the 2000 Act) add an organization to Sch 2, remove an organization from that Schedule, or amend it in some other way.

6.25 The Home Secretary may exercise his power to add to or amend the Schedule in respect of an organization only if he believes that it is concerned in terrorism, according to s 4 of the 2000 Act. An organization is concerned in terrorism if, by s 5, it:

(a) commits or participates in acts of terrorism;

(b) prepares for terrorism;

(c) promotes or encourages terrorism; or

(d) is otherwise concerned in terrorism.

Section 21 of the 2006 Act adds to this framework, stating that 'promotes or **6.26**
encourages terrorism' (s 3(5)(c) of the 2000 Act), above, includes any case in
which the activities of an organization include the unlawful glorification of the
commission or preparation (whether in the past, in the future, or generally) of
acts of terrorism; or are carried out in a manner that ensures that the organization is associated with statements containing any such glorification (the new
s 3(5A)).

Further definition is provided by the insertion of s 3(5B), so that the 'glorifica- **6.27**
tion' of any conduct is unlawful if there are persons who may become aware
of it who could reasonably be expected to infer that what is being glorified, is
being glorified as conduct that should be emulated in existing circumstances, or
conduct that is illustrative of a type of conduct that should be so emulated.

This is in identical terms to s 1(3) of the substantive offence of 'encourage- **6.28**
ment' created by the 2006 Act, discussed in Chapter 2. It will be no easier for the
Home Secretary to grapple with this test than a jury. Section 3(5C), like s 20(2)
for Part 1, says that that 'glorification' includes any form of praise or celebration,
and cognate expressions are to be construed accordingly; 'statement' includes a
communication without words consisting of sounds or images or both.

It is noteworthy that these three new subsections (5A, 5B, and 5C) were late **6.29**
amendments, after the Report stage of the Bill. Previously the Bill proposed
merely to add the following definition to s 5 of the 2000 Act:

The cases in which an organisation promotes or encourages terrorism for the purposes of
subsection (5)(c) include any case in which activities of the organisation indirectly
encourage terrorism, within the meaning of 'indirect encouragement' as specified in
section 1(3) of the Terrorism Act 2006.

This referred back to the originals 1(3) which has itself been amplified. The
intention behind these late amendments was to further define what is meant by
'indirect encouragement', the effect is unwieldy and difficult to apply.

D. NAME CHANGES UNDER THE 2006 ACT

As we have already noted, the Secretary of State may (pursuant to s 3(3) of the **6.30**
2000 Act) add an organization to the proscribed list in Sch 2, remove an organization from it, or amend that Schedule. The 2006 Act gives him an even broader
discretion, to treat organizations that do not appear in the Schedule as if they
were included, pursuant to s 22. This provision adds a number of new subsections to s 3 of the 2000 Act.

6.31   The effect of these amendments is that the Home Secretary can deem that an organization which does appear in the Schedule is also known under a name that does not, or is in reality indistinguishable from one that does not so appear. The name which is not specified in the Act is then treated as if it were in fact included. The purpose is to catch those organizations that deliberately change or rename themselves so as to avoid proscription. It will also encompass groups that splinter into factions, as paramilitary groups in Northern Ireland have tended to do over the last four decades. A problem arises in that similarly-named organizations may in fact be rivals, and the splintering may have been caused by the fact that they have a wholly different purpose and leadership.

6.32   An order under these provisions is subject to the negative resolution procedure. By contrast, an order amending Sch 2 is subject to the affirmative resolution procedure.

6.33   The Government has clearly stated its intention: a principal purpose of the 2006 Act is, 'to allow us to deal, by order, with proscribed groups which change their name. It clearly cannot be desirable for a proscribed group to seek to evade the consequences of proscription simply by changing its name.'[3]

6.34   Thus, the new s 3(6)(a) of the 2000 Act allows the Home Secretary to provide, by order, that where he believes that an organization listed in Sch 2 is operating wholly or partly under a name that is not specified in that Schedule (whether as well as or instead of under the specified name), the name not specified in the Schedule will be treated as if it was so named. This covers the situation where the (fictitious) Cardiff Dragons for a Free Wales, having been named in the Schedule, make a deliberate decision to mobilize under the name Celtic Dragons. The Secretary of State's order that the Celtic Dragons be treated as if they were named in the Schedule can be made either on the basis that the Cardiff Dragons have changed permanently, or merely that they have decided to mobilize for a specific event, for example, a bombing campaign on St David's Day, under the new name though the old organization subsists.

6.35   It is submitted that the order should be based on the fact that the same people/administration are shared by both organizations, or at least that one is 'wholly or partly' included in the other. This is an imprecise test. What if the membership secretary of the Cardiff Dragons organizes half of the Cardiff members for the bombing campaign but recruits the same number again from brigades of international anarchists? It is submitted that the Secretary of State would be justified in holding that this was the Cardiff Dragons 'partly' operating as the Celtic Dragons, albeit with outside help. In the absence of the involvement of an executive member, or a substantial shared membership, the order would not be justified. The issue is, how big a part is 'partly'?

6.36   Plainly it will not suffice that a new group arises with the same objectives, albeit that they be geographically similar. In the example used, the Swansea

---

[3] *Hansard*, HL, vol 675, col 1387 (21 November 2005) per Baroness Scotland.

Jacks for a Free Wales may dislike groups from Cardiff and its rule as much as that of Westminster, though both groups share the greater aim of independence from England. Nor will such an order be justified when one member leaves to start a splinter organization; there have been bloody feuds within paramilitary organizations in Northern Ireland when groups have fragmented. The interests of warring factions may be opposed for the duration of the conflict, and their memberships and organizations distinct.

Further, the new s 3(6)(b) of the 2000 Act gives the Secretary of State the **6.37** power to order that an unspecified name is to be treated as a name appearing in the Schedule where he believes that 'an organisation that is operating under a name that is not so specified is otherwise for all practical purposes the same as an organisation so listed'. This covers the loose association or coalition that is the model for certain so-called Islamic groups. The difficulty arises in determining when a loose association becomes so disparate that it is not proper to classify it as an organization. The London bombings of July 2005 may have been the work of a small group of individuals which had no substantial links to an international organization, though its members and other groups may have had objectives in common. If this is correct the suicide bombers were never members of a proscribed organization.

The 2000 and 2006 Acts only catch acts perpetrated by a defendant while both **6.38** the order made under the above subsections and the listing of the specified name in Sch 2 are in force: s 6(7) of the 2000 Act, as now amended. By way of a fictitious example, it is only an offence to be a member of the unspecified (ie not named in the Schedule) Celtic Dragons at a time when there is an order in force that the organization is also known as, or is for all practical purposes the same as, the Cardiff Dragons, and at that time the Cardiff Dragons are named in the Schedule.

The Secretary of State may at any time, by order, revoke an order under s 3(6) **6.39** that an unspecified name should be treated as if it were included in the Schedule: s 3(8) of the 2000 Act, as now amended. It would be prudent to take this course if, for example, it became plain that a splinter group was no longer acting in concert with the parent organization. In this event both organizations could be listed separately.

It is noteworthy that nothing in the new s 3(6) to (8) prevents the establish- **6.40** ment of liability by proof that an organization is in reality the same as an organization listed in Sch 2, even though it was not operating under a name specified in Sch 2, nor was named in an order under s 3(6): s 3(9) of the 2000 Act, as amended. Thus, there is no technical defence available where the Secretary of State has failed or neglected to list (or order that an organization is treated as if listed) in the Schedule, where in fact the organization in question is the same as the one so listed.

Taking an example, suppose the Schedule includes 'Cardiff Dragons for a **6.41** Free Wales'. XY is charged under s 11(1) of the 2000 Act with being a member of that organization. At his trial the evidence is that the listed organization is based at an identified address, and that the membership secretary is called XY. Further, the defendant was arrested in possession of a membership card in the name of XY, bearing the identified address, XY's correct date of birth, and the title 'membership secretary'. XY takes the point that the slogan on his membership card reads 'Cardiff Dragons—fighting for a free Wales'. He claims to belong to a group simply called the 'Cardiff Dragons' and that its struggle for a free Principality is its central purpose but not part of its name. The two words 'Cardiff Dragons' do not appear in that simple way on the Schedule. Moreover, the Secretary of State has not ordered that a group called 'Cardiff Dragons—fighting for a free Wales' should be treated (s 3(6) of the 2000 Act) as a listed organization. Neither of these facts provides a bar to XY's conviction. On the evidence he is part of the same organization as one listed in the Schedule.

E. PROSCRIBED GROUPS

6.42 There follows the list of proscribed organizations under Terrorism Act 2000, Sch 2, as amended, with notes.[4]

Schedule 2—Proscribed Organisations [5]

The Irish Republican Army

Cumann na mBan

Fianna na hEireann

The Red Hand Commando

Saor Eire

The Ulster Freedom Fighters

The Ulster Volunteer Force

The Irish National Liberation Army

The Irish People's Liberation Organisation

The Ulster Defence Association

The Loyalist Volunteer Force

---

[4] This Schedule is printed as amended by the Terrorism Act 2000 (Proscribed Organisations) (Amendment) Order 2001 (SI 2001/1261); and the Terrorism Act 2000 (Proscribed Organisations) (Amendment) Order 2002 (SI 2002/2724).

[5] Note: The entry for The Orange Volunteers refers to the organization which uses that name and in the name of which a statement described as a press release was published on 14 October 1998.

The entry for Jemaah Islamiyah refers to the organization using that name that is based in southeast Asia, members of which were arrested by the Singapore authorities in December 2001 in connection with a plot to attack US and other Western targets in Singapore.

The Continuity Army Council

The Orange Volunteers

The Red Hand Defenders

Al-Qa'ida

Egyptian Islamic Jihad

Al-Gama'at al-Islamiya

Armed Islamic Group (Groupe Islamique Armée) (GIA)

Salafist Group for Call and Combat (Groupe Salafiste pour la Prédication et le Combat) (GSPC)

Babbar Khalsa

International Sikh Youth Federation

Harakat Mujahideen

Jaish e Mohammed

Lashkar e Tayyaba

Liberation Tigers of Tamil Eelam (LTTE)

Hizballah External Security Organisation

Hamas-Izz al-Din al-Qassem Brigades

Palestinian Islamic Jihad–Shaqaqi

Abu Nidal Organisation

Islamic Army of Aden

Mujaheddin e Khalq

Kurdistan Workers' Party (Partiya Karekeren Kurdistan) (PKK)

Revolutionary Peoples' Liberation Party-Front (Devrimci Halk Kurtulus Partisi-Cephesi) (DHKP-C)

Basque Homeland and Liberty (Euskadi ta Askatasuna) (ETA)

17 November Revolutionary Organisation (N17)

Abu Sayyaf Group

Asbat Al-Ansar

The Islamic Movement for Uzbekistan

Jemaah Islamiyah

The following groups were added to the list by SI 2005/2892: **6.43**

Al Ittihad Al Islamia

Ansar Al Islam

Ansar Al Sunna

Groupe Islamique Combattant Marocain

Harakat-ul-Jihad-ul-Islami

Harakat-ul-Jihad-ul-Islami (Bangladesh)

Harakat-ul-Mujahideen/Alami

Hezb-e Islami Gulbuddin

Islamic Jihad Union

Jamaat ul-Furquan

Jundallah

Khuddam ul-islam

Lashkar-e Jhangvi

Libyan Islamic Fighting Group

Sipah-e Sahaba Pakistan

At the time of going to print, the Home Office says it is keeping 'under review' the status of Hizb ut-Tahir (HT) and Al Muhajiroun groups.

F. DEPROSCRIPTION

1. Overview of Changes Introduced by the 2006 Act

6.44   Section 22(3) to (7) of the 2006 Act make amendments to the scheme of appeal and review of proscription orders. Section 4 of the 2000 Act has always allowed those who have an interest in the proscription of an organization to apply to the Secretary of State to have it deproscribed. Section 22(3) and (4) amend the old s 4 so as to allow similar applications to be made in respect of an order that a name be treated as another name for a listed organization. This is an obvious requirement of fairness; otherwise an unspecified group would be less able to challenge the categorization than one listed.

6.45   Similarly, s 22(5) of the 2006 Act extends the right to appeal to POAC, if the Secretary of State refuses to revoke an order following an application under s 4. An appeal is also available against the POAC's decision under s 6 of the 2000 Act. Again, these are consequential amendments.

6.46   If an appeal is successful under s 5 of the 2000 Act, as amended, the Secretary of State must make an order as provided for in the new s 5(5A) of the 2000 Act, now inserted by s 22(6) of the 2006 Act. Section 22(7) inserts new provisions into s 7 of the 2000 Act and it sets out the effect of a successful appeal on a conviction that was dependent on the proscription of an organization. The practical effects of these changes are considered below.

2. Application to the Secretary of State

6.47   The 2006 Act extends the right to apply for deproscription so as to include organizations (and anyone affected by the fact of an organization's proscription) caught by the wider ambit of s 3 of the 2000 Act, as now amended. So groups (and individuals affected) that are to be treated as if they are listed in the Schedule have the same rights to apply and appeal against that categorization as groups expressly listed: by s 22(3) to (6) of the 2006 Act.

Thus the unspecified Celtic Dragons may apply to the Secretary of State (s 4 **6.48** of the 2000 Act) for an order that they are no longer to be treated as if they were in the Schedule; in the same way as the specified Cardiff Dragons were able (and still are able) to apply for deproscription. At first sight their arguments would be slightly different in that the (unspecified) Celtic Dragons would aim to show they were not in reality the (specified) Cardiff Dragons. By contrast, the named Cardiff Dragons would be arguing against the merits of proscription as a terrorist group.

It should be noted that by virtue of s 10 of the 2000 Act, there is a limited **6.49** immunity from prosecution so that applicants are not discouraged from applying for (or appealing against a refusal of) deproscription. Evidence given in relation to such proceedings 'shall not be admissible as evidence in proceedings for an offence under any of sections 11 to 13, 15 to 19 and 56' of the 2000 Act. This does not provide immunity should the details of more general criminal conduct emerge. In reality any active member of a proscribed organization will be reluctant to challenge the categorization. Whether or not his own evidence is admissible against him, to come forward would alert the Security and Intelligence Services. Admissions against interest are liable to be admitted in evidence in proceedings before immigration tribunals.

3. Appeal Against Refusal by the Secretary of State

If such a group or 'person affected' cannot persuade the Secretary of State to **6.50** deproscribe it or he has an appeal to POAC where an application under s 4 has been refused: s 5(2) of the 2000 Act. The Commission must allow an appeal against a refusal to deproscribe an organization if it considers that the decision to refuse was flawed when looked at in the light of the principles applicable on an application for judicial review: s 5(3) of the 2000 Act.

Where the Commission allows an appeal under this section by or in respect of **6.51** an organization, it may make an order, in which case the Secretary of State shall 'as soon as is reasonably practicable' (s 5(5)) lay before Parliament, in accordance with that section, the draft of an order under the section, removing the organization from the list in Sch 2, or providing that it is no longer to be treated as if it is a name for a listed organization.

A party to an appeal under s 5 which POAC has determined may bring a **6.52** further appeal on a question of law (under s 6 of the 2000 Act) to the Court of Appeal if the first appeal was heard in England and Wales; the Court of Session if the first appeal was heard in Scotland; or the Court of Appeal in Northern Ireland if the first appeal was heard in Northern Ireland. Such an appeal under s 6(2) may be brought only with the permission of the Commission, or where the Commission refuses permission, of the court to which the appeal would be brought.

6.53 An order of the Commission (s 5) shall not require the Secretary of State to take any action until the final determination or disposal of an appeal under this section (including any appeal to the House of Lords).

6.54 A successful appeal in relation to deproscription will have the obvious effect on the conviction of an individual for the substantive offences discussed above. Plainly, a person convicted of an offence of membership of a proscribed organization is not guilty if it subsequently transpires that at the material time it should not have been a proscribed organization. The regime is set out fully in s 7 of the 2000 Act, and is amended to take into account the now wider ambit of s 3 so as to include offences in respect of an organization treated as if it were an organization named in the Schedule, by virtue of s 22(7) of the 2006 Act.

6.55 The regime relating to such convictions applies where an appeal under s 5 has been allowed in respect of an organization, or an order has been made under s 3(3)(b) in respect of the organization in accordance with an order of the Commission under s 5(4) (and, if the order was made in reliance on s 123(5), a resolution has been passed by each House of Parliament under s 123(5)(b)). The important criteria are that a person has been convicted of an offence in respect of the organization under any of ss 11 to 13, 15 to 19, and 56, and crucially that the activity to which the charge referred took place on or after the date of the refusal to deproscribe against which the appeal under s 5 was brought. It is no defence to say that since a defendant was convicted of membership of the proscribed Cardiff Dragons, that group had had recourse to lawful protest only and should now be deproscribed. The conviction is only open to challenge under this regime if the defendant's membership began after the erroneous decision to proscribe.

6.56 If such an individual was convicted on indictment he may appeal against the conviction to the Court of Appeal, and the Court of Appeal must allow the appeal: s 7(2) of the 2000 Act. A person may appeal against a conviction by virtue of s 7(2) whether or not he has already appealed against the conviction. Such an appeal must be brought within the period of 28 days beginning with the date on which the order mentioned in s 7(1)(b) comes into force, and is to be treated as an appeal under s 1 of the Criminal Appeal Act 1968 (but it does not require leave).

6.57 If the person was convicted by a Magistrates' Court, he may appeal against the conviction to the Crown Court, and the Crown Court must allow the appeal. He may appeal against a conviction by virtue of this regime whether or not he pleaded guilty, whether or not he has already appealed against the conviction, and whether or not he has made an application in respect of the conviction under s 111 of the Magistrates' Courts Act 1980 (case stated). Such an appeal must be brought within the period of 21 days beginning with the date on which the order mentioned in s 7(1)(b) comes into force, and will be treated as an appeal under s 108(1)(b) of the Magistrates' Courts Act 1980.

4. Human Rights

If a party to proceedings in relation to proscription wishes to assert that his **6.58**
human rights have been infringed (contrary to s 6(1) of the Human Rights Act
1998), he should raise the argument before POAC, which is the appropriate
court under s 7(1) of the 1998 Act by virtue of s 9 of the 2000 Act. This is
amended by s 22(9) of the 2006 Act, so that similar redress is available to parties
under the expanded s 3 (organizations treated as if their name appeared on the
Schedule).

5. The Nature and Limitations of POAC

POAC provides welcome judicial scrutiny of executive action, with limitations. **6.59**
The statutory basis of POAC is detailed in Sch 3 to the Terrorism Act 2000 (as
amended by SI 2001/443).

The most fundamental limitation (s 5(3) of the 2000 Act) is that the Commis- **6.60**
sion will decide proceedings in accordance with the principles applicable on a
claim for judicial review. A requirement for the re-hearing of the facts de novo
would have provided greater protection and scrutiny.

Potential heads of challenge to the refusal of the Secretary of State to depro- **6.61**
scribe are likely to be limited. Arguments could be mounted on the basis of
jurisdictional errors of substance, other fundamental procedural errors (orders
being properly signed and served by the appropriate Minister), and abuse of
discretion. National security interests will weigh heavily.

The structure of POAC is similar to that of the Special Immigration Appeals **6.62**
Commission ('SIAC'), first introduced by the Special Immigration Appeals Act
1997. Most notably the use of 'special advocates' (by para 7, Sch 3 to the 2000
Act) is common to both, representing but not responsible to (or taking instructions from) the particular party affected by proscription. This allows the special
advocate, but not the affected party, to have access to sensitive material, for
example, the fruits of intercepts under the Regulation of Investigatory Powers
Act 2000. There is express provision allowing for the reasons for proscription to
be withheld from the affected party (para 5(4), Sch 3). This is extended by
s 22(11) of the 2006 Act to include the withholding of full particulars of reasons
from those within the increased remit of s 3 (organizations treated as if they are
named on Sch 2).

Each sitting panel of POAC must consist of three members (para 4(3)(a)), at **6.63**
least one of whom must be a person who holds or has held high judicial office
(within the meaning of the Appellate Jurisdiction Act 1876), (para 4(3)(b)).

A criticism of POAC is that its members lack the tenure of others in high **6.64**
judicial office: this does not give the appearance of robust impartiality.

7

ARREST AND DETENTION
WITHOUT CHARGE

A. OVERVIEW

A constable may, under s 41 of the 2000 Act, arrest without warrant a person **7.01** whom he reasonably suspects of being a terrorist. Such a suspect is now liable to be detained at a police station and questioned by virtue of ss 23 to 25 of the 2006 Act for a total period of 28 days (the Government having initially proposed a period of 90 days). This is a change of fundamental importance in our criminal law.

Within 48 hours of the terrorist explosions in the centre of Birmingham **7.02** city, in which 22 people were killed, the Prevention of Terrorism (Temporary Provisions) Act 1974 ('the 1974 Act') was enacted. Section 7 of that Act gave power to a constable to arrest without warrant a person 'whom he reasonably suspects to be' guilty of various offences relating to proscribed organizations, or exclusion orders, as introduced by ss 1 and 3 of that Act, or a person 'concerned in the commission, preparation or instigation of acts of terrorism'. That person might be detained for no more than 48 hours, but the Secretary of State was empowered to extend that period by another five days.

That Act was renewed annually. In 1988, the European Court of Human **7.03** Rights held in *Brogan v United Kingdom*[1] that this power of detention, under the scheme of the 1974 Act, as modified by the Prevention of Terrorism Act 1976 and renewed, was in breach of Art 5.3 of the European Convention on Human Rights for want of judicial oversight. Article 5 reads:

1. Everyone has the right to liberty and security of person. No one shall be deprived of his liberty save in the following cases and in accordance with a procedure prescribed by law;
   (a) the lawful detention of a person after conviction by a competent court;
   (b) the lawful arrest or detention of a person for non-compliance with the lawful order of a court or in order to secure the fulfilment of any obligation prescribed by law;
   (c) the lawful arrest or detention of a person effected for any purpose of bringing him before the competent legal authority on reasonable suspicion of having committed an offence or when it is reasonably considered necessary to prevent his committing an offence or fleeing after having done so;
   [. . .]
   (e) the lawful arrest or detention of a person to prevent his effecting an unauthorised entry into the country or of a person against whom action is being taken with a view to deportation or extradition.

The Government took recourse to the power to make a derogation from the Convention, which was subsequently upheld as valid in *Brannigan and McBride v United Kingdom*.[2]

7.04 However, the provisions of s 41 of and Sch 8 to the 2000 Act were intended, in part, to be compliant with Art 5 by introducing judicial supervision, while retaining the seven-day maximum period. By s 306 of the Criminal Justice Act 2003, the 2000 Act was amended so as to extend the period from 7 to 14 days.

7.05 The extended period beyond 14 days' detention is to be reviewed by a High Court judge. The application to extend the period of detention may now be made by Crown prosecutors, in addition to police officers above the rank of superintendent. The grounds for extending the period of detention of terrorist subjects now include awaiting the results of forensic enquiry or analysis.

7.06 The role of the review officer remains intact, as established by the 2000 Act.

B. ARREST WITHOUT WARRANT OF TERRORIST SUSPECTS

7.07 The power set out in s 41 is broad. It does not require contemplation of a specific offence at the time of arrest, and does not require disclosure to the accused or his representatives as detailed as would follow arrest under the normal criminal justice regime.

7.08 A terrorist is, by virtue of s 40 of the 2000 Act, a person who either has committed an offence under ss 11, 12, 15–18, 54, and 56–63 of the 2000 Act; or

---

[1] (1989) 11 EHRR 539.
[2] (1994) 17 EHRR 539.

'is or has been concerned in the commission, preparation or instigation of acts of terrorism' (a definition essentially identical to that first set out in the 1974 Act). In s 1 of the 2000 Act, 'terrorism' means the use or threat of action where the action falls within s 1(2), where the use or threat is designed to influence the government or to intimidate the public or a section of the public, and where the use or threat is made for the purpose of advancing a political, religious, or ideological cause.

Action falls within s 1(2) if it involves serious violence against a person, or serious damage to property, or if it endangers life, creates a serious risk to health or safety, or is designed seriously to interfere with or disrupt an electronic system.   **7.09**

The use or threat of action falling within s 1(2) which involves the use of firearms or explosives is terrorism whether or not s 1(1)(b) is satisfied; so that campaigns using firearms or explosives are categorized as terrorist offences whether or not the action is designed to influence the government or influence people.   **7.10**

For these purposes of the definition, 'action' includes action outside the United Kingdom. The reference to any person or to property is a reference to any person, or to property, wherever situated. The reference to the public includes the public of a country other than the United Kingdom, and 'the government' means the government of the United Kingdom, of a part of the United Kingdom or of a country other than the United Kingdom. In the 2000 Act, a reference to action taken for the purposes of terrorism includes a reference to action taken for the benefit of a proscribed organization.   **7.11**

The test of 'reasonable suspicion' is similar to the requirement of the general power of arrest for arrestable offences as set out in ss 24 and 25 of the Police and Criminal Evidence Act 1984 ('the 1984 Act').   **7.12**

This power to arrest someone reasonably suspected of being a 'terrorist' will not be in breach of Art 5.1(c) of the ECHR for lack of certainty. The point was taken in relation to a similar provision in the case of *Brogan v United Kingdom*[3] under the Prevention of Terrorism (Temporary Provisions) Act 1976, the successor to the 1974 Act. The long 2000 Act definition is extended by s 34 of the 2006 Act to include actions and threats designed to influence not merely a government but 'an international governmental organisation', including, presumably, the United Nations, the European Union, and NATO.   **7.13**

This intention is evident in a letter of 25 October 2005 from Rt Hon Charles Clarke MP, Home Secretary, to members of the Joint Committee on Human Rights, 'We are making one slight change to that definition in the Bill to ensure that threat to international organisations, such as the United Nations, as well as to national governments is covered.'[4]   **7.14**

---

[3] (1989) 11 EHRR 539, para 50.
[4] HC 561–11, 2005, Ev 59.

7.15 Later in the letter he explained:

My view, therefore, is that we need to stick with the definition that we have. An important safeguard is that any prosecutions for offences in Part 1 of the Terrorism Bill require the consent of the Director of Public Prosecutions or Attorney General which will ensure that prosecutions which are not in the public interest do not take place.

C. DETENTION

7.16 In the absence of authorization for continued detention, a terror suspect must be released after 48 hours in custody. The first stage of an extension arises under a 'warrant of further detention' (para 29, Sch 8 to the 2000 Act) for an initial maximum period of seven days from the time of arrest. A subsequent extension is by way of 'extension of warrant' to a maximum of 28 days from arrest, under para 36, as inserted by s 25(3) of the 2006 Act.

7.17 The power to detain initially is found in s 41(3) of the 2000 Act which provides that, subject to s 41(4) to (7), a person detained must, unless detained under any other power, be released not later than the end of the period of 48 hours beginning with the time of his arrest under this section. If he was being detained under Sch 7 to the 2000 Act (Port and Border Controls) when he was arrested under this section, the clock begins to run from the time when his examination under that Schedule began. The maximum period is also 48 hours.

7.18 An officer 'independent' of the enquiry must review the detention of a terror suspect. If, on a review of a person's detention under Part II of Sch 8 to the 2000 Act, the review officer does not authorize continued detention, the person must, unless detained in accordance with s 41(5) or (6), or under any other power, be released: s 41(4) of the 2000 Act. Where a police officer intends to make an application for a warrant under para 29 of Sch 8 (Warrant of Extension of Detention) to the 2000 Act to extend a person's detention, he may be detained pending the making of the application: s 41(5).

7.19 In the event that an application is made under para 29 (Warrant of Extension) or para 36 (Application to Extend Warrant) of Sch 8 in respect of a person's detention, he may also be detained pending the conclusion of hearings on the application: s 41(6). It is submitted that those detained for extended periods are entitled to expeditious hearings.

7.20 Where an application under paras 29 or 36 is granted in respect of a person's detention, it is obvious that he may be detained, subject to para 37 of that Schedule (the conditions set out in the warrant no longer applying), for the period specified in the warrant: s 41(7). Moreover, the refusal of an application to extend a person's detention under paras 29 or 36 of Sch 8 does not prevent his continued detention in accordance with this section: s 41(8), so that he can be detained in any event for the balance of the period authorized already.

7.21 A person who has the powers of a constable in one part of the United Kingdom may exercise the power in any part of the United Kingdom: s 41(9).

This gives additional flexibility to the police, though in practice the investigation of terrorism will normally be carried out by specialist units.

1. People Who May Apply for an Extension

Previously, only a police officer of at least the rank of superintendent could make such an application. Section 23(2) of the 2006 Act extends the categories of persons who may apply to extend the detention of a terrorist suspect, from a police officer of at least the rank of superintendent, to: **7.22**

(a) in England and Wales, a Crown prosecutor;

(b) in Scotland, the Lord Advocate or a procurator fiscal;

(c) in Northern Ireland, the Director of Public Prosecutions for Northern Ireland;

(d) in any part of the United Kingdom, a police officer of at least the rank of superintendent.

2. Warrant of Further Detention: Paragraph 29 of Schedule 8

Such a warrant may allow detention for a period up to seven days from the time of arrest. The role of the 'review officer' ceases when a warrant of further detention is issued. The presumption is that the extension will be for a period of seven days (para 29(3)) unless the application is for a shorter period or the court does not think it appropriate to extend for seven days. **7.23**

Any authorized person may apply to a 'judicial authority' for the issue of a warrant of further detention, beyond the initial 48 hours, under para 29(1). **7.24**

Such a warrant authorizes the further detention under s 41 of a specified person for a specified period, and must state the time at which it is issued: para 29(2). **7.25**

This specified period is a maximum of seven days, starting from the time of the person's arrest under s 41, or, if he was being detained under Sch 7 (Port and Border Control) when he was arrested under s 41, from the time when his examination under that Schedule began: para 29(3). **7.26**

The 2006 Act inserts a new subparagraph (3A) into para 29(3), stating that the judicial authority may issue a warrant of further detention for a shorter period than seven days. This may be issued if either the application specifies a shorter period or the judicial authority so rules. **7.27**

3. 'Judicial Authority'

In Part III of Sch 8 to the 2000 Act, 'judicial authority' means, by para 29(4): **7.28**

(a) in England and Wales, . . . a District Judge (Magistrates' Courts) who is designated for the purpose of this Part by the Lord Chancellor [Lord Chief Justice of England and Wales after consulting the Lord Chancellor];

(b) in Scotland, the sheriff; and

(c) in Northern Ireland, a county court judge, or a resident magistrate who is designated for the purpose of this Part by the Lord Chancellor.

The Lord Chief Justice may nominate a judicial office holder (as defined in s 109(4) of the Constitutional Reform Act 2005) to exercise his functions under subparagraph (4)(a).

4. 'Senior Judge'

7.29 For the purposes of para 36, a 'senior judge' means a judge of the High Court, or the Scottish equivalent in an appropriate case: para 36(7).

5. Extension of Warrant of Detention: Paragraph 36 of Schedule 8

7.30 Extensions of the warrant of detention have an absolute aggregate maximum of 28 days from the time of arrest. Each individual extension beyond the first 14 days can be for no longer than 7 days each. Applications can be made by the same list of people as set out above, namely, police officers of at least the rank of superintendent and Crown prosecutors. Again, the presumption is that the period of extension will be for 7 days (Sch 8, para 36) as amended, unless the application is for a shorter period or the tribunal does not think such a period is appropriate.

7.31 The tribunal to whom the application is made will either be a 'judicial authority' or a 'senior judge'. The basic rule is that there is no need to take the application before a High Court judge provided that the period of extension sought is not greater than 14 days from the time of arrest: para 36(1A). The exception is where a senior judge has already been seized of such an application in the proceedings: para 36(1A(b)).

7.32 After two weeks' detention it is necessary to seek an extension from a High Court judge. Paragraph 36(2) provides that where the period specified is extended, the warrant shall be endorsed with a note setting out the new period.

7.33 Warrants may be extended for up to 7 days at a time, within the aggregate maximum of 28 days: new para 36(3). Time begins to run from the end of the period specified in the original warrant, or the end of the most recent extension: para 36(3A).

7.34 There is a discretion (para 36(3AA)) in the judicial authority or senior judge to extend or further extend the period specified in a warrant by a shorter period than is required by (para 36(3A)), if the application is for a shorter period or the tribunal thinks it appropriate to extend for a shorter period than requested. A practical example would be if the court is assured that forensic results will be available within 48 hours of the expiry of detention. The tribunal might in any event be satisfied that there are circumstances that would make it inappropriate for the period of the extension to be as long as the period requested.

A judicial authority may adjourn the hearing of an application under para 36(1) only if the hearing is adjourned to a date before the expiry of the period specified in the warrant: para 36(5). It would defeat the safeguards set out in the Act if the hearing could be adjourned while a detainee was in custody. **7.35**

D. RIGHTS OF A DETAINED TERROR SUSPECT

The regime under Part I of Sch 8 to the 2000 Act continues under the 2006 Act. **7.36**

A detained person is deemed to be in legal custody throughout the period of his detention: Sch 8, para 5 to the 2000 Act. Schedule 8 sets out the places at which suspects may be detained (police stations and other places designated by the Secretary of State, para 1). It makes provision for taking steps reasonably necessary to identify the detainee by photography and measurement, but not through the taking of samples (para 2). **7.37**

1. Right to Have a Person Informed of the Fact of Detention

A detained person has the right to have one named person informed that he is being held at a police station: Sch 8, para 6(1). The person named must be a friend of the detained person, a relative, or a person who is known to him or who is likely to take an interest in his welfare: para 6(2). There are exceptions to this general rule, set out below. Where a detained person is transferred from one police station to another, he is entitled to exercise the right under this paragraph in respect of the police station to which he is transferred: para 6(3). **7.38**

2. Right to Consult a Solicitor

A person detained under Sch 7 or s 41 at a police station in England, Wales, or Northern Ireland is entitled, if he so requests, to consult a solicitor as soon as is reasonably practicable, privately and at any time: Sch 8, para 7(1). Where a request is made under para 7(1), the request and the time at which it was made must be recorded: para 7(2). **7.39**

3. Rights May Be Delayed

An officer of at least the rank of superintendent may authorize a delay (para 8(1)) in informing the person named by a detained person under para 6 and/or in permitting a detained person to consult a solicitor under para 7. Save that where a person is detained under s 41 he must be permitted to exercise his rights under paras 6 and 7 within 48 hours of his arrest. **7.40**

7.41 An officer may give an authorization under para 8(1) only if he has reasonable grounds for believing (para 8(3) and (4)) that one or more of the following consequences will occur:

(a) interference with or harm to evidence of a serious arrestable offence;

(b) interference with or physical injury to any person;

(c) the alerting of persons who are suspected of having committed a serious arrestable offence but who have not been arrested for it;

(d) the hindering of the recovery of property obtained as a result of a serious arrestable offence or in respect of which a forfeiture order could be made under s 23;

(e) interference with the gathering of information about the commission, preparation, or instigation of acts of terrorism;

(f) the alerting of a person and thereby making it more difficult to prevent an act of terrorism; and

(g) the alerting of a person and thereby making it more difficult to secure a person's apprehension, prosecution, or conviction in connection with the commission, preparation, or instigation of an act of terrorism.

7.42 An officer may also delay access to these rights where he has reasonable grounds for believing that (para 8(5)):

(a) the detained person has benefited from his criminal conduct; and

(b) the recovery of the value of the property constituting the benefit will be hindered by—

(i) informing the named person of the detained person's detention,

(ii) the exercise of the right under para 7 to consult a solicitor.

7.43 For these purposes the question whether a person has benefited from his criminal conduct is to be decided in accordance with Part 2 of the Proceeds of Crime Act 2002.

7.44 If an authorization to delay is given orally, the person giving it must confirm it in writing as soon as is reasonably practicable: para 8(6). The detained person must be told the reason for the delay as soon as is reasonably practicable, and the reason must be recorded as soon as is reasonably practicable: para 8(7).

7.45 Where the reason for authorizing delay ceases to subsist there 'may be no further delay in permitting the exercise of the right in the absence of a further authorisation': para 8(8).

7.46 'Serious arrestable offence' has the meaning given by s 116 of the 1984 Act (in relation to England and Wales) and by para 87 of the Police and Criminal Evidence (Northern Ireland) Order 1989 (in relation to Northern Ireland); but it also includes [references to a 'serious offence' are (in relation to England and Wales) to an indictable offence, and (in relation to Northern Ireland) to a serious arrestable offence within the meaning of paragraph 87 of the Police and Criminal Evidence (Northern Ireland) Order 1989; but also include]—

(a) an offence under any of the provisions mentioned in s 40(1)(a) of this Act, and

(b) an attempt or conspiracy to commit an offence under any of the provisions mentioned in s 40(1)(a).

This provision is written as amended by the Proceeds of Crime Act 2002, **7.47** s 456 and Sch 11, para 39(1) and (2); and as amended, as from a day to be appointed, by the Serious Organised Crime and Police Act 2005, s 111 and Sch 7, para 48 (insertion of words in square brackets).

4. Overheard Consultation with a Solicitor

A detained person who wishes to exercise the right under para 7 may only be **7.48** allowed to consult a solicitor in the sight and hearing of a qualified officer: Sch 8, para 9(1). Such a direction under this paragraph may be given where the person is detained at a police station in England or Wales, by an officer of at least the rank of Commander or Assistant Chief Constable, or where the person is detained at a police station in Northern Ireland, by an officer of at least the rank of Assistant Chief Constable: para 9(2).

A direction may be given only if the officer giving it has reasonable grounds **7.49** for believing that, unless the direction is given, the exercise of the right by the detained person will have any of the consequences specified.

In this provision 'a qualified officer' means a police officer who is of at least **7.50** the rank of Inspector, is of the uniformed branch of the force of which the officer giving the direction is a member, and in the opinion of the officer giving the direction, has no connection with the detained person's case: para 9(4). A direction under this paragraph shall cease to have effect once the reason for giving it ceases to subsist: para 9(5).

Such a supervised consultation will seldom be of any practical value to a **7.51** detainee; it would plainly be inappropriate for the lawyer to take instructions within the sight and hearing of the investigating authorities. The benefit of such consultation will not extend beyond the communication of basic messages and support, and information as to the conditions in which the detained person is being held.

The provisions of the 2000 Act in relation to the taking of fingerprints and **7.52** samples are not amended by the 2006 Act.

5. The Role of the Review Officer

A person's detention must be periodically reviewed by a review officer: Sch 8, **7.53** para 21(1). The first review shall be carried out as soon as is reasonably practicable after the time of the person's arrest: para 21(2). Subsequent reviews shall, subject to para 22, be carried out at intervals of not more than 12 hours: para 21(3).

No review of a person's detention shall be carried out after a warrant extend- **7.54** ing his detention has been issued under Sch 8, Part III: para 21(4); in other words, there is no role for the reviewing officer once a para 29 warrant of further detention is issued, nor when that warrant is extended under para 36.

7.55 A review may be postponed (para 22) if at the latest time at which it may be carried out in accordance with para 21:

(a) the detained person is being questioned by a police officer and an officer is satisfied that an interruption of the questioning to carry out the review would prejudice the investigation in connection with which the person is being detained;
(b) no review officer is readily available; or
(c) it is not practicable for any other reason to carry out the review.

7.56 Where a review is postponed it shall be carried out as soon as is reasonably practicable. For the purposes of ascertaining the time within which the next review is to be carried out, a postponed review shall be deemed to have been carried out at the latest time at which it could have been carried out in accordance with para 21.

7.57 A review officer may authorize a person's continued detention only if satisfied that it is necessary (para 23(1)) as amended by s 24(1) the 2006 Act which adds (subparagraph (ba)):

(a) to obtain relevant evidence whether by questioning him or otherwise;
(b) to preserve relevant evidence;
(ba) pending the result of an examination or analysis of any relevant evidence or of anything the examination or analysis of which is to be or is being carried out with a view to obtaining relevant evidence;
(c) pending a decision whether to apply to the Secretary of State for a deportation notice to be served on the detained person;
(d) pending the making of an application to the Secretary of State for a deportation notice to be served on the detained person;
(e) pending consideration by the Secretary of State whether to serve a deportation notice on the detained person; or
(f) pending a decision whether the detained person should be charged with an offence.

7.58 The addition of para 23(1)(ba) was made in contemplation of the need to analyse forensic samples of DNA, handwriting, and fingerprints. It is also a useful provision for prosecuting authorities awaiting the results of mobile phone billing or cell site analysis. This is a very wide provision indeed; it is difficult to conceive of a case where there would not be outstanding enquiries to be made 'with a view to obtaining relevant evidence' from at least one mobile telephone or forensic sample. Such, in the experience of practitioners, is the workload of experts that this justification is likely to subsist throughout the 28-day extended period of detention before charge.

7.59 By virtue of para 23(1)(a) or (b) above, the review officer must not authorize continued detention unless he is satisfied that the investigation in connection with which the person is detained is being conducted diligently and expeditiously (para 23(2)). Although the review officer must be unconnected with the investigation, some may be sceptical at the likelihood of a police officer releasing a terror suspect on the ground that a fellow officer is acting without expedition.

The review officer must not authorize continued detention by virtue of para 23(1)(c) to (f) unless he is satisfied that the process pending the completion of which detention is necessary is being conducted diligently and expeditiously. **7.60**

'Relevant evidence' means evidence which relates to the commission by the detained person of an offence under any of the provisions mentioned in s 40(1)(a) of the 2000 Act, the substantive terrorist offences; or is evidence which indicates that the detained person falls within s 40(1)(b), 'is or has been concerned in the commission, preparation or instigation of acts of terrorism.' (See also the 2000 Act, s 1.) **7.61**

6. Selecting the Review Officer

The review officer must be an officer who has not been directly involved in the investigation in connection with which the person is detained (para 24(1)). In the case of a review carried out within the period of 24 hours beginning with the time of arrest, the review officer shall be an officer of at least the rank of Inspector (para 24(2)). For subsequent reviews the review officer shall be an officer of at least the rank of superintendent (para 24(3)). **7.62**

Paragraph 25 of Sch 8 applies where the review officer is of a rank lower than superintendent and the officer of higher rank gives directions relating to the detained person, and those directions are at variance with the performance by the review officer of a duty imposed on him under this Schedule. In this event the review officer must refer the matter at once to an officer of at least the rank of superintendent to resolve the issue. **7.63**

7. Representations

Under para 26(1) of Sch 8, before determining whether to authorize a person's continued detention, a review officer must give either of the following persons an opportunity to make representations about the detention: the detained person or a solicitor representing him who is available at the time of the review. Representations may be oral or written. However, the review officer may refuse to hear oral representations from the terror suspect if the officer considers that the detainee is unfit to make representations because of his condition or behaviour. **7.64**

If a review officer authorizes continued detention he must inform the detained person of any of his rights under paras 6 and 7 which he has not yet exercised (to inform someone of his custody and consult a solicitor), and where the exercise of any of his rights under either of those paragraphs is being delayed in accordance with the provisions of para 8, of the fact that it is being so delayed (para 27(1)). **7.65**

Where a review of a person's detention is being carried out at a time when his exercise of a right under either of those paragraphs is being delayed the review **7.66** officer must consider whether the reason or reasons for which the delay was authorized continue to subsist, and if in his opinion the reason or reasons have ceased, he must inform the officer who authorized the delay of his opinion, unless he was that officer (para 27(2)).

7.67 A review officer carrying out a review must keep a written record of the outcome of the review and, if applicable, the grounds upon which continued detention is authorized; the reason for postponement of the review; the fact that the detained person has been informed as required under para 27(1); the officer's conclusion on the matter considered under para 27(2); and all other decisions in respect of custody under this regime (para 28(1)).

7.68 The record made by the review officer must be made in the presence of the detained person, and the officer must also inform him at that time whether he (the review officer) is authorizing continued detention, and if he is, of his grounds (para 28(2)).

7.69 Common sense exceptions apply to this requirement to make entries in the record in the presence of the terror suspect. There is no such requirement in circumstances when, at the time when the record is made, the detained person is incapable of understanding what is said to him, violent, or likely to become violent, or in urgent need of medical attention (para 28(3)).

E. JUDICIAL GROUNDS FOR EXTENDING DETENTION

7.70 The major innovation of the 2006 Act is, by ss 24(2) et seq, to confer on a judge a power to authorize extended detention pending the outcome of forensic enquiry.

7.71 A judicial authority may issue a warrant of further detention if it is satisfied that there are reasonable grounds to believe that such detention is necessary for one of the following reasons, where the investigation is being conducted diligently and expeditiously: Sch 8, para 32; to obtain relevant evidence whether by questioning him or otherwise to preserve relevant evidence; or pending the result of an examination or analysis of any relevant evidence or of anything the examination or analysis of which is to be or is being carried out with a view to obtaining relevant evidence.

7.72 There is a transitional provision; s 24(6) of the 2006 Act states that the amendments in this section do not apply in a case where the arrest (or Sch 7 examination) took place before commencement.

F. RELEASE

7.73 Section 23(11) of the 2006 Act replaces the old Sch 8, para 37 (detention-conditions), with a provision that requires a person in charge of a detainee to release the person if any of the grounds of further detention no longer subsists.

A duty is imposed on an officer coming to this conclusion who is not in charge 7.74
of a detainee to inform the officer who has custody, and another duty is imposed
on that officer to release upon notification (para 37(3)).

A transitional provision (2000 Act, s 23(12)) provides that this section does 7.75
not apply to those arrested (or interviewed under Sch 7) before commencement
of the same, in which case the old rules apply.

The safeguards are that an authorization may be given only if the person 7.76
giving it considers it expedient for the prevention of acts of terrorism. There are
detailed rules about who may authorize such areas and places (see s 44(4)). For
example, an authorization may be given where the specified area or place is
the whole or part of the Metropolitan Police district, by a police officer for the
district who is of at least the rank of Commander of the Metropolitan Police. In
any event, if an authorization is given orally, the person giving it shall confirm it
in writing as soon as is reasonably practicable.

There is a detailed new regime for the search of premises, considered in 7.77
Chapter 8.

G. 'SUNSET' SECTION

Section 25 of the 2006 Act provides that the regime of extended maximum 7.78
detention period will end or be renewed a year after commencement. It was
the Government's stated intention that 'The power to hold people for up
to 28 days prior to charge in terrorist cases will lapse and the limit will
revert to 14 days unless there is an annual renewal vote in both Houses of
Parliament.'[5]

The precise mechanics are as follows. The effect of s 25 of the 2006 Act is that, 7.79
in respect of the extended maximum aggregate pre-charge detention in terrorist
cases (to 28 days), the amendments made by s 23 will cease to apply one year
after their commencement unless continued in force by an order made by the
Secretary of State. In other words, if the Secretary of State does not make an
order the maximum period of detention will revert to 14 days. This order is
subject to the affirmative resolution procedure, that is, it must be approved by a
resolution of both Houses of Parliament.

Section 25(1) states that s 25 will apply if more than a year has passed since 7.80
the commencement of s 23, and an order is not in force disapplying this section.
Section 25(2) provides that the Secretary of State may make an order (by statutory instrument) disapplying this section for up to a period of one year. The
power can be used on more than one occasion. Section 25(3) further sets out
that, if no order disapplying this section is made under s 25(2), the maximum
period that an individual can be detained under the 2000 Act is limited to 14 days.

---

[5] *Hansard*, HL, vol 675, col 1387 (21 November 2005) per Baroness Scotland.

It further provides that in this event the necessary modifications to paras 36 and 37 of Sch 8, as set out in s 25(4), will have effect.

7.81 The overall effect of those amendments is that if the maximum period of detention reverts to 14 days, all applications for extension of detention will be made to a judicial authority. This is consistent, as under the provisions inserted into Sch 8 to the 2000 Act by s 23 of the 2006 Act, a 'senior judge' is only concerned in applications for extension of detention beyond 14 days. If it is not possible to extend detention beyond 14 days there is no need for such a senior judge to be involved. Section 25(5) provides that in the case of an individual who has been detained for a period longer than 14 days under the 2000 Act at any point in time at which this section applies, the person having custody of that individual must release him forthwith, even if his detention had been authorized to continue for longer at a time prior to this section applying. Section 25(6) states that the order disapplying s 25 of the 2006 Act will be subject to the affirmative resolution procedure, requiring a resolution of both Houses of Parliament.

7.82 In the light of the history of the 1974 Act it seems likely that the sun will be slow in setting on the provisions of the 2006 Act.

H. COMMENTARY

7.83 The Police and Criminal Evidence Act 1984 was intended to provide a comprehensive code for the treatment and detention of persons accused of serious criminal offences, though the Prevention of Terrorism (Temporary Provisions) Acts continued as a wholly separate scheme applicable to a much more limited class of offences. So long as the maximum period of police detention permitted under the latter statutory scheme remained seven days, as it did from 1974 until its repeal in 2000, and from 2000 to 2003 under the 2000 Act, the fact that there were differences between the two schemes was of little practical significance. Now that the period of maximum detention has been raised in two stages from 7 to 28 days the distinctions between the two statutory schemes are very important.

7.84 Under s 37(1) of the 1984 Act, before amendment in 2003 (discussed below), the custody officer had to consider after arrest whether he had 'sufficient evidence to charge that person for the offence for which he was arrested'. If not, he had to release him on bail or without bail, unless he had 'reasonable grounds for believing that his detention without being charged is necessary to secure or preserve evidence relating to an offence for which he is in custody or to obtain such evidence by questioning him.' This test applies to further decisions, taken either by a senior officer or a Magistrates' Court, to extend detention up to the maximum period of 96 hours that a person may be kept at the police station.

7.85 Code C, para 16.1 of the 2003 Codes of Practice issued by the Secretary of State under s 66 of the 1984 Act reads:

when the officer in charge of the investigation reasonably believes there is sufficient evidence to provide a realistic prospect of the detainee's conviction (see paragraph 11.6), he shall without delay and subject to the following qualification inform the custody officer who will be responsible for considering whether or not the detainee should be charged.

The Courts have not always insisted that evidence obtained by interviews after **7.86** it has become clear there is a sufficient basis to charge should be excluded in evidence,[6] but the limited circumstances in which questioning is permitted while a suspect is detained are nonetheless clear. Under the scheme of the 1974 and 2000 Acts, however, it is irrelevant whether there is sufficient evidence to permit a charge. The provisions of the 2000 Act are in fact silent about the timing of any charge. Paragraphs 23(1) and 32(1) of Sch 8 provide that one of the conditions of further detention is the necessity 'to obtain further evidence whether by questioning him or otherwise', but this is not limited to the necessity of finding evidence in order to charge, or evidence relevant to the offence for which the person has been arrested; the decision maker could still consider it 'necessary' even if there is an abundance of evidence against the suspect already.

The other striking difference between the two schemes is to be found in the **7.87** provisions relating to legal advice. The 2000 Act provisions for delaying access to legal advice and for withholding the right to a private consultation are open to abuse. The Terrorism Act 2000 (Code of Practice on Audio Recording of Interviews) Order 2001 (SI 2001/159) and the Terrorism Act 2000 (Code of Practice on Audio Recording of Interviews) (No 2) Order 2001 (SI 2001/189) require that any interview be audio-recorded according to the Code. The Secretary of State was obliged to create such a Code by Sch 8, para 3. (He was also given a discretion by para 3(4) of Sch 8 to make an order as to video recording of such interviews, but has not yet done so.)

In spite of the tape-recording requirement, it seems inevitable, if these provi- **7.88** sions are used with any frequency, that assertions will be made by the police, as regularly occurred before the 1984 Act was introduced, that a person confessed through his cell door; as he was being taken to the shower; when the tape had expired, etc. It will be deeply frustrating for juries to have no independent means of discovering where the truth will lie, and, as before, there will be a tendency in the jury in grave or emotional cases to conclude that it has no practical alternative but to trust the account of the police, for fear of releasing a dangerous man.

These new amendments appear almost to be designed to facilitate mistreat- **7.89** ment and to exert psychological pressure upon suspected persons. Other purposes have been set out above. Most of the supposed objectives of the new regime could be accomplished while the defendant was remanded to prison in the

---

[6] See, for example, *R v McGuiness* [1998] Crim LR 502; *R v Pointer* [1997] Crim LR 676; cf *R v Coleman, Knight and Hochenberg* (CA, 20 October 1995) (94/4814/X4).

conventional way after charge. It is extremely difficult to envisage circumstances in which 'reasonable grounds' could exist for suspecting that a person was a terrorist, but the police would not have sufficient evidence to charge him within the time constraints allowed by the 1984 Act. The 20 years in which that scheme has operated has not shown that an extended period is necessary in, for example, grave charges of murder, serious or complex fraud, or drug trafficking.

7.90   Further, little evidence is required to charge a person in any event, and less in the case terrorism allegations than cases of conventional crime, as is obvious from the breadth of the offences created by the 2000 and 2006 Acts.

7.91   The common law made no formal difference between the material relevant for arrest and for 'charge'. In fact, a person arrested did not need to be the subject of a formal 'charge' by police at all, since he was 'charged' on arrest. See, for example, *Christie v Leachinsky*.[7] As Lord Devlin put it in *The Criminal Prosecution in England:* 'The police have no power to detain anyone unless they charge him with a specified crime and arrest him accordingly.'[8] At common law the defendant could be taken directly to the Magistrates' Court on arrest, though the Judges' Rules recognized from 1912 that there may have been some differences between the cautions appropriate to arrest and the act of formal charging, when that occurred in fact at a police station. Rule 5(3) of the Magistrates' Courts Rules 1952 recognized this:

After the evidence for the prosecution has been given, the court shall, unless it decides not to commit for trial, cause the charge to be written down, if this had not already been done, and read it to the accused, and shall explain it to him in ordinary language.

7.92   In the two decades before the enactment of the 1984 Act, it became common for the police to detain people for several days before charging them, a development tolerated and condoned by the criminal courts, which had previously shown an aversion to the use of evidence emerging from such detention, ever since the days of the Star Chamber. In a few notorious cases the periods extended to a week. A number of authorities illustrate this increased tolerance.[9] The false notion became current that there was a substantial difference between the standard of material required for an arrest, and that required for charge. The use of confession evidence became regular in crime on indictment, and in serious cases of terrorism, murder, armed robbery, etc, the use of actual or imputed confessions became the central and standard feature of most trials on indictment.

7.93   The new belief that different standards were necessary for charging underlay the statutory consent to periods of pre-charge detention in the 1984 Act.

---

[7] [1947] AC 573.
[8] (OUP, 1960), p 68.
[9] For example, *Commissioners of Excise v Harz and Power* [1967] 1 AC 760; *DPP v Ping Lin* [1976] AC 574; *R v Sang* [1980] AC 402; *R v Rennie* (1982) 74 Cr App R 207.

However, the changes to s 37 of the 1984 Act effected by s 28 of, and Sch 2 **7.94** to, the Criminal Justice Act 2003 show in this limited respect a return to the common law/Lord Devlin approach. Under s 37A of the 1984 Act, as amended, the Director of Public Prosecutions may issue guidance to custody officers in the matter of decisions as to charge. The Director has now given guidance and formulated a threshold test, and made the appropriate expertise available to the police at all times under the 'CPS Direct' scheme.

Whereas the normal test as to whether a person should be charged is whether **7.95** there is enough evidence to provide a reasonable prospect of conviction,[10] there is now a 'threshold test' in cases where it is inappropriate to release a suspect on bail. In such cases (s 6 of the Code) a person may be charged if:

there is at least a reasonable suspicion against the person of having committed an offence (in accordance with Article 5 of the European Convention on Human Rights) and that at that stage it is in the public interest to proceed.

The evidential decision in each case will require consideration of a number of factors including: the evidence available at the time and the likelihood and nature of further evidence being obtained; the reasonableness for believing that evidence will become available; the time that it will take and the steps being taken to gather it; the impact of the expected evidence on the case; and the charges the totality of the evidence will support.

It is for this reason that it is not necessary, for want of formal evidence, to **7.96** release a person without charge if he has been arrested under the 2000 or 2006 Acts. Would it not be possible, at the very least, to charge him with the offence of preparation of terrorist acts, contrary to s 5[11] of the 2006 Act?

It is submitted that the real reason for the creation of the 28-day rule must **7.97** have been to facilitate interrogation. The consequences of unregulated interrogation as it developed between 1960 and 1984 included a long and deplorable succession of miscarriages of justice, and the quashing of convictions from 1989 onwards (the 'Birmingham Six' and innumerable others) convicted on the basis of dubious confessions obtained many years earlier.

Because the provisions of the 1984 Act have been generally successful, the **7.98** dangers of the misuse of police station confessions are less immediate to modern criminal lawyers. The Judges Rules of 1964, a reformulation of the 1912 Rules contained the following summary of the common law approach,[12] which until the 1960s made pointless any period of police detention extending beyond the earliest time it was practical to take suspects to court:

It is a fundamental principle of the admissibility in evidence against any person equally of any answer given by that person to a question put by a police officer, or of any

---

[10] See s 5 of the Code for Crown Prosecutors, issued annually under the provisions of s 10 of the Prosecution of Offences Act 1985; <www.cps.gov.uk>.
[11] As discussed in Chapter 3.
[12] See, for example, *Ibrahim v R* [1914] AC 559.

statement made by that person, that it shall have been voluntary in the sense that it has not been obtained from him by fear or prejudice or hope of advantage exercised or held out by a person in authority or by oppression.

7.99   The provisions of the 2000 and 2006 Acts, providing for long periods of pre-trial detention, are dangerous. The supervising judges will have no detailed knowledge of the circumstances of an investigation, and will be heavily reliant on the persons applying for continued and extended detention. The new provisions may well lead to a return to the discredited standards and practice of the criminal justice system that developed and flourished in the two decades before 1984. In spite of the judicial protections, terrorist suspects will be deeply vulnerable.

8

STOP, SEARCH, SEIZURE, DETENTION
OF CASH

A. STOP AND SEARCH OF PERSONS

1. Basic Powers

In order to appreciate the importance of the incrementally increased powers **8.01** conferred on police officers by the 2006 Act, it will be necessary in this Chapter to consider both the fresh powers created by the 2006 Act and the powers of search and seizure enacted in the 2000 Act, which the 2006 Act enlarges.

A controversial power derives from s 44 of the 2000 Act. This section permits **8.02** any constable in uniform to stop a vehicle in an area or at a place specified in an authorization and to search the vehicle, the driver of the vehicle, a passenger in the vehicle, and anything in or on the vehicle or carried by the driver or a passenger. The authorization must be given by an Assistant Chief Constable, or a Commander in the Metropolitan Police (s 44(5)). Section 44(2) stipulates that an authorization under the subsection authorizes any constable in uniform to stop a pedestrian in an area or at a place specified in the authorization and to search him, and anything carried by him. This was the section under which Mr Walter Wolfgang (aged 82) was detained at the 2005 Labour Party Conference, having heckled the Foreign Secretary, shouting 'That's a lie!' He was bundled out of the hall and when he tried to re-enter was briefly detained under s 44.

8.03   A fear was expressed to the Joint Human Rights Committee during the passage of the Bill,[1] in relation to this power:

As with so much else in this Bill, we fear that these extensions to existing powers will act as a stalking horse for the other areas of the law, beyond terrorism, and will be used ultimately, for instance, against those engaged in legitimate domestic protest.

B. SEARCH OF PREMISES

8.04   Powers of search and seizure in relation to terrorist investigations are set out in detail in Sch 5 to the 2000 Act. Those powers were modelled generally on the scheme set out in Part I of and Sch 1 to the Police and Criminal Evidence Act 1984 ('the 1984 Act').

8.05   The 1984 Act provided, by s 8, for the grant to a constable of a warrant to search for evidential material for particular premises if various conditions were satisfied. By s 11 of that Act, 'excluded material' means personal records that a person has acquired or created in the course of any trade, business, profession, or other occupation, or for the purpose of any paid or unpaid office and which he holds in confidence; human tissue or tissue fluid that has been taken for medical diagnosis or treatment and which a person holds in confidence; and journalistic material which consists of documents, or records other than documents, and which a person holds in confidence.

8.06   By s 14 of the 1984 Act, 'special procedure material' means journalistic material that is not 'excluded material'; and material acquired or created in the course of any trade, business, profession, or other occupation, or for the purpose of any paid or unpaid office and which is held subject to an express undertaking of confidence or an obligation of confidence imposed by any enactment.

8.07   Schedule 1 to the 1984 Act created a two-tier system by which sensitive material of this kind could be obtained. One was by way of applying, inter partes, for a notice under para 4 of that Schedule, requiring the person occupying the premises to provide it to the constable. The more intrusive form of judicial order was a warrant, to be granted only if (paras 1–4 of Sch 1) service of a notice would or might be effectual for the reasons specified. This two-tier technique has appeared in other statutes, such as s 2 of the Criminal Justice Act 1987, applicable to cases of serious or complex fraud.

8.08   Applications for intrusive warrants under Sch 1 to the 1984 Act should be 'substantially the last resort': per Lord Bingham in *R v Crown Court at Lewis, ex p Hill*.[2] This case is also authority for the proposition that in ex parte applications for warrants of this kind, the applicant has a duty of full and frank

---

[1] HC 561-II Ev 97.
[2] (1991) 93 Cr App R 60. See also *R v Central Criminal Court, ex p Propend Finance Property Ltd* [1996] 2 Cr App R 26.

disclosure. Lack of candour may lead to the quashing of a warrant. Warrants obtained improperly are liable to be quashed in proceedings for judicial review.

The reason for applying the principle in criminal proceedings has been expressed in this way: **8.09**

Generations of justices have, or I would hope have, been brought up to recognise that the issue of a search warrant is a very serious interference with the liberty of the subject and a step which would only be taken after the most mature careful consideration of all the facts of the case.[3]

Previously, the doctrine was much more developed in civil proceedings: **8.10**

It is perfectly well settled that a person who makes an ex parte application to the court—that is to say, in the absence of the person who will be affected by that which the court is asked to do[4]—is under an obligation to the court to make the fullest possible disclosure of all material facts within his knowledge, and if he does not make that fullest possible disclosure, then he cannot obtain any advantage from the proceedings, and he will be deprived of any advantage he may have already obtained by means of the order which has thus wrongly been obtained by him. That is perfectly plain and requires no authority to justify it.[5]

For an example of the importance of the duty of full and frank disclosure in a different area of criminal procedure, an application for a search warrant in a criminal case brought in aid of a foreign government, see *R v Crown Court at Southwark, ex p Gross*.[6]   **8.11**

1. All Premises Warrants

The regime established by the 2000 Act is amended by the 2006 Act, in particular in relation to warrants to allow police to search 'all premises' belonging to an individual.   **8.12**

A number of terms that are used in ss 26 and 27 of the 2006 Act are defined in the 2000 Act. 'Premises' is defined in s 121 of the latter as including any place and in particular including a vehicle, an offshore installation within the meaning given in s 44 of the Petroleum Act 1998, and a tent or moveable structure. 'Vehicle' is given definition by s 121 as including an aircraft, hovercraft, train, or vessel. Section 44 of the Petroleum Act 1998 covers a variety of installations that are maintained in the water or on the foreshore or other land that is intermittently covered with water and which do not have a link with dry land such as oil   **8.13**

---

[3] *Williams v Summerfield* [1972] 2 QB 512, 581, per Lord Widgery CJ.
[4] ibid.
[5] *R v Kensington Income Tax Commissioners, ex p Princess Edmond de Polignac* [1917] 1 KB 486, 509, per Warrington LJ, cited with approval by Donaldson J in *Bank Mellat v Nikpour* [1985] FSR 87, 90 in the context of an application for a Mareva injunction. Donaldson J added: 'The rule requiring full disclosure seems to me to be of fundamental importance.'
[6] CO/1759/98; [1998] COD 45.

or gas rigs. 'Dwelling' is defined in s 121 of the 2000 Act as a building or part of a building used as a dwelling and a vehicle which is habitually stationary and is used as a dwelling.

8.14   Section 26(2) and (3) of the 2006 Act amend para 1 of Sch 5 to the 2000 Act so as to provide that search warrants under that Schedule may authorize the searching not just of named premises but also any premises occupied or controlled by a specified person (known as an 'all premises' warrant).

8.15   Section 26(4) of the 2006 Act amends para 1(5) of Sch 5 to the 2000 Act so as to provide that an all premises warrant may be granted where it is not reasonably practicable to specify in the application for the warrant all the premises which the person to which the application relates occupies or controls and which might need to be searched. This subsection also makes a number of consequential changes.

8.16   Section 26(5) of the 2006 Act amends the 2000 Act so as to provide that para 2 of Sch 5 applies only to specific premises warrants; s 26(6) inserts para 2A into Sch 5 for 'all premises warrants' that corresponds to para 2. Paragraph 2 cannot apply to all premises warrants; it refers to an application not relating to residential premises and, in the case of all premises warrants, the premises to which it relates will not be known at the time of the application.

8.17   If the magistrate is not convinced of the necessity of the warrant he may (under para 2A, inserted by s 26(6) of the 2006 Act) nevertheless grant it if the other conditions are met, provided that the application is made by a police officer of at least the rank of superintendent, the warrant is not to be executed in respect of residential premises and the warrant is executed within 24 hours of being issued. The new paragraph includes a definition of 'residential premises' as meaning any premises which the constable exercising the power to enter and search has reasonable grounds for believing are used wholly or mainly as a dwelling.

8.18   Section 26(7) and (8) amend para 11 of Sch 5 to the 2000 Act, which allows for applications for search warrants involving 'excluded material' or 'special procedure material' following an order under para 5, or where it is not appropriate to make such an order, for access to and production of such material, to allow all premises warrants to be made in such cases. ('Excluded material' and 'special procedure material' have the same meaning as under ss 11 and 14 respectively of the 1984 Act: Sch 5, para 4.)

8.19   Section 26(9) and (10) amend para 12 of Sch 5 to the 2000 Act, which sets out the conditions for granting a warrant under para 11. The tests for an all premises warrant are the same as for a specific premises warrant, modified to take account of the fact that there are no premises to be specified.

8.20   Thus, a constable may apply to a Circuit Judge for a warrant to search any premises for the purpose of a terrorist investigation: Sch 5, para 1 to the 2000 Act. The new provision gives a broader definition of the premises that may be entered. The new power is to enter premises which are (para 2A of Sch 5, as amended):

(a) one or more sets of premises specified in the application (in which case the application is for a 'specific premises warrant'); or

(b) any premises occupied or controlled by a person specified in the application, including such sets of premises as are so specified (in which case the application is for an 'all premises warrant').

This is plainly wider than the corresponding non-terrorist police power. The police may now apply for an 'all premises warrant' allowing them to enter each and every premises belonging to a specified person. This would be regarded as an extraordinarily wide authorization if issued against any successful businessman or private landlord. It could be used as an effective instrument of harassment by the police against such an individual. It is, however, subject to the judicial restraint set out in s 26(4)(c). **8.21**

Such warrants will be issued by a judge if certain criteria, as set out in the amended para 1(5) are satisfied. The test is whether the warrant is sought for the purposes of a terrorist investigation, whether there are reasonable grounds for believing that there is material on relevant premises which is likely to be of substantial value, whether by itself or together with other material, to a terrorist investigation and which does not consist of or include 'excluded material', and whether the issue of a warrant is likely to be necessary in the circumstances of the case. **8.22**

These 2006 Act provisions are based on ss 113 and 114 of the Serious Organised Crime and Police Act 2005 ('SOCPA') which amended the 1984 Act so as to allow all premises warrants to be granted under that Act. Some critics have questioned whether the new powers are therefore otiose. **8.23**

The Joint Committee on Human Rights received a submission from the British Irish Rights Watch[7] that: **8.24**

In view of the extensive search powers already contained in Schedule 5 of the 2000 Act, and the specific 'all premises' warrant provisions in sections 113 and 114 of the Serious Organised Crime and Police Act 2005, the provisions in this proposed Clause seem redundant.

The 2006 Act adds the following, by virtue of s 26(4)(c): **8.25**

in the case of an application for an all premises warrant, that it is not reasonably practicable to specify in the application all the premises which the person so specified occupies or controls and which might need to be searched.

There is potential for abuse here. Applications are made ex parte. Judicial supervision must ensure rigorous application of the test as to whether it is 'reasonably practicable' to specify all the premises that might need to be searched. Given that the subject may have been under intensive surveillance the court should be slow to accede to requests for warrants in these general terms. **8.26**

---

[7] HL Paper 75-II Ev 07.

8.27   The rest of the regime brought into force under para 1 of the 2000 Act remains unchanged.

8.28   A warrant authorizes police to enter the premises to search them and any person found there, and to seize and retain any relevant material which is found therein (para 1(2)). Material is relevant if the constable has reasonable grounds for believing that it is likely to be of substantial value, whether by itself or together with other material, to a terrorist investigation, and it must be seized in order to prevent it from being concealed, lost, damaged, altered, or destroyed (para 1(3)).

8.29   There are express statutory limits to the powers granted under such warrants: para 1(4). No authorization exists for the seizure and retention of items subject to legal professional privilege, or for a constable to require a person to remove any clothing in public except for headgear, footwear, an outer coat, a jacket, or gloves.

2. Warrants as to Which Special Conditions are Satisfied

8.30   The previous regime (under Sch 5, para 2 to the 2000 Act) under which a warrant would still issue even where the justice of the peace was not satisfied that a para 1 warrant was 'likely to be necessary in the circumstances of the case' but where other conditions were satisfied, has been further extended by 2006 Act: s 26(5) and (6).

8.31   Prior to the 2006 Act, the only conditions to be met for the issue of such a warrant were that the application was made by a police officer of at least the rank of superintendent, and that the application did not relate to residential premises. The justice could grant the application if satisfied of the matters referred to in para 1(5)(a) and (b), that is, that the warrant was for the purposes of a terrorist investigation and the reasonable grounds for belief that the evidence found would be of substantial value, as set out above. For these purposes 'residential premises' means any premises which the officer making the application has reasonable grounds for believing are used wholly or mainly as a dwelling: para 2(4).

8.32   The limitation placed on such warrants was that they were exercisable only within the period of 24 hours beginning with the time when the warrant was issued.

8.33   The new para 2A (inserted by s 26(6) of the 2006 Act) provides that such a 24-hour warrant may issue, in the absence of a finding that a para 1 warrant is likely to be necessary in the circumstances. The only requirements are that the application is made by a police officer of at least the rank of superintendent, and although the justice to whom the application is made is not satisfied of the 'necessary in the circumstances' test referred to in para 1(5)(c), the justice may grant the application if satisfied of the matters referred to in para 1(5)(a), (b), and (d); namely, the requirements of 'terrorist investigation', 'material likely to be of substantial value', and 'not reasonably practicable to name all the premises it will be necessary to search'. These tests are set out in more detail above.

As before, this type of warrant cannot issue in respect of residential premises, **8.34** and must be executed within 24 hours: new para 2A(3).

The definition of 'residential premises' is retained (new para 2A(4)), save that **8.35** it applies to the opinion of the officer exercising the power granted and not merely the officer making the application for a warrant.

3. Excluded or Special Procedure Material: Search

Under the 2000 Act, Sch 5, para 11 established a regime for applications for **8.36** search warrants involving excluded or special procedure material. This is now amended by the 2006 Act.

There is a mirror image extension in the same terms as the amendment to the **8.37** scope of para 1 warrants above, their application is no longer restricted to 'the premises specified in the warrant' but now expanded to include (para 11(3)(A)):

(a) one or more sets of premises specified in the application (in which case the application is for a 'specific premises warrant'); or
(b) any premises occupied or controlled by a person specified in the application, including such sets of premises as are so specified (in which case the application is for an 'all premises warrant').

A Circuit Judge or a District Judge (Magistrates' Courts) may now grant an **8.38** application for an all premises warrant under para 11 if he is satisfied that an order made under para 5 has not been complied with, and that the person specified in the application is also specified in the order: new para 12(2A).

Moreover, the same tribunals may also grant an application for an all pre- **8.39** mises warrant under para 11 if satisfied that there are reasonable grounds for believing that there is material on premises to which the application relates which consists of or includes 'excluded material' or 'special procedure material' but does not include items subject to legal professional privilege, and that the conditions in para 11(3) and (4) are met: new para 12(2B).

The condition mentioned, para 11(3), is that the warrant is sought for **8.40** the purposes of a terrorist investigation, and the material is likely to be of substantial value, whether by itself or together with other material, to a terrorist investigation.

The second condition, set out at para 12(4), is that it is not appropriate to **8.41** make an order under para 5 in relation to the material because it is not practicable to communicate with any person entitled to produce the material, it is not practicable to communicate with any person entitled to grant access to the material or entitled to grant entry to the premises on which the material is situated, or that a terrorist investigation may be seriously prejudiced unless a constable can secure immediate access to the material. These provisions are similar to those in Sch 1 to the 1984 Act.

C. SEIZURE OF TERRORIST PUBLICATIONS

1. Overview

8.42 The 2006 Act introduces a new regime of warrants to allow investigators to enter and search premises and then to seize terrorist publications found therein. Section 28 of the 2006 Act gives this new power to magistrates, and the detailed provisions are set out in Sch 2 to the 2006 Act.

8.43 If a justice of the peace is satisfied that there are reasonable grounds for suspecting that articles to which this section applies are likely to be found on any premises, he may issue a warrant authorizing a constable to enter and search the premises; and to seize anything found there which the constable has reason to believe is such an article (s 28).

8.44 This provision applies to an article if it is likely to be the subject of conduct amounting to the substantive offence of 'dissemination of terrorist publications' under s 2 of the 2006 Act (Sch 2, para 2(2)).

8.45 Section 2 of the 2006 Act provides the following guidance as to what is a 'terrorist publication'; the same test is applied to the issue of a warrant under s 28 and Sch 2. A judgment must be made as to whether the article contains matter which is likely (s 2):

(3) [. . .]
    (a) to be understood, by some or all of the persons to whom it is or may become available as a consequence of that conduct, as a direct or indirect encouragement or other inducement to them to the commission, preparation or instigation of acts of terrorism; or
    (b) to be useful in the commission or preparation of such acts and to be understood, by some or all of those persons, as contained in the publication, or made available to them, wholly or mainly for the purpose of being so useful to them.

(4) For the purposes of this section matter that is likely to be understood by a person as indirectly encouraging the commission or preparation of acts of terrorism includes any matter which—
    (a) glorifies the commission or preparation (whether in the past, in the future or generally) of such acts; and
    (b) is matter from which that person could reasonably be expected to infer that what is being glorified is being glorified as conduct that should be emulated by him in existing circumstances.

8.46 The question whether a publication is a terrorist publication in relation to particular conduct is to be determined as at the time of that conduct; and having regard both to the contents of the publication as a whole and to the circumstances in which that conduct occurs: s 2(5) of the 2006 Act.

2. The Use of the Power under Section 28

Any officer acting under a s 28 warrant may use 'such force as is reasonable in the circumstances for exercising that power': s 28(3). **8.47**

A publication seized under the authority of a s 28 warrant may be removed by a constable to such place as he thinks fit; and must be retained there in the custody of a constable until returned or otherwise disposed of in accordance with the Act: s 28(4). **8.48**

The power to forfeit and destroy, or otherwise dispose of, seized terrorist publications is found in s 28(5). The Director of Public Prosecutions must lay the information. **8.49**

This power is to be exercised in accordance with the detailed regime in Sch 2 to the 2006 Act. **8.50**

The following provisions of Sch 2 apply when an article has been seized under the authority of a s 28 warrant and it is being retained in the custody of a constable ('the relevant constable'): para 1. **8.51**

This officer must give notice of the article's seizure to every person whom he believes to have been the owner of the article, or one of its owners, at the time of the seizure. If there is no such person or it is not reasonably practicable to give him notice, every person whom the relevant constable believes to have been an occupier at that time of the premises where the article was seized from must be notified: para 2. **8.52**

The notice must set out what has been seized and the grounds for the seizure. The notice may be given to a person only by delivering it to him personally, addressing it to him, and leaving it for him at the appropriate address or sending it to him at that address by post: para 2(3). **8.53**

Where the owner is not ascertainable it is sufficient to leave or post a notice addressed to 'the occupier' at the address from which the publications were seized: para 2(4). These provisions are similar to those in s 16 of the 1984 Act. **8.54**

Liberty to derogate from the terms of the Act is permitted by para 2(5) of Sch 2 to the 2006 Act. This provides that an article may be treated or condemned as forfeited under this Schedule only if the requirements of this paragraph have been complied with in the case of that article; or it was not reasonably practicable for them to be complied with. Let us consider the example of an anti-war rally in Parliament Square which turns to violence. An officer finds a bundle of leaflets urging people to storm the gates of Parliament at 5pm to create a diversion, while a bomber approaches Downing Street at 4.30pm. As a matter of common sense and expediency the officer should inform a superior officer, then throw the bundle of leaflets away and continue to police the riot, even though that would not be compliant with his duties under the Schedule. There is no guidance in the Act as to the limits of the exception set out in para 2(5). **8.55**

The Schedule makes detailed provision for determining the 'appropriate address' to which the notice should be sent: para 2(6) and (7) refer to: **8.56**

(a) in the case of a body corporate, its registered or principal office in the United Kingdom;

(b) in the case of a firm, the principal office of the partnership;

(c) in the case of an unincorporated body or association, the principal office of the body or association; and

(d) in any other case, his usual or last known place of residence in the United Kingdom or his last known place of business in the United Kingdom.

8.57   Whereas in the case of a company registered outside the United Kingdom, a firm carrying on business outside the United Kingdom, or an unincorporated body or association with offices outside the United Kingdom, the references in this paragraph to its principal office include references to its principal office within the United Kingdom (if any).

3. Defending Against Forfeiture: Giving Notice of Claim

8.58   A person claiming that the seized article is not liable to forfeiture must give 'notice of his claim' to a constable at any police station in the police area in which the premises where the seizure took place are located. Oral notice is not sufficient: Sch 2 to the 2006 Act, para 3 refers. An efficient means of communication as between police stations in a given area is obviously required.

8.59   Time is limited in respect of serving a notice of claim; it will not be effective if it is served more than one month after the day of the giving of the notice of seizure; or if no such notice has been given, the day of the seizure: para 4(1).

8.60   To comply with these provisions a notice of claim must specify the name and address of the claimant; and in the case of a claimant who is outside the United Kingdom, the name and address of a solicitor in the United Kingdom who is authorized to accept service, and to act, on behalf of the claimant: para 4(2).

8.61   Service on a solicitor as specified above is taken to be service on the claimant for the purposes of any proceedings under this schedule: para 4(3).

8.62   Paragraph 4(4) deals with the precise method for calculating when the time begins to run in a case in which notice of the seizure was given to different persons on different days. The reference in this paragraph to the day on which that notice was given means, in relation to a person to whom notice of the seizure was given, the day on which that notice was given to that person. In relation to any other person, time runs from the day on which notice of the seizure was given to the last person to be given such a notice.

4. Automatic Forfeiture

8.63   Failure to give an adequate notice of claim within the one-month time limit leads to automatic forfeiture: para 5, Sch 2 to the 2005 Act.

5. Forfeiture by the Court in Other Cases

The consequence of complying with the notice of claim requirements is that **8.64** the matter is resolved by a court, if indeed the police wish to pursue the question of forfeiture. If they no longer seek forfeiture the articles must be returned. There is no express sanction against the police who fail to make safe return, though usual civil claims would lie in a case where the material was 'lost' rather than forfeited.

Where a notice of claim in respect of an article is duly given in accordance **8.65** with paras 3 and 4, the relevant constable must decide whether to take proceedings to ask the court to condemn the article as forfeited: para 6(1) of Sch 2. The decision whether to take such proceedings must be made as soon as reasonably practicable after the giving of the notice of claim: para 6(2).

The test applied by the court has two limbs. If the relevant constable takes **8.66** such proceedings and the court finds that the article was liable to forfeiture at the time of its seizure, and is not satisfied that its forfeiture would be inappropriate, the court must condemn the article as forfeited: para 6(3).

There are plainly two lines of defence available: the first is that the article was **8.67** never liable to forfeiture at the material time. This will involve arguments about the nature of the publication, that is falls without the definitions at s 2(3) of the 2006 Act, above.

Secondly, the defence may seek to raise the 'forfeiture would be inappropriate' **8.68** limb. It is an inherently vague test. When might forfeiture be inappropriate? If the offending article is itself of intrinsic value, for example a painting with a slogan, the court may be satisfied by offers of renovation and/or censorship from the current owner. An end of terrace house in Northern Ireland with a mural glorifying terrorism when offered for sale would stretch the definition of 'publication'. If it passed the first test, one would argue forfeiture was less appropriate than the application of a few coats of paint.

There is ambiguity as to where the burden of proof lies. The wording of **8.69** para 6(3) may suggest the burden is on the police to show that the article is a terrorist publication, 'If that constable takes proceedings and the court finds that the article was liable to forfeiture at the time of its seizure.'

By contrast the second test is that (para 6(3)(b)) the court 'is not satisfied **8.70** that its forfeiture would be inappropriate.' On the face of it this appears to place a burden on the defence, who must satisfy the court of the inappropriateness of forfeiture.

Although the emphasis in para 6 is on the police electing to take court pro- **8.71** ceedings, the clear wording of para 8 shows that the person from whom the article has been seized is the 'claimant' and the nature of proceedings is civil, see below.

Some assistance is to be found in paras 14 and 15: 'Provisions as to proof'. **8.72** They provide that the 'fact, form and manner of the seizure is to be taken, without further evidence and unless the contrary is shown, to have been as set forth in the process.' This places a burden it appears, on the balance of probabilities, on the person whose property has been seized to dispute the details of the manner and timing of its seizure: para 14.

8.73   The condemnation by a court of an article as forfeited under Sch 2 is proved by the production of either the order of condemnation; or a certified copy of the order purporting to be signed by an officer of the court by which the order was made. This is a matter of standard formality; otherwise the matter would be re-opened in its entirety at the convenience of a claimant, potentially long after the event.

8.74   If a constable takes such proceedings and the court finds in favour of the defence, either on the ground that the article was not liable to forfeiture at the time of its seizure, or the court is satisfied that its forfeiture would be inappropriate, the court must order the return of the article to the person who appears to the court to be entitled to it: para 6(4).

8.75   In the event that the relevant constable decides not to take proceedings for condemnation in a case in which a notice of claim has been given, he must return the article to the person who appears to him to be the owner of the article, or to one of the persons who appear to him to be owners of it: para 6(5). Such an article must be returned as soon as reasonably practicable after the decision not to take proceedings for condemnation: para 6(6).

6. Nature of Forfeiture Proceedings

8.76   These are civil proceedings and may be instituted (para 7):

(a) in England or Wales, either in the High Court or in a magistrates' court;
(b) in Scotland, either in the Court of Session or in the sheriff court; and
(c) in Northern Ireland, either in the High Court or in a court of summary jurisdiction.

8.77   Proceedings under this Schedule in a Magistrates' Court in England or Wales (or sheriff court in Scotland, summary court in Northern Ireland) may be instituted in a particular court only if it has jurisdiction in relation to the place where the article to which they relate was seized: para 8.

8.78   In proceedings by virtue of this Schedule commenced in England and Wales or Northern Ireland, the claimant or his solicitor must make a statement on oath that, at the time of the seizure, the seized article was, or was to the best of his knowledge and belief, the property of the claimant: para 9(1). This plainly describes the person whose property has been seized as the 'claimant' and is consistent with the heading 'notice of claim'. There are special provisions for determining who should make the oath in the case of companies, partnerships, and jointly held property. These are fully set out in para 16: a secretary or other officer binds the company, any one partner the partnership, any two joint owners where there are more than five, etc.

8.79   In any 2006 Act, Sch 2 proceedings in the High Court, the court may require the claimant to give such security for the costs of the proceedings as may be determined; and the claimant must comply with any such requirement. If a requirement of this paragraph is not complied with, the court must find against the claimant: para 9(3).

7. Appeals

An appeal lies from the Magistrates' Court to the Crown Court (para 10(1)), or **8.80** in Northern Ireland from the summary court to the county court (para 10(2)), presumably by way of hearing de novo. Moreover, this paragraph expressly preserves the right to require the statement of a case for the opinion of the High Court: para 10(3).

Where an appeal is made (whether by case stated or otherwise) against the **8.81** decision of the lower court, the disputed article must be left in the custody of a constable pending the final resolution: para 11.

8. Effect of Forfeiture and Disposal of Unclaimed Property

Where an article is treated or condemned as forfeited under this Schedule, the **8.82** forfeiture is to be treated as having taken effect as from the time of the seizure: para 12, Sch 2 to the 2006 Act.

Where the article seized under the authority of a warrant under s 28 of the **8.83** 2006 Act is required to be returned to a person, para 13(1) of Sch 2 states that if the article is (without having been returned) still in the custody of a constable after the end of the period of 12 months beginning with the day after the requirement to return it arose, and it is not practicable to dispose of the article by returning it immediately to the person to whom it is required to be returned, the constable may dispose of it in any manner he thinks fit. It is hoped this power will not be used as a convenient shield for police non-compliance with the Schedule. It remains to be seen what will be held as legitimate bars to return; the fact that the owner of the disputed article is now on remand for a terrorist offence, or serving a sentence, perhaps. This would not stop the return of a pamphlet through the postal service, but a whole print run would be problematic. In this case the solicitor should offer safe storage.

9. Saving for Owner's Rights

Third party rights are expressly preserved in relation to the imposition of a **8.84** requirement on the police to return an article to a person, and the actual return of an article to a person: para 17, Sch 2 to the 2006 Act. An example would be the seizure of 10,000 leaflets advertising a demonstration organized by the separatist Cardiff Dragons, due to take place on 1 April. They are printed on 14 March and delivered to the Dragons' HQ. Standard business terms would allow 28 days for payment. Police seize the leaflets on 28 March. A court orders their return on 14 April. The printer requires payment but the leaflets were kept by police until the date of the march had passed. The Dragons must pay their printers; the contract is enforceable as it was not unlawful. It is to be hoped the police do not use this provision to stifle protest and financially to embarrass legitimate organizations.

D. SEARCH OF VEHICLES

8.85 The 2006 Act gives investigators increased powers to stop and search vehicles. Officers did not previously enjoy a general power to search vehicles that were themselves on ships or aircraft. Thus, s 29 of the 2006 Act extends para 8(1) of Sch 7 to the 2000 Act so as to allow an examining officer to search a vehicle, at a port, which is found on a ship or aircraft, or which the examining officer reasonably believes has been or is about to be on a ship or aircraft, for the purposes of determining whether a person the examining officer is questioning under para 2 of Sch 7 falls within s 40(1)(b) of the 2000 Act. This is achieved by the insertion of new subparagraphs (e) and (f) into para 8, Sch 7 to the 2000 Act. A person comes within s 40(1)(b) of the 2000 Act if he is or has been concerned in the commission, preparation, or instigation of acts of terrorism. An 'examining officer' for these purposes can be a police constable, an immigration officer, or a customs officer. Before the 2006 Act, an examining officer did not have the right to search vehicles in such circumstances, even though he did have the power to search vehicles in the Northern Ireland border area (see para 8(2) of Sch 7). It is noteworthy that the definition of vehicle in s 121 of the 2000 Act (which provides that 'vehicle' includes an aircraft, hovercraft, train, or vessel) does not extend to Sch 7.

E. STOP AND SEARCH IN INTERNAL WATERS

8.86 The s 44 power of stop and search is further extended by the 2006 Act to include internal waters (lakes, rivers, etc) that are adjacent to the specified place. So that, if the conference complex in Brighton includes a boating lake on its periphery, and the complex is a s 44 designated place during Labour Party Conferences, the police will have the power to stop and search a protestor who heckles the Foreign Secretary from a boat on the lake as well as from the auditorium. This is a logical extension which closes a significant lacuna. Thus, s 30 of the 2006 Act amends ss 44 and 45 of the 2000 Act. Section 44 provides that an authorization may be given for a particular police area or part of a police area and under that authorization a constable may stop a vehicle in the area and search the vehicle, the driver of the vehicle, a passenger in the vehicle, and anything on or in the vehicle or carried by the driver or a passenger. Section 30(2) adds a new subsection to s 44 so as to enable an authorization to include internal waters adjacent to any area or place specified under s 44(4), or part of such internal waters. Section 30(3) and (4) make consequential amendments to ss 44 and 45 to ensure that 'driver' in those sections has a logical meaning in the context of a vehicle which is not a car. Thus 'driver' is defined in s 52 of the 2000 Act as including the person who was driving the vehicle when it was left on a road, if it was left on a road. Under s 45 of the 2000 Act a constable may seize an article found during a search under s 44.

F. APPLICATIONS FOR EXTENDED DETENTION OF SEIZED CASH

Section 35 of the 2006 Act amends Sch 1 to the Anti-Terrorism, Crime and **8.87** Security Act 2001. The major change is that the hearing of the first application to extend the period for which the cash is detained may now be conducted in private without the person whose cash has been taken being present, represented, or informed in advance. Schedule 1 to the 2001 Act sets out the scheme for the forfeiture of terrorist cash. Under para 2 of that Schedule an authorized officer may seize any cash if he has reasonable grounds for suspecting that it is terrorist cash. 'Terrorist cash' is defined as cash that is intended to be used for terrorist purposes, cash which consists of resources of a proscribed organization, and property that is earmarked as terrorist property. Once terrorist cash has been seized, para 3 of the Schedule governs the length of time it can be detained. In the first instance the cash can be detained for 48 hours after which the authorized officer must apply to a Magistrates' Court (or a sheriff in Scotland) to extend the period of detention. The first application for extension can also be made, outside Scotland, to a justice of the peace (pursuant to para 3(3)). Section 35 of the 2006 Act adds a new subparagraph to para 3, providing that where first application for extension of detention of terrorist cash is made to a justice of the peace it can be heard without notice being given to the person affected by the order or that person's legal representative and can be heard in private in the absence of the affected person and his legal representative. There is a limited safeguard against unfairness in that the person affected will have the opportunity to challenge the making of the order at a later date because he will be served with a copy of it (para 3(4)) and can apply for it to be discharged (para 5). Section 35(2) of the 2006 Act provides that this amendment will not be retrospective, and applies to applications made after commencement only. The rationale for this modification is to avoid 'tipping-off' terrorists that their cash has been seized in the early stage of an investigation.

9

INVESTIGATORY POWERS

A. AMENDMENT OF THE INTELLIGENCE SERVICES ACT 1994

Under the Intelligence Services Act 1994 ('ISA'), the Secret Intelligence Service, **9.01** and the Government Communications Headquarters ('GCHQ') were made subject to a statutory regime. The purpose of this Act included the making of provision for the issue of warrants and authorizations enabling action to be taken by the Secret Services. It also established a procedure for the investigation of complaints about the Secret Intelligence Service and the GCHQ. The ISA established an Intelligence and Security Committee to oversee the two Services and GCHQ. Most pertinently, the ISA made provision for the issue of warrants, by the Secretary of State, authorizing entry on to property and interference with 'wireless telegraphy': s 5.

Crucially, an express exception was made, by s 5(3) that a warrant authorizing **9.02** the taking of action in support of the prevention or detection of serious crime 'may not relate to property in the British Islands', defined below.

The 2006 Act amends this regime. Section 31 adds to the categories of persons **9.03** who are authorized to issue warrants on behalf of the Secretary of State. In an urgent case, where the Secretary of State has given prior authority to specified senior officials, such people may issue such a warrant by their own hand provided that the warrant is so endorsed. This is a further extension of the power of the executive arm of government to issue warrants authorizing intrusive action by agents of the state.

A restriction is placed on this new power of senior specified officials. Tests of **9.04** proportionality are imported from s 7 of the ISA (by s 31(3) of the 2006 Act). The Intelligence Service must only be authorized to do acts which are necessary to its function and in circumstances where the likely consequences will be 'reasonable'. A further requirement is placed on senior specified officials by the new s 6(1)(b) of the ISA in that when an official issues such a warrant he must inform the Secretary of State about it 'as soon as practicable after issuing it'. This is clearly aimed at providing political accountability. A more general safeguard is the scrutiny of the Intelligence and Security Committee of both Houses of Parliament (established by the ISA, s 10).

9.05   The 2006 Act amends s 6(2)(b) of the ISA so that such warrants issued by senior officials lapse after the fifth working day, rather than after the second working day as before. The same extension is made in relation to warrants for acts done abroad, by s 7(6)(b) of the ISA. The Secretary of State has the power to renew these warrants under his own hand, by virtue of s 7(7).

9.06   The regime in relation to acts done abroad is extended to include acts done on property which is in fact within the United Kingdom, when a mistake has been made about where the property is located: s 31(6). The effect of this amendment is that the Intelligence Service will not be liable in domestic criminal or civil law merely because they should have obtained a s 5 (general) warrant rather than a s 7 (acts done outside the British Islands) warrant, where there has been a mistake about the location of the property in question. Where the conditions set out in the new s 7(10) of the ISA are satisfied, a legal fiction arises that although the property was within the British Islands at the material time, 'this section shall have effect as if the act were done outside the British Islands'. The 'British Islands' are defined by the Interpretation Act of 1978 as the United Kingdom, the Channel Islands, and the Isle of Man.

9.07   This section applies to acts done on property which is in fact within the British Islands but which is mistakenly believed to be abroad: s 7(11) of the ISA. This would include, by way of an example, the remote detonation of a small device to disable the headlights of a lorry which in fact had disembarked at Dover but which the Intelligence Service thought was in northern France driving to Calais.

9.08   This legal fiction also applies where it was mistakenly believed at the time of issue of the warrant that the property was abroad but it has since become apparent that the property is in fact within the jurisdiction, provided that the act is done before the end of the fifth working day from the point at which the mistake is realized: ss 7(12) et seq of the ISA.

B. INTERCEPTION WARRANTS

9.09   The Regulation of Investigatory Powers Act 2000 ('RIPA') creates offences in relation to unlawful and unauthorized interceptions of public postal and telecommunication systems. Section 5 makes provision for 'interception warrants' to issue at the request of various agencies of the state. This regime is modified by the 2006 Act. The main purpose of the RIPA was to ensure that the particular investigatory powers are used in accordance with human rights. These powers are the interception of communications, the acquisition of communications data (for example, telephone billing data), intrusive surveillance (on residential premises or in private vehicles), covert surveillance in the course of specific operations, the use of covert human intelligence sources (that is, agents, informants, and undercover officers), and access to encrypted data. For each of these specific powers, the RIPA seeks to ensure that the law clearly covers the purposes for which they may be used, which investigatory authorities can use the powers, who should authorize each use of the power, the use that can be made of the material gained, independent judicial oversight, and a means of redress for the individual.

Section 32(2) of the 2006 Act inserts a new s 9(6)(ab) into the RIPA. The **9.10** Secretary of State may now renew an interception warrant at any time before the end of a six-month period from the date of issue, provided that it was issued in the interests of national security or to safeguard the economic well-being of the United Kingdom. This is an extension of the three months 'relevant period' within which renewal could be made prior to amendment. The amendment brings the duration of the initial interception warrant issued in the interests of national security or for the purpose of safeguarding the economic wellbeing of the United Kingdom into conformity with the duration of any such warrant when renewed. Before the 2006 Act, these warrants lasted only for three months when first issued, but could be renewed for a six-months period. This amendment provides that both initial and renewed warrants will now last for a maximum of six months.

Under the original regime there had been an understandable 'prohibition on **9.11** the modification of scheduled parts of a warrant by the person to whom the warrant is addressed or his subordinates': s 10(6) of the RIPA. This provision is substituted by s 32(3) of the 2006 Act. Such an official may now authorize modification to the warrant provided that the instrument is endorsed with a statement that it was issued or renewed because it was believed to be necessary in the interests of national security. Such a modification ceases to have effect at the end of the fifth working day after it is made: s 10(9)(b) of the RIPA, as amended by s 32(4).

The RIPA provides for extra safeguards in the case of 'certificated warrants' **9.12** in relation to 'telephone taps' under s 8(4). This regime is relaxed by the 2006 Act, s 32(5), (6), and (7). The safeguards appear in s 16 of the RIPA. Whereas previously a warrant could only authorize interception during a maximum period of three months, this is now extended to six months in cases where the examination has been certified as being in the interests of national security: s 16(3A) of the RIPA.

A further relaxation is granted in national security cases, by s 32(7) of the **9.13** 2006 Act. Where there has been a change of circumstances since the issue of the warrant, the person to whom it is addressed may consider intercept material beyond the ordinary scope of the warrant for a period of five days (as opposed to one day under the original regime, provided he has written authorization from a senior official: s 16(5A) of the RIPA as amended. The approach is to avoid placing undue burdens on investigators in matters of national security.

9.14   The 2006 Act stopped far short of making the contents of intercepts admissible evidence, possibly because investigating authorities were fearful that wide disclosure of unused material might be sought. Many complicated Public Interest Immunity applications would follow if the contents of 'wire-taps' were admissible at a criminal trial. Clive Walker has argued in evidence to the Joint Committee:

> It would assist in many cases to have intercept evidence as admissible. No serious debate on the issue can be held without information. As a first step, the Home Office should publish the reports from the inquiries held to date, including the most recent held in 2004. It should be explained why the normal procedures for dealing with public interest immunity cannot satisfactorily deal with any concerns.[1]

C. DISCLOSURE NOTICES FOR THE PURPOSES OF TERRORIST INVESTIGATIONS

9.15   The investigatory powers of the DPP, etc conferred by the Serious Organised Crime and Police Act 2005 ('SOCPA') are extended to the field of 'terrorist investigations' by s 33(1) and (2) of the 2006 Act. Here 'terrorist investigations' are enquiries into the commission, preparation, or instigation of acts of terrorism, any act or omission which appears to have been for the purposes of terrorism and which consists in or involves the commission, preparation, or instigation of an offence, or the commission, preparation, or instigation of an offence under the 2000 Act under Part 1 of the 2006 Act other than an offence under s 1 or s 2 of that Act.

9.16   In general terms, s 33 of the 2006 Act extends the regime contained in Part 2, Chapter 1 of the SOCPA under which a disclosure notice may be issued by the Investigating Authority, requiring those on whom such a notice is served to provide specific information as set out in the notice. There is a draconian penalty attached in that refusal to provide information is an offence, punishable by imprisonment for up to 51 weeks, or a fine. In addition it is an offence to provide false or misleading information, punishable by imprisonment for up to two years, or a fine, or both.

9.17   Section 33(1) of the 2006 Act amends s 60(1) of the SOCPA to extend the powers of the Investigating Authority to enable the issuing of disclosure notices in terrorist investigations. Prior to this a disclosure notice could only be issued in connection with the investigation of specific offences. Section 33(2) inserts a definition of 'terrorist investigation' into s 60 of the SOCPA.

9.18   Section 33(3) of the 2006 Act modifies s 62 of the SOCPA to the effect that a disclosure notice may be given where the Investigating Authority believes that a person has information that relates to a terrorist investigation. There must also

---

[1] HC 561-II Ev 171.

be reasonable grounds for believing both that the person to whom the notice is issued has relevant information and that any information provided is likely to be of substantial value to that investigation. As discussed in relation to arrest on 'reasonable grounds', the belief must be a genuine one, though it may be based on hearsay or informant evidence, and may fall short of evidence requiring a case to answer.

Section 33(4) of the 2006 Act inserts definitions of 'act of terrorism', 'terror- **9.19**
ism', and 'terrorist investigation' into s 70 of the SOCPA for the purpose of the disclosure notice provisions. The first two of these terms are defined in the 2000 Act. The definition of terrorist investigation is set out in s 60(7) of the SOCPA (as inserted by subsection (2) of this section).

In summary, the regime of 'disclosure notices' is the most significant of these **9.20**
investigatory powers, whereby the investigating authority can require a person to answer questions and provide documents: ss 62 and 63 of the SOCPA. There are restrictions on this power to require disclosure, most notably in respect of privileged documents and information: s 64. Moreover, the use to which answers and documents disclosed may be put is very restricted. A statement made in response to such a requirement is not admissible evidence against him in criminal proceedings: s 65. The only exception is for offences of perjury and similar.

10

PART 3—REVIEW OF TERROR LEGISLATION

The Secretary of State must appoint a person to review the operation of the **10.01** provisions of the 2000 Act and of Part 1 of the 2006 Act, by virtue of s 36 of the 2006 Act. This replaces s 126 of the 2000 Act which provided for the annual review of that initial legislation. It is curious that Part 2 of the 2006 Act is not expressly subject to the same review, though extended detention and the pro-scription powers all derive from the 2000 Act and are therefore indirectly within the remit of review.

There is no stipulation as to the qualifications or standing required in a candi- **10.02** date for the post. He will be appointed by the Home Secretary to review powers exercised by his own department in many cases. Lord Carlile of Berriew QC is the reviewer of the 2000 Act.

Section 36(2) of the 2006 Act says that such a person may carry out such **10.03** reviews from time to time and the outcome of such a review must be reported to the Secretary of State. Under s 36(3) and (4) an initial review and report must be completed in the year following the laying before Parliament of the last report under s 126 of the 2000 Act. Subsequent reviews and reports must be conducted and produced at least annually. It is difficult to imagine the need arising for a report more than once a year, though pressure may be increased in the wake of terrorist attacks.

The Secretary of State must lay a copy of any report before Parliament: **10.04** s 36(5). There is no express requirement that the full unabridged report must be placed before Parliament, thought the implication is that the same document is forwarded. This will prevent the reviewer from including sensitive information in his report to the Home Secretary.

Section 36(6) allows for the reimbursing of the reviewer for costs incurred in **10.05** the course of his duties and for the payment of an allowance. There is no indication in the statute as to whether this is a full-time post.

APPENDIX 1

The Terrorism Act 2000

The extracts from this Act reprinted here are those which (a) create criminal offences which are referred to in the body of the book and are in some cases amended by the 2006 Act; and (b) are provisions relating to detention, search, and seizure which are amended by the 2006 Act.

PART I
INTRODUCTORY

1 Terrorism: interpretation

(1) In this Act "terrorism" means the use or threat of action where—
    (a) the action falls within subsection (2),
    (b) the use or threat is designed to influence the government [or an international governmental organisation][1] or to intimidate the public or a section of the public, and
    (c) the use or threat is made for the purpose of advancing a political, religious or ideological cause.

(2) Action falls within this subsection if it—
    (a) involves serious violence against a person,
    (b) involves serious damage to property,
    (c) endangers a person's life, other than that of the person committing the action,
    (d) creates a serious risk to the health or safety of the public or a section of the public, or
    (e) is designed seriously to interfere with or seriously to disrupt an electronic system.

(3) The use or threat of action falling within subsection (2) which involves the use of firearms or explosives is terrorism whether or not subsection (1)(b) is satisfied.

(4) In this section—
    (a) "action" includes action outside the United Kingdom,
    (b) a reference to any person or to property is a reference to any person, or to property, wherever situated,
    (c) a reference to the public includes a reference to the public of a country other than the United Kingdom, and
    (d) "the government" means the government of the United Kingdom, of a Part of the United Kingdom or of a country other than the United Kingdom.

(5) In this Act a reference to action taken for the purposes of terrorism includes a reference to action taken for the benefit of a proscribed organisation.

---

[1] Words in square brackets inserted by the 2006 Act, s.34.

PART II
PROSCRIBED ORGANISATIONS

Procedure

3 Proscription

(1) For the purposes of this Act an organisation is proscribed if—
    (a) it is listed in Schedule 2, or
    (b) it operates under the same name as an organisation listed in that Schedule.

(2) Subsection (1)(b) shall not apply in relation to an organisation listed in Schedule 2 if its entry is the subject of a note in that Schedule.

(3) The Secretary of State may by order—
    (a) add an organisation to Schedule 2;
    (b) remove an organisation from that Schedule;
    (c) amend that Schedule in some other way.

(4) The Secretary of State may exercise his power under subsection (3)(a) in respect of an organisation only if he believes that it is concerned in terrorism.

(5) For the purposes of subsection (4) an organisation is concerned in terrorism if it—
    (a) commits or participates in acts of terrorism,
    (b) prepares for terrorism,
    (c) promotes or encourages terrorism, or
    (d) is otherwise concerned in terrorism.

[(5A) The cases in which an organisation promotes or encourages terrorism for the purposes of subsection (5)(c) include any case in which activities of the organisation—
    (a) include the unlawful glorification of the commission or preparation (whether in the past, in the future or generally) of acts of terrorism; or
    (b) are carried out in a manner that ensures that the organisation is associated with statements containing any such glorification.

(5B) The glorification of any conduct is unlawful for the purposes of subsection (5A) if there are persons who may become aware of it who could reasonably be expected to infer that what is being glorified, is being glorified as—
    (a) conduct that should be emulated in existing circumstances, or
    (b) conduct that is illustrative of a type of conduct that should be so emulated.

(5C) In this section—

"glorification" includes any form of praise or celebration, and cognate expressions are to be construed accordingly;

"statement" includes a communication without words consisting of sounds or images or both.][2]

(6) Where the Secretary of State believes—
    (a) that an organisation listed in Schedule 2 is operating wholly or partly under a name that is not specified in that Schedule (whether as well as or instead of under the specified name), or
    (b) that an organisation that is operating under a name that is not so specified is otherwise for all practical purposes the same as an organisation so listed,

---

[2] As inserted by the 2006 Act, s.21.

he may, by order, provide that the name that is not specified in that Schedule is to be treated as another name for the listed organisation.

(7) Where an order under subsection (6) provides for a name to be treated as another name for an organisation, this Act shall have effect in relation to acts occurring while—

    (a) the order is in force, and

    (b) the organisation continues to be listed in Schedule 2,

as if the organisation were listed in that Schedule under the other name, as well as under the name specified in the Schedule.

(8) The Secretary of State may at any time by order revoke an order under subsection (6) or otherwise provide for a name specified in such an order to cease to be treated as a name for a particular organisation.

(9) Nothing in subsections (6) to (8) prevents any liability from being established in any proceedings by proof that an organisation is the same as an organisation listed in Schedule 2, even though it is or was operating under a name specified neither in Schedule 2 nor in an order under subsection (6).

4 Deproscription: application

(1) An application may be made to the Secretary of State for an order under section 3(3) or (8)—

    (a) removing an organisation from Schedule 2, or

    (b) providing for a name to cease to be treated as a name for an organisation listed in that Schedule.

(2) An application may be made by—

    (a) the organisation, or

    (b) any person affected by the organisation's proscription [or by the treatment of the name as a name for the organisation].[3]

(3) The Secretary of State shall make regulations prescribing the procedure for applications under this section.

(4) The regulations shall, in particular—

    (a) require the Secretary of State to determine an application within a specified period of time, and

    (b) require an application to state the grounds on which it is made.

5 Deproscription: appeal

(1) There shall be a commission, to be known as the Proscribed Organisations Appeal Commission.

(2) Where an application under section 4 has been refused, the applicant may appeal to the Commission.

(3) The Commission shall allow an appeal against a refusal to deproscribe an organisation or to provide for a name to cease to be treated as a name for an organisation if it considers that the decision to refuse was flawed when considered in the light of the principles applicable on an application for judicial review.

(4) Where the Commission allows an appeal under this section [. . .], it may make an order under this subsection.

---

[3] Words inserted by the 2006 Act, s.22(4).

(5) Where an order is made under subsection (4) in respect of an appeal against a refusal to deproscribe an organisation, the Secretary of State shall as soon as is reasonably practicable—

    (a) lay before Parliament, in accordance with section 123(4), the draft of an order under section 3(3)(b) removing the organisation from the list in Schedule 2, or

    (b) make an order removing the organisation from the list in Schedule 2 in pursuance of section 123(5).

[(5A) Where an order is made under subsection (4) in respect of an appeal against a refusal to provide for a name to cease to be treated as a name for an organisation, the Secretary of State shall, as soon as is reasonably practicable, make an order under section 3(8) providing that the name in question is to cease to be so treated in relation to that organisation.][4]

(6) Schedule 3 (constitution of the Commission and procedure) shall have effect.

6 Further appeal

(1) A party to an appeal under section 5 which the Proscribed Organisations Appeal Commission has determined may bring a further appeal on a question of law to—

    (a) the Court of Appeal, if the first appeal was heard in England and Wales,

    (b) the Court of Session, if the first appeal was heard in Scotland, or

    (c) the Court of Appeal in Northern Ireland, if the first appeal was heard in Northern Ireland.

(2) An appeal under subsection (1) may be brought only with the permission—

    (a) of the Commission, or

    (b) where the Commission refuses permission, of the court to which the appeal would be brought.

(3) An order under section 5(4) shall not require the Secretary of State to take any action until the final determination or disposal of an appeal under this section (including any appeal to the *House of Lords* Supreme Court).

7 Appeal: effect on conviction, &c

(1) This section applies where—

    (a) an appeal under section 5 has been allowed in respect of an organisation,

    (b) an order has been made under section 3(3)(b) in respect of the organisation in accordance with an order of the Commission under section 5(4) (and, if the order was made in reliance on section 123(5), a resolution has been passed by each House of Parliament under section 123(5)(b)),

    (c) a person has been convicted of an offence in respect of the organisation under any of sections 11 to 13, 15 to 19 and 56, and

    (d) the activity to which the charge referred took place on or after the date of the refusal to deproscribe against which the appeal under section 5 was brought.

[(1A) This section also applies where—

    (a) an appeal under section 5 has been allowed in respect of a name treated as the name for an organisation,

    (b) an order has been made under section 3(8) in respect of the name in accordance with an order of the Commission under section 5(4),

    (c) a person has been convicted of an offence in respect of the organisation under any of sections 11 to 13, 15 to 19 and 56, and

---

[4] As inserted by the 2006 Act, s.22(6).

(d) the activity to which the charge referred took place on or after the date of the refusal, against which the appeal under section 5 was brought, to provide for a name to cease to be treated as a name for the organisation.][5]

(2) If the person mentioned in subsection (1)(c) [or (1A)(c)] was convicted on indictment—

    (a) he may appeal against the conviction to the Court of Appeal, and

    (b) the Court of Appeal shall allow the appeal.

(3) A person may appeal against a conviction by virtue of subsection (2) whether or not he has already appealed against the conviction.

(4) An appeal by virtue of subsection (2)—

    (a) must be brought within the period of 28 days beginning with the date on which the order mentioned in subsection (1)(b) [or (1A)(b)] comes into force, and

    (b) shall be treated as an appeal under section 1 of the Criminal Appeal Act 1968 (but does not require leave).

(5) If the person mentioned in subsection (1)(c) or [(1A)(c)] was convicted by a magistrates' court—

    (a) he may appeal against the conviction to the Crown Court, and

    (b) the Crown Court shall allow the appeal.

(6) A person may appeal against a conviction by virtue of subsection (5)—

    (a) whether or not he pleaded guilty,

    (b) whether or not he has already appealed against the conviction, and

    (c) whether or not he has made an application in respect of the conviction under section 111 of the Magistrates' Courts Act 1980 (case stated).

(7) An appeal by virtue of subsection (5)—

    (a) must be brought within the period of 21 days beginning with the date on which the order mentioned in subsection (1)(b) or [(1A)(b)][6] comes into force, and

    (b) shall be treated as an appeal under section 108(1)(b) of the Magistrates' Courts Act 1980.

(8) In section 133(5) of the Criminal Justice Act 1988 (compensation for miscarriage of justice) after paragraph (b) there shall be inserted—
"or

    (c) on an appeal under section 7 of the Terrorism Act 2000."

Offences

11 Membership

(1) A person commits an offence if he belongs or professes to belong to a proscribed organisation.

(2) It is a defence for a person charged with an offence under subsection (1) to prove—

    (a) that the organisation was not proscribed on the last (or only) occasion on which he became a member or began to profess to be a member, and

    (b) that he has not taken part in the activities of the organisation at any time while it was proscribed.

(3) A person guilty of an offence under this section shall be liable—

---

[5] Inserted by the 2006 Act, s.22(7).
[6] All words in square brackets inserted by the 2006 Act, s.22(8).

(a) on conviction on indictment, to imprisonment for a term not exceeding ten years, to a fine or to both, or

(b) on summary conviction, to imprisonment for a term not exceeding six months, to a fine not exceeding the statutory maximum or to both.

(4) In subsection (2) "proscribed" means proscribed for the purposes of any of the following—

(a) this Act;

(b) the Northern Ireland (Emergency Provisions) Act 1996;

(c) the Northern Ireland (Emergency Provisions) Act 1991;

(d) the Prevention of Terrorism (Temporary Provisions) Act 1989;

(e) the Prevention of Terrorism (Temporary Provisions) Act 1984;

(f) the Northern Ireland (Emergency Provisions) Act 1978;

(g) the Prevention of Terrorism (Temporary Provisions) Act 1976;

(h) the Prevention of Terrorism (Temporary Provisions) Act 1974;

(i) the Northern Ireland (Emergency Provisions) Act 1973.

12 Support

(1) A person commits an offence if—

(a) he invites support for a proscribed organisation, and

(b) the support is not, or is not restricted to, the provision of money or other property (within the meaning of section 15).

(2) A person commits an offence if he arranges, manages or assists in arranging or managing a meeting which he knows is—

(a) to support a proscribed organisation,

(b) to further the activities of a proscribed organisation, or

(c) to be addressed by a person who belongs or professes to belong to a proscribed organisation.

(3) A person commits an offence if he addresses a meeting and the purpose of his address is to encourage support for a proscribed organisation or to further its activities.

(4) Where a person is charged with an offence under subsection (2)(c) in respect of a private meeting it is a defence for him to prove that he had no reasonable cause to believe that the address mentioned in subsection (2)(c) would support a proscribed organisation or further its activities.

(5) In subsections (2) to (4)—

(a) "meeting" means a meeting of three or more persons, whether or not the public are admitted, and

(b) a meeting is private if the public are not admitted.

(6) A person guilty of an offence under this section shall be liable—

(a) on conviction on indictment, to imprisonment for a term not exceeding ten years, to a fine or to both, or

(b) on summary conviction, to imprisonment for a term not exceeding six months, to a fine not exceeding the statutory maximum or to both.

13 Uniform

(1) A person in a public place commits an offence if he—

(a) wears an item of clothing, or

(b) wears, carries or displays an article,

in such a way or in such circumstances as to arouse reasonable suspicion that he is a member or supporter of a proscribed organisation.

(2) A constable in Scotland may arrest a person without a warrant if he has reasonable grounds to suspect that the person is guilty of an offence under this section.

(3) A person guilty of an offence under this section shall be liable on summary conviction to—
   (a) imprisonment for a term not exceeding six months,
   (b) a fine not exceeding level 5 on the standard scale, or
   (c) both.

Information and evidence

37 Powers

Schedule 5 (power to obtain information, &c) shall have effect.

PART V
COUNTER-TERRORIST POWERS

Suspected terrorists

40 Terrorist: interpretation

(1) In this Part "terrorist" means a person who—
   (a) has committed an offence under any of sections 11, 12, 15 to 18, 54 and 56 to 63, or
   (b) is or has been concerned in the commission, preparation or instigation of acts of terrorism.

(2) The reference in subsection (1)(b) to a person who has been concerned in the commission, preparation or instigation of acts of terrorism includes a reference to a person who has been, whether before or after the passing of this Act, concerned in the commission, preparation or instigation of acts of terrorism within the meaning given by section 1.

41 Arrest without warrant

(1) A constable may arrest without a warrant a person whom he reasonably suspects to be a terrorist.

(2) Where a person is arrested under this section the provisions of Schedule 8 (detention: treatment, review and extension) shall apply.

(3) Subject to subsections (4) to (7), a person detained under this section shall (unless detained under any other power) be released not later than the end of the period of 48 hours beginning—
   (a) with the time of his arrest under this section, or
   (b) if he was being detained under Schedule 7 when he was arrested under this section, with the time when his examination under that Schedule began.

(4) If on a review of a person's detention under Part II of Schedule 8 the review officer does not authorise continued detention, the person shall (unless detained in accordance with subsection (5) or (6) or under any other power) be released.

(5) Where a police officer intends to make an application for a warrant under paragraph 29 of Schedule 8 extending a person's detention, the person may be detained pending the making of the application.

(6) Where an application has been made under paragraph 29 or 36 of Schedule 8 in respect of a person's detention, he may be detained pending the conclusion of proceedings on the application.

(7) Where an application under paragraph 29 or 36 of Schedule 8 is granted in respect of a person's detention, he may be detained, subject to paragraph 37 of that Schedule, during the period specified in the warrant.

(8) The refusal of an application in respect of a person's detention under paragraph 29 or 36 of Schedule 8 shall not prevent his continued detention in accordance with this section.

(9) A person who has the powers of a constable in one Part of the United Kingdom may exercise the power under subsection (1) in any Part of the United Kingdom.

42 Search of premises

(1) A justice of the peace may on the application of a constable issue a warrant in relation to specified premises if he is satisfied that there are reasonable grounds for suspecting that a person whom the constable reasonably suspects to be a person falling within section 40(1)(b) is to be found there.

(2) A warrant under this section shall authorise any constable to enter and search the specified premises for the purpose of arresting the person referred to in subsection (1) under section 41.

(3) In the application of subsection (1) to Scotland—
   (a) "justice of the peace" includes the sheriff, and
   (b) the justice of the peace or sheriff can be satisfied as mentioned in that subsection only by having heard evidence on oath.

43 Search of persons

(1) A constable may stop and search a person whom he reasonably suspects to be a terrorist to discover whether he has in his possession anything which may constitute evidence that he is a terrorist.

(2) A constable may search a person arrested under section 41 to discover whether he has in his possession anything which may constitute evidence that he is a terrorist.

(3) A search of a person under this section must be carried out by someone of the same sex.

(4) A constable may seize and retain anything which he discovers in the course of a search of a person under subsection (1) or (2) and which he reasonably suspects may constitute evidence that the person is a terrorist.

(5) A person who has the powers of a constable in one Part of the United Kingdom may exercise a power under this section in any Part of the United Kingdom.

Power to stop and search

44 Authorisations

(1) An authorisation under this subsection authorises any constable in uniform to stop a vehicle in an area or at a place specified in the authorisation and to search—
   (a) the vehicle;
   (b) the driver of the vehicle;
   (c) a passenger in the vehicle;
   (d) anything in or on the vehicle or carried by the driver or a passenger.

(2) An authorisation under this subsection authorises any constable in uniform to stop a pedestrian in an area or at a place specified in the authorisation and to search—
   (a) the pedestrian;

(b) anything carried by him.

(3) An authorisation under subsection (1) or (2) may be given only if the person giving it considers it expedient for the prevention of acts of terrorism.

(4) An authorisation may be given—

(a) where the specified area or place is the whole or part of a police area outside Northern Ireland other than one mentioned in paragraph (b) or (c), by a police officer for the area who is of at least the rank of assistant chief constable;

(b) where the specified area or place is the whole or part of the metropolitan police district, by a police officer for the district who is of at least the rank of commander of the metropolitan police;

(c) where the specified area or place is the whole or part of the City of London, by a police officer for the City who is of at least the rank of commander in the City of London police force;

(d) where the specified area or place is the whole or part of Northern Ireland, by a member of the Police Service of Northern Ireland who is of at least the rank of assistant chief constable.

[(4ZA) The power of a person mentioned in subsection (4) to give an authorisation specifying an area or place so mentioned includes power to give such an authorisation specifying such an area or place together with—

(a) the internal waters adjacent to that area or place; or

(b) such area of those internal waters as is specified in the authorisation.][7]

(4A) In a case (within subsection (4)(a), (b) or (c)) in which the specified area or place is in a place described in section 34(1A), an authorisation may also be given by a member of the British Transport Police Force who is of at least the rank of assistant chief constable.

(4B) In a case in which the specified area or place is a place to which section 2(2) of the Ministry of Defence Police Act 1987 applies, an authorisation may also be given by a member of the Ministry of Defence Police who is of at least the rank of assistant chief constable.

(4BA) In a case in which the specified area or place is a place in which members of the Civil Nuclear Constabulary have the powers and privileges of a constable, an authorisation may also be given by a member of that Constabulary who is of at least the rank of assistant chief constable.

(4C) But an authorisation may not be given by—

(a) a member of the British Transport Police Force [. . .]

(b) a member of the Ministry of Defence Police, or

(c) a member of the Civil Nuclear Constabulary,

in any other case.

(5) If an authorisation is given orally, the person giving it shall confirm it in writing as soon as is reasonably practicable.

[(5A) In this section—

"driver", in relation to an aircraft, hovercraft or vessel, means the captain, pilot or other person with control of the aircraft, hovercraft or vessel or any member of its crew and, in relation to a train, includes any member of its crew;

---

[7] Inserted by the 2006 Act, s.30(2).

"internal waters" means waters in the United Kingdom that are not comprised in any police area.]⁸

45 Exercise of power

(1) The power conferred by an authorisation under section 44(1) or (2)—
  (a) may be exercised only for the purpose of searching for articles of a kind which could be used in connection with terrorism, and
  (b) may be exercised whether or not the constable has grounds for suspecting the presence of articles of that kind.

(2) A constable may seize and retain an article which he discovers in the course of a search by virtue of section 44(1) or (2) and which he reasonably suspects is intended to be used in connection with terrorism.

(3) A constable exercising the power conferred by an authorisation may not require a person to remove any clothing in public except for headgear, footwear, an outer coat, a jacket or gloves.

(4) Where a constable proposes to search a person or vehicle by virtue of section 44(1) or (2) he may detain the person or vehicle for such time as is reasonably required to permit the search to be carried out at or near the place where the person or vehicle is stopped.

(5) Where—
  (a) a vehicle or pedestrian is stopped by virtue of section 44(1) or (2), and
  (b) the driver of the vehicle or the pedestrian applies for a written statement that the vehicle was stopped, or that he was stopped, by virtue of section 44(1) or (2),
  the written statement shall be provided.

(6) An application under subsection (5) must be made within the period of 12 months beginning with the date on which the vehicle or pedestrian was stopped.

[(7) In this section "driver" has the same meaning as in section 44.]⁹

46 Duration of authorisation

(1) An authorisation under section 44 has effect, subject to subsections (2) to (7), during the period—
  (a) beginning at the time when the authorisation is given, and
  (b) ending with a date or at a time specified in the authorisation.

(2) The date or time specified under subsection (1)(b) must not occur after the end of the period of 28 days beginning with the day on which the authorisation is given.

[(2A) An authorisation under section 44(4BA) does not have effect except in relation to times when the specified area or place is a place where members of the Civil Nuclear Constabulary have the powers and privileges of a constable.]¹⁰

(3) The person who gives an authorisation shall inform the Secretary of State as soon as is reasonably practicable.

(4) If an authorisation is not confirmed by the Secretary of State before the end of the period of 48 hours beginning with the time when it is given—
  (a) it shall cease to have effect at the end of that period, but

---

⁸ Inserted by the 2006 Act, s.33.
⁹ As inserted by the 2006 Act, s.30(4).
¹⁰ Inserted by the Energy Act 2004, s.57(3).

(b) its ceasing to have effect shall not affect the lawfulness of anything done in reliance on it before the end of that period.

(5) Where the Secretary of State confirms an authorisation he may substitute an earlier date or time for the date or time specified under subsection (1)(b).

(6) The Secretary of State may cancel an authorisation with effect from a specified time.

(7) An authorisation may be renewed in writing by the person who gave it or by a person who could have given it; and subsections (1) to (6) shall apply as if a new authorisation were given on each occasion on which the authorisation is renewed.

47 Offences

(1) A person commits an offence if he—
   (a) fails to stop a vehicle when required to do so by a constable in the exercise of the power conferred by an authorisation under section 44(1);
   (b) fails to stop when required to do so by a constable in the exercise of the power conferred by an authorisation under section 44(2);
   (c) wilfully obstructs a constable in the exercise of the power conferred by an authorisation under section 44(1) or (2).

(2) A person guilty of an offence under this section shall be liable on summary conviction to—
   (a) imprisonment for a term not exceeding six months,
   (b) a fine not exceeding level 5 on the standard scale, or
   (c) both.

Parking

48 Authorisations

(1) An authorisation under this section authorises any constable in uniform to prohibit or restrict the parking of vehicles on a road specified in the authorisation.

(2) An authorisation may be given only if the person giving it considers it expedient for the prevention of acts of terrorism.

(3) An authorisation may be given—
   (a) where the road specified is outside Northern Ireland and is wholly or partly within a police area other than one mentioned in paragraphs (b) or (c), by a police officer for the area who is of at least the rank of assistant chief constable;
   (b) where the road specified is wholly or partly in the metropolitan police district, by a police officer for the district who is of at least the rank of commander of the metropolitan police;
   (c) where the road specified is wholly or partly in the City of London, by a police officer for the City who is of at least the rank of commander in the City of London police force;
   (d) where the road specified is in Northern Ireland, by a member of the Police Service of Northern Ireland who is of at least the rank of assistant chief constable.

(4) If an authorisation is given orally, the person giving it shall confirm it in writing as soon as is reasonably practicable.

49 Exercise of power

(1) The power conferred by an authorisation under section 48 shall be exercised by placing a traffic sign on the road concerned.

(2) A constable exercising the power conferred by an authorisation under section 48 may suspend a parking place.

(3) Where a parking place is suspended under subsection (2), the suspension shall be treated as a restriction imposed by virtue of section 48—

    (a) for the purposes of section 99 of the Road Traffic Regulation Act 1984 (removal of vehicles illegally parked, &c) and of any regulations in force under that section, and

    (b) for the purposes of Articles 47 and 48 of the Road Traffic Regulation (Northern Ireland) Order 1997 (in relation to Northern Ireland).

50 Duration of authorisation

(1) An authorisation under section 48 has effect, subject to subsections (2) and (3), during the period specified in the authorisation.

(2) The period specified shall not exceed 28 days.

(3) An authorisation may be renewed in writing by the person who gave it or by a person who could have given it; and subsections (1) and (2) shall apply as if a new authorisation were given on each occasion on which the authorisation is renewed.

51 Offences

(1) A person commits an offence if he parks a vehicle in contravention of a prohibition or restriction imposed by virtue of section 48.

(2) A person commits an offence if—

    (a) he is the driver or other person in charge of a vehicle which has been permitted to remain at rest in contravention of any prohibition or restriction imposed by virtue of section 48, and

    (b) he fails to move the vehicle when ordered to do so by a constable in uniform.

(3) It is a defence for a person charged with an offence under this section to prove that he had a reasonable excuse for the act or omission in question.

(4) Possession of a current disabled person's badge shall not itself constitute a reasonable excuse for the purposes of subsection (3).

(5) A person guilty of an offence under subsection (1) shall be liable on summary conviction to a fine not exceeding level 4 on the standard scale.

(6) A person guilty of an offence under subsection (2) shall be liable on summary conviction to—

    (a) imprisonment for a term not exceeding 51 weeks,

    (b) a fine not exceeding level 4 on the standard scale, or

    (c) both.

52 Interpretation

In sections 48 to 51—

"disabled person's badge" means a badge issued, or having effect as if issued, under any regulations for the time being in force under section 21 of the Chronically Sick and Disabled Persons Act 1970 (in relation to England and Wales and Scotland) or section 14 of the Chronically Sick and Disabled Persons (Northern Ireland) Act 1978 (in relation to Northern Ireland);

"driver" means, in relation to a vehicle which has been left on any road, the person who was driving it when it was left there;

"parking" means leaving a vehicle or permitting it to remain at rest;

"traffic sign" has the meaning given in section 142(1) of the Road Traffic Regulation Act 1984 (in relation to England and Wales and Scotland) and in Article 28 of the Road Traffic Regulation (Northern Ireland) Order 1997 (in relation to Northern Ireland);

"vehicle" has the same meaning as in section 99(5) of the Road Traffic Regulation Act 1984 (in relation to England and Wales and Scotland) and Article 47(4) of the Road Traffic Regulation (Northern Ireland) Order 1997 (in relation to Northern Ireland).

Port and border controls

53 Port and border controls

(1) Schedule 7 (port and border controls) shall have effect.

(2) The Secretary of State may by order repeal paragraph 16 of Schedule 7.

(3) The powers conferred by Schedule 7 shall be exercisable notwithstanding the rights conferred by section 1 of the Immigration Act 1971 (general principles regulating entry into and staying in the United Kingdom).

PART VI
MISCELLANEOUS

Terrorist offences

54 Weapons training

(1) A person commits an offence if he provides instruction or training in the making or use of—

  (a) firearms,

  [(aa) radioactive material or weapons designed or adapted for the discharge of any radioactive material,][11]

  (b) explosives, or

  (c) chemical, biological or nuclear weapons.

(2) A person commits an offence if he receives instruction or training in the making or use of—

  (a) firearms,

  [(aa) radioactive material or weapons designed or adapted for the discharge of any radioactive material,][12]

  (b) explosives, or

  (c) chemical, biological or nuclear weapons.

(3) A person commits an offence if he invites another to receive instruction or training and the receipt—

  (a) would constitute an offence under subsection (2), or

  (b) would constitute an offence under subsection (2) but for the fact that it is to take place outside the United Kingdom.

(4) For the purpose of subsections (1) and (3)—

  (a) a reference to the provision of instruction includes a reference to making it available either generally or to one or more specific persons, and

---

[11] As inserted by the 2001 Act, s.120(1).
[12] ibid.

(b) an invitation to receive instruction or training may be either general or addressed to one or more specific persons.

(5) It is a defence for a person charged with an offence under this section in relation to instruction or training to prove that his action or involvement was wholly for a purpose other than assisting, preparing for or participating in terrorism.

(6) A person guilty of an offence under this section shall be liable—

    (a) on conviction on indictment, to imprisonment for a term not exceeding ten years, to a fine or to both, or

    (b) on summary conviction, to imprisonment for a term not exceeding six months, to a fine not exceeding the statutory maximum or to both.

(7) A court by or before which a person is convicted of an offence under this section may order the forfeiture of anything which the court considers to have been in the person's possession for purposes connected with the offence.

(8) Before making an order under subsection (7) a court must give an opportunity to be heard to any person, other than the convicted person, who claims to be the owner of or otherwise interested in anything which can be forfeited under that subsection.

(9) An order under subsection (7) shall not come into force until there is no further possibility of it being varied, or set aside, on appeal (disregarding any power of a court to grant leave to appeal out of time).

55 Weapons training: interpretation

In section 54—

"biological weapon" means a biological agent or toxin (within the meaning of the Biological Weapons Act 1974) in a form capable of use for hostile purposes or anything to which section 1(1)(b) of that Act applies,

"chemical weapon" has the meaning given by section 1 of the Chemical Weapons Act 1996, and

"radioactive material" means radioactive material capable of endangering life or causing harm to human health.[13]

56 Directing terrorist organisation

(1) A person commits an offence if he directs, at any level, the activities of an organisation which is concerned in the commission of acts of terrorism.

(2) A person guilty of an offence under this section is liable on conviction on indictment to imprisonment for life.

57 Possession for terrorist purposes

(1) A person commits an offence if he possesses an article in circumstances which give rise to a reasonable suspicion that his possession is for a purpose connected with the commission, preparation or instigation of an act of terrorism.

(2) It is a defence for a person charged with an offence under this section to prove that his possession of the article was not for a purpose connected with the commission, preparation or instigation of an act of terrorism.

(3) In proceedings for an offence under this section, if it is proved that an article—

    (a) was on any premises at the same time as the accused, or

---

[13] Definitions in this section as amended by the 2001 Act, s.120(2)(b).

(b) was on premises of which the accused was the occupier or which he habitually used otherwise than as a member of the public,

the court may assume that the accused possessed the article, unless he proves that he did not know of its presence on the premises or that he had no control over it.

(4) A person guilty of an offence under this section shall be liable—

    (a) on conviction on indictment, to imprisonment for a term not exceeding 15 years, to a fine or to both, or

    (b) on summary conviction, to imprisonment for a term not exceeding six months, to a fine not exceeding the statutory maximum or to both.

58 Collection of information

(1) A person commits an offence if—

    (a) he collects or makes a record of information of a kind likely to be useful to a person committing or preparing an act of terrorism, or

    (b) he possesses a document or record containing information of that kind.

(2) In this section "record" includes a photographic or electronic record.

(3) It is a defence for a person charged with an offence under this section to prove that he had a reasonable excuse for his action or possession.

(4) A person guilty of an offence under this section shall be liable—

    (a) on conviction on indictment, to imprisonment for a term not exceeding 10 years, to a fine or to both, or

    (b) on summary conviction, to imprisonment for a term not exceeding six months, to a fine not exceeding the statutory maximum or to both.

(5) A court by or before which a person is convicted of an offence under this section may order the forfeiture of any document or record containing information of the kind mentioned in subsection (1)(a).

(6) Before making an order under subsection (5) a court must give an opportunity to be heard to any person, other than the convicted person, who claims to be the owner of or otherwise interested in anything which can be forfeited under that subsection.

(7) An order under subsection (5) shall not come into force until there is no further possibility of it being varied, or set aside, on appeal (disregarding any power of a court to grant leave to appeal out of time).

Inciting terrorism overseas

59 England and Wales

(1) A person commits an offence if—

    (a) he incites another person to commit an act of terrorism wholly or partly outside the United Kingdom, and

    (b) the act would, if committed in England and Wales, constitute one of the offences listed in subsection (2).

(2) Those offences are—

    (a) murder,

    (b) an offence under section 18 of the Offences against the Person Act 1861 (wounding with intent),

    (c) an offence under section 23 or 24 of that Act (poison),

    (d) an offence under section 28 or 29 of that Act (explosions), and

    (e) an offence under section 1(2) of the Criminal Damage Act 1971 (endangering life by damaging property).

(3) A person guilty of an offence under this section shall be liable to any penalty to which he would be liable on conviction of the offence listed in subsection (2) which corresponds to the act which he incites.

(4) For the purposes of subsection (1) it is immaterial whether or not the person incited is in the United Kingdom at the time of the incitement.

(5) Nothing in this section imposes criminal liability on any person acting on behalf of, or holding office under, the Crown.

60 Northern Ireland

(1) A person commits an offence if—
   (a) he incites another person to commit an act of terrorism wholly or partly outside the United Kingdom, and
   (b) the act would, if committed in Northern Ireland, constitute one of the offences listed in subsection (2).

(2) Those offences are—
   (a) murder,
   (b) an offence under section 18 of the Offences against the Person Act 1861 (wounding with intent),
   (c) an offence under section 23 or 24 of that Act (poison),
   (d) an offence under section 28 or 29 of that Act (explosions), and
   (e) an offence under Article 3(2) of the SI 1977/426 (NI 4). Criminal Damage (Northern Ireland) Order 1977 (endangering life by damaging property).

(3) A person guilty of an offence under this section shall be liable to any penalty to which he would be liable on conviction of the offence listed in subsection (2) which corresponds to the act which he incites.

(4) For the purposes of subsection (1) it is immaterial whether or not the person incited is in the United Kingdom at the time of the incitement.

(5) Nothing in this section imposes criminal liability on any person acting on behalf of, or holding office under, the Crown.

61 Scotland

(1) A person commits an offence if—
   (a) he incites another person to commit an act of terrorism wholly or partly outside the United Kingdom, and
   (b) the act would, if committed in Scotland, constitute one of the offences listed in subsection (2).

(2) Those offences are—
   (a) murder,
   (b) assault to severe injury, and
   (c) reckless conduct which causes actual injury.

(3) A person guilty of an offence under this section shall be liable to any penalty to which he would be liable on conviction of the offence listed in subsection (2) which corresponds to the act which he incites.

(4) For the purposes of subsection (1) it is immaterial whether or not the person incited is in the United Kingdom at the time of the incitement.

(5) Nothing in this section imposes criminal liability on any person acting on behalf of, or holding office under, the Crown.

Terrorist bombing and finance offences

62 Terrorist bombing: jurisdiction

(1) If—

    (a) a person does anything outside the United Kingdom as an act of terrorism or for the purposes of terrorism, and

    (b) his action would have constituted the commission of one of the offences listed in subsection (2) if it had been done in the United Kingdom,

  he shall be guilty of the offence.

(2) The offences referred to in subsection (1)(b) are—

    (a) an offence under section 2, 3 or 5 of the Explosive Substances Act 1883 (causing explosions, &c),

    (b) an offence under section 1 of the Biological Weapons Act 1974 (biological weapons), and

    (c) an offence under section 2 of the Chemical Weapons Act 1996 (chemical weapons).

63 Terrorist finance: jurisdiction

(1) If—

    (a) a person does anything outside the United Kingdom, and

    (b) his action would have constituted the commission of an offence under any of sections 15 to 18 if it had been done in the United Kingdom,

  he shall be guilty of the offence.

(2) For the purposes of subsection (1)(b), section 18(1)(b) shall be read as if for "the jurisdiction" there were substituted "a jurisdiction".

103 Terrorist information

(1) A person commits an offence if—

    (a) he collects, makes a record of, publishes, communicates or attempts to elicit information about a person to whom this section applies which is of a kind likely to be useful to a person committing or preparing an act of terrorism, or

    (b) he possesses a document or record containing information of that kind.

(2) This section applies to a person who is or has been—

    (a) a constable,

    (b) a member of Her Majesty's Forces,

    (c) the holder of a judicial office,

    (d) an officer of any court, or

    (e) employed in the prison service in Northern Ireland.

(3) In this section "record" includes a photographic or electronic record.

(4) If it is proved in proceedings for an offence under subsection (1)(b) that a document or record—

    (a) was on any premises at the same time as the accused, or

    (b) was on premises of which the accused was the occupier or which he habitually used otherwise than as a member of the public,

  the court may assume that the accused possessed the document or record, unless he proves that he did not know of its presence on the premises or that he had no control over it.

(5) It is a defence for a person charged with an offence under this section to prove that he had a reasonable excuse for his action or possession.

(6) A person guilty of an offence under this section shall be liable—
  (a) on conviction on indictment, to imprisonment for a term not exceeding 10 years, to a fine or to both, or
  (b) on summary conviction, to imprisonment for a term not exceeding six months, to a fine not exceeding the statutory maximum or to both.

(7) A court by or before which a person is convicted of an offence under this section may order the forfeiture of any document or record containing information of the kind mentioned in subsection (1)(a).

(8) Before making an order under subsection (7) a court must give an opportunity to be heard to any person, other than the convicted person, who claims to be the owner of or otherwise interested in anything which can be forfeited under that subsection.

(9) An order under subsection (8) shall not come into force until there is no further possibility of it being varied, or set aside, on appeal (disregarding any power of a court to grant leave to appeal out of time).

118 Defences

(1) Subsection (2) applies where in accordance with a provision mentioned in subsection (5) it is a defence for a person charged with an offence to prove a particular matter.

(2) If the person adduces evidence which is sufficient to raise an issue with respect to the matter the court or jury shall assume that the defence is satisfied unless the prosecution proves beyond reasonable doubt that it is not.

(3) Subsection (4) applies where in accordance with a provision mentioned in subsection (5) a court—
  (a) may make an assumption in relation to a person charged with an offence unless a particular matter is proved, or
  (b) may accept a fact as sufficient evidence unless a particular matter is proved.

(4) If evidence is adduced which is sufficient to raise an issue with respect to the matter mentioned in subsection (3)(a) or (b) the court shall treat it as proved unless the prosecution disproves it beyond reasonable doubt.

(5) The provisions in respect of which subsections (2) and (4) apply are—
  (a) sections 12(4), 39(5)(a), 54, 57, 58, 77 and 103 of this Act, and
  (b) sections 13, 32 and 33 of the Northern Ireland (Emergency Provisions) Act 1996 (possession and information offences) as they have effect by virtue of Schedule 1 to this Act.

SCHEDULE 5

TERRORIST INVESTIGATIONS: INFORMATION

PART I

ENGLAND AND WALES AND NORTHERN IRELAND

Searches

1 (1) A constable may apply to a justice of the peace for the issue of a warrant under this paragraph for the purposes of a terrorist investigation.

  (2) A warrant under this paragraph shall authorise any constable—
    (a) to enter [premises mentioned in sub-paragraph (2A)],[14]

---

[14] Inserted by the 2006 Act, s.26(1)(2).

    (b) to search the premises and any person found there, and

    (c) to seize and retain any relevant material which is found on a search under paragraph (b).

[(2A) The premises referred to in sub-paragraph (2)(a) are—

    (a) one or more sets of premises specified in the application (in which case the application is for a "specific premises warrant"); or

    (b) any premises occupied or controlled by a person specified in the application, including such sets of premises as are so specified (in which case the application is for an "all premises warrant").][15]

  (3) For the purpose of sub-paragraph (2)(c) material is relevant if the constable has reasonable grounds for believing that—

    (a) it is likely to be of substantial value, whether by itself or together with other material, to a terrorist investigation, and

    (b) it must be seized in order to prevent it from being concealed, lost, damaged, altered or destroyed.

  (4) A warrant under this paragraph shall not authorise—

    (a) the seizure and retention of items subject to legal privilege, or

    (b) a constable to require a person to remove any clothing in public except for headgear, footwear, an outer coat, a jacket or gloves.

  (5) Subject to paragraph 2, a justice may grant an application under this paragraph if satisfied—

    (a) that the warrant is sought for the purposes of a terrorist investigation,

    (b) that there are reasonable grounds for believing that there is material on [premises to which the application relates] which is likely to be of substantial value, whether by itself or together with other material, to a terrorist investigation and which does not consist of or include excepted material (within the meaning of paragraph 4 below) [. . .]

    (c) that the issue of a warrant is likely to be necessary in the circumstances of the case, [and

    (d) in the case of an application for an all premises warrant, that it is not reasonably practicable to specify in the application all the premises which the person so specified occupies or controls and which might need to be searched].[16]

2 (1) This paragraph applies where an application for a specific premises warrant is made under paragraph 1 and—

    (a) the application is made by a police officer of at least the rank of superintendent,

    (b) the application does not relate to residential premises, and

    (c) the justice to whom the application is made is not satisfied of the matter referred to in paragraph 1(5)(c).

  (2) The justice may grant the application if satisfied of the matters referred to in paragraph 1(5)(a) and (b).

  (3) Where a warrant under paragraph 1 is issued by virtue of this paragraph, the powers under paragraph 1(2)(a) and (b) are exercisable only within the period of 24 hours beginning with the time when the warrant is issued.

---

[15] As inserted by the 2006 Act, s.26(3).

[16] All words in square brackets in this subsection are as substituted and inserted by the 2006 Act, s.26(4).

(4) For the purpose of sub-paragraph (1) "residential premises" means any premises which the officer making the application has reasonable grounds for believing are used wholly or mainly as a dwelling.

[2A (1) This paragraph applies where an application for an all premises warrant is made under paragraph 1 and—

(a) the application is made by a police officer of at least the rank of superintendent, and

(b) the justice to whom the application is made is not satisfied of the matter referred to in paragraph 1(5)(c).

(2) The justice may grant the application if satisfied of the matters referred to in paragraph 1(5)(a), (b) and (d).

(3) Where a warrant under paragraph 1 is issued by virtue of this paragraph, the powers under paragraph 1(2)(a) and (b) are exercisable only—

(a) in respect of premises which are not residential premises, and

(b) within the period of 24 hours beginning with the time when the warrant is issued.

(4) For the purpose of sub-paragraph (3) "residential premises", in relation to a power under paragraph 1(2)(a) or (b), means any premises which the constable exercising the power has reasonable grounds for believing are used wholly or mainly as a dwelling.][17]

3 (1) Subject to sub-paragraph (2), a police officer of at least the rank of superintendent may by a written authority signed by him authorise a search of specified premises which are wholly or partly within a cordoned area.

(2) A constable who is not of the rank required by sub-paragraph (1) may give an authorisation under this paragraph if he considers it necessary by reason of urgency.

(3) An authorisation under this paragraph shall authorise any constable—

(a) to enter the premises specified in the authority,

(b) to search the premises and any person found there, and

(c) to seize and retain any relevant material (within the meaning of paragraph 1(3)) which is found on a search under paragraph (b).

(4) The powers under sub-paragraph (3)(a) and (b) may be exercised—

(a) on one or more occasions, and

(b) at any time during the period when the designation of the cordoned area under section 33 has effect.

(5) An authorisation under this paragraph shall not authorise—

(a) the seizure and retention of items subject to legal privilege;

(b) a constable to require a person to remove any clothing in public except for headgear, footwear, an outer coat, a jacket or gloves.

(6) An authorisation under this paragraph shall not be given unless the person giving it has reasonable grounds for believing that there is material to be found on the premises which—

(a) is likely to be of substantial value, whether by itself or together with other material, to a terrorist investigation, and

(b) does not consist of or include excepted material.

---

[17] As inserted by the 2006 Act, s.26(6).

(7) A person commits an offence if he wilfully obstructs a search under this paragraph.

(8) A person guilty of an offence under sub-paragraph (7) shall be liable on summary conviction to—

    (a) imprisonment for a term not exceeding 51 weeks,

    (b) a fine not exceeding level 4 on the standard scale, or

    (c) both.

Excepted material

4 In this Part—

    (a) "excluded material" has the meaning given by section 11 of the Police and Criminal Evidence Act 1984,

    (b) "items subject to legal privilege" has the meaning given by section 10 of that Act, and

    (c) "special procedure material" has the meaning given by section 14 of that Act;

and material is "excepted material" if it falls within any of paragraphs (a) to (c).

Excluded and special procedure material: production & access

5 (1) A constable may apply to a Circuit Judge or a District Judge (Magistrates' Courts) for an order under this paragraph for the purposes of a terrorist investigation.

    (2) An application for an order shall relate to particular material, or material of a particular description, which consists of or includes excluded material or special procedure material.

    (3) An order under this paragraph may require a specified person—

        (a) to produce to a constable within a specified period for seizure and retention any material which he has in his possession, custody or power and to which the application relates;

        (b) to give a constable access to any material of the kind mentioned in paragraph (a) within a specified period;

        (c) to state to the best of his knowledge and belief the location of material to which the application relates if it is not in, and it will not come into, his possession, custody or power within the period specified under paragraph (a) or (b).

    (4) For the purposes of this paragraph—

        (a) an order may specify a person only if he appears to the Circuit judge or the District Judge (Magistrates' Courts) to have in his possession, custody or power any of the material to which the application relates, and

        (b) a period specified in an order shall be the period of seven days beginning with the date of the order unless it appears to the judge that a different period would be appropriate in the particular circumstances of the application.

    (5) Where a Circuit Judge or a District Judge (Magistrates' Courts) makes an order under sub-paragraph (3)(b) in relation to material on any premises, he may, on the application of a constable, order any person who appears to the judge to be entitled to grant entry to the premises to allow any constable to enter the premises to obtain access to the material.

6 (1) A Circuit Judge or a District Judge (Magistrates' Courts) may grant an application under paragraph 5 if satisfied—

    (a) that the material to which the application relates consists of or includes excluded material or special procedure material,

   (b) that it does not include items subject to legal privilege, and

   (c) that the conditions in sub-paragraphs (2) and (3) are satisfied in respect of that material.

(2) The first condition is that—

   (a) the order is sought for the purposes of a terrorist investigation, and

   (b) there are reasonable grounds for believing that the material is likely to be of substantial value, whether by itself or together with other material, to a terrorist investigation.

(3) The second condition is that there are reasonable grounds for believing that it is in the public interest that the material should be produced or that access to it should be given having regard—

   (a) to the benefit likely to accrue to a terrorist investigation if the material is obtained, and

   (b) to the circumstances under which the person concerned has any of the material in his possession, custody or power.

7 (1) An order under paragraph 5 may be made in relation to—

   (a) material consisting of or including excluded or special procedure material which is expected to come into existence within the period of 28 days beginning with the date of the order;

   (b) a person who the Circuit judge or the District Judge (Magistrates' Courts) thinks is likely to have any of the material to which the application relates in his possession, custody or power within that period.

(2) Where an order is made under paragraph 5 by virtue of this paragraph, paragraph 5(3) shall apply with the following modifications—

   (a) the order shall require the specified person to notify a named constable as soon as is reasonably practicable after any material to which the application relates comes into his possession, custody or power,

   (b) the reference in paragraph 5(3)(a) to material which the specified person has in his possession, custody or power shall be taken as a reference to the material referred to in paragraph (a) above which comes into his possession, custody or power, and

   (c) the reference in paragraph 5(3)(c) to the specified period shall be taken as a reference to the period of 28 days beginning with the date of the order.

(3) Where an order is made under paragraph 5 by virtue of this paragraph, paragraph 5(4) shall not apply and the order—

   (a) may only specify a person falling within sub-paragraph (1)(b), and

   (b) shall specify the period of seven days beginning with the date of notification required under sub-paragraph (2)(a) unless it appears to the judge that a different period would be appropriate in the particular circumstances of the application.

8 (1) An order under paragraph 5—

   (a) shall not confer any right to production of, or access to, items subject to legal privilege, and

   (b) shall have effect notwithstanding any restriction on the disclosure of information imposed by statute or otherwise.

(2) Where the material to which an application under paragraph 5 relates consists of information contained in a computer—

    (a) an order under paragraph 5(3)(a) shall have effect as an order to produce the material in a form in which it can be taken away and in which it is visible and legible, and

    (b) an order under paragraph 5(3)(b) shall have effect as an order to give access to the material in a form in which it is visible and legible.

9 (1) An order under paragraph 5 may be made in relation to material in the possession, custody or power of a government department.

  (2) Where an order is made by virtue of sub-paragraph (1)—

    (a) it shall be served as if the proceedings were civil proceedings against the department, and

    (b) it may require any officer of the department, whether named in the order or not, who may for the time being have in his possession, custody or power the material concerned, to comply with the order.

  (3) In this paragraph "government department" means an authorised government department for the purposes of the Crown Proceedings Act 1947.

10 (1) An order of a Circuit judge or a District Judge (Magistrates' Courts) under paragraph 5 shall have effect as if it were an order of the Crown Court.

  (2) Criminal Procedure Rules may make provision about proceedings relating to an order under paragraph 5.

  (3) In particular, the rules may make provision about the variation or discharge of an order.

Excluded or special procedure material: search

11 (1) A constable may apply to a Circuit judge or a District Judge (Magistrates' Courts) for the issue of a warrant under this paragraph for the purposes of a terrorist investigation.

  (2) A warrant under this paragraph shall authorise any constable—

    (a) to enter [premises mentioned in sub-paragraph (3A)],

    (b) to search the premises and any person found there, and

    (c) to seize and retain any relevant material which is found on a search under paragraph (b).

  (3) A warrant under this paragraph shall not authorise—

    (a) the seizure and retention of items subject to legal privilege;

    (b) a constable to require a person to remove any clothing in public except for headgear, footwear, an outer coat, a jacket or gloves.

  [(3A) The premises referred to in sub-paragraph (2)(a) are—

    (a) one or more sets of premises specified in the application (in which case the application is for a "specific premises warrant"); or

    (b) any premises occupied or controlled by a person specified in the application, including such sets of premises as are so specified (in which case the application is for an "all premises warrant").][18]

  (4) For the purpose of sub-paragraph (2)(c) material is relevant if the constable has reasonable grounds for believing that it is likely to be of substantial value, whether by itself or together with other material, to a terrorist investigation.

12 (1) A Circuit Judge or a District Judge (Magistrates' Courts) may grant an application [for a specific premises warrant][19] under paragraph 11 if satisfied that an

---

[18] All words in square brackets are as substituted or inserted by the 2006 Act, s.26(7).

[19] As inserted by the 2006 Act, s.26(9).

order made under paragraph 5 in relation to material on the premises specified in the application has not been complied with.

(2) A Circuit judge or a District Judge (Magistrates' Courts) may also grant an application for a specific premises warrant under paragraph 11 if satisfied that there are reasonable grounds for believing that—

    (a) there is material on premises specified in the application which consists of or includes excluded material or special procedure material but does not include items subject to legal privilege, and

    (b) the conditions in sub-paragraphs (3) and (4) are satisfied.

[(2A) A Circuit judge or a District Judge (Magistrates' Courts) may grant an application for an all premises warrant under paragraph 11 if satisfied—

    (a) that an order made under paragraph 5 has not been complied with, and

    (b) that the person specified in the application is also specified in the order.

(2B) A Circuit judge or a District Judge (Magistrates' Courts) may also grant an application for an all premises warrant under paragraph 11 if satisfied that there are reasonable grounds for believing—

    (a) that there is material on premises to which the application relates which consists of or includes excluded material or special procedure material but does not include items subject to legal privilege, and

    (b) that the conditions in sub-paragraphs (3) and (4) are met.][20]

(3) The first condition is that—

    (a) the warrant is sought for the purposes of a terrorist investigation, and

    (b) the material is likely to be of substantial value, whether by itself or together with other material, to a terrorist investigation.

(4) The second condition is that it is not appropriate to make an order under paragraph 5 in relation to the material because—

    (a) it is not practicable to communicate with any person entitled to produce the material,

    (b) it is not practicable to communicate with any person entitled to grant access to the material or entitled to grant entry to [premises to which the application for the warrant relates],[21] or

    (c) a terrorist investigation may be seriously prejudiced unless a constable can secure immediate access to the material.

Explanations

13 (1) A constable may apply to a Circuit judge or a District Judge (Magistrates' Courts) for an order under this paragraph requiring any person specified in the order to provide an explanation of any material—

    (a) seized in pursuance of a warrant under paragraph 1 or 11, or

    (b) produced or made available to a constable under paragraph 5.

(2) An order under this paragraph shall not require any person to disclose any information which he would be entitled to refuse to disclose on grounds of legal professional privilege in proceedings in the High Court.

(3) But a lawyer may be required to provide the name and address of his client.

---

[20] As inserted by the 2006 Act, s.26(10).
[21] As substituted by the 2006 Act, s.26(11).

(4) A statement by a person in response to a requirement imposed by an order under this paragraph—

    (a) may be made orally or in writing, and

    (b) may be used in evidence against him only on a prosecution for an offence under paragraph 14.

(5) Paragraph 10 shall apply to orders under this paragraph as it applies to orders under paragraph 5.

14 (1) A person commits an offence if, in purported compliance with an order under paragraph 13, he—

    (a) makes a statement which he knows to be false or misleading in a material particular, or

    (b) recklessly makes a statement which is false or misleading in a material particular.

(2) A person guilty of an offence under sub-paragraph (1) shall be liable—

    (a) on conviction on indictment, to imprisonment for a term not exceeding two years, to a fine or to both, or

    (b) on summary conviction, to imprisonment for a term not exceeding six months, to a fine not exceeding the statutory maximum or to both.

Urgent cases

15 (1) A police officer of at least the rank of superintendent may by a written order signed by him give to any constable the authority which may be given by a search warrant under paragraph 1 or 11.

(2) An order shall not be made under this paragraph unless the officer has reasonable grounds for believing—

    (a) that the case is one of great emergency, and

    (b) that immediate action is necessary.

(3) Where an order is made under this paragraph particulars of the case shall be notified as soon as is reasonably practicable to the Secretary of State.

(4) A person commits an offence if he wilfully obstructs a search under this paragraph.

(5) A person guilty of an offence under sub-paragraph (4) shall be liable on summary conviction to—

    (a) imprisonment for a term not exceeding *three months* 51 weeks,

    (b) a fine not exceeding level 4 on the standard scale, or

    (c) both.

16 (1) If a police officer of at least the rank of superintendent has reasonable grounds for believing that the case is one of great emergency he may by a written notice signed by him require any person specified in the notice to provide an explanation of any material seized in pursuance of an order under paragraph 15.

(2) Sub-paragraphs (2) to (4) of paragraph 13 and paragraph 14 shall apply to a notice under this paragraph as they apply to an order under paragraph 13.

(3) A person commits an offence if he fails to comply with a notice under this paragraph.

(4) It is a defence for a person charged with an offence under sub-paragraph (3) to show that he had a reasonable excuse for his failure.

(5) A person guilty of an offence under sub-paragraph (3) shall be liable on summary conviction to—

    (a) imprisonment for a term not exceeding six months,

(b) a fine not exceeding level 5 on the standard scale, or

(c) both.

Supplementary

17 For the purposes of sections 21 and 22 of the Police and Criminal Evidence Act 1984 (seized material: access, copying and retention)—

    (a) a terrorist investigation shall be treated as an investigation of or in connection with an offence, and

    (b) material produced in pursuance of an order under paragraph 5 shall be treated as if it were material seized by a constable.

    (f) the reference in paragraph 17 to sections 21 and 22 of the Police and Criminal Evidence Act 1984 shall be taken as a reference to Articles 23 and 24 of the Police and Criminal Evidence (Northern Ireland) Order 1989, and

    (g) references to "a Circuit Judge" shall be taken as references to a Crown Court judge.

SCHEDULE 8

DETENTION

Section 41 and Schedule 7, para 6

PART I

TREATMENT OF PERSONS DETAINED UNDER SECTION 41 OR SCHEDULE 7

Place of detention

1 (1) The Secretary of State shall designate places at which persons may be detained under Schedule 7 or section 41.

    (2) In this Schedule a reference to a police station includes a reference to any place which the Secretary of State has designated under sub-paragraph (1) as a place where a person may be detained under section 41.

    (3) Where a person is detained under Schedule 7, he may be taken in the custody of an examining officer or of a person acting under an examining officer's authority to and from any place where his attendance is required for the purpose of—

        (a) his examination under that Schedule,

        (b) establishing his nationality or citizenship, or

        (c) making arrangements for his admission to a country or territory outside the United Kingdom.

    (4) A constable who arrests a person under section 41 shall take him as soon as is reasonably practicable to the police station which the constable considers the most appropriate.

    (5) In this paragraph "examining officer" has the meaning given in Schedule 7.

    (6) Where a person is arrested in one Part of the United Kingdom and all or part of his detention takes place in another Part, the provisions of this Schedule which apply to detention in a particular Part of the United Kingdom apply in relation to him while he is detained in that Part.

Identification

2 (1) An authorised person may take any steps which are reasonably necessary for—

    (a) photographing the detained person,

    (b) measuring him, or

    (c) identifying him.

 (2) In sub-paragraph (1) "authorised person" means any of the following—

    (a) a constable,

    (b) a prison officer,

    (c) a person authorised by the Secretary of State, and

    (d) in the case of a person detained under Schedule 7, an examining officer (within the meaning of that Schedule).

 (3) This paragraph does not confer the power to take—

    (a) fingerprints, non-intimate samples or intimate samples (within the meaning given by paragraph 15 below), or

    (b) relevant physical data or samples as mentioned in section 18 of the Criminal Procedure (Scotland) Act 1995 as applied by paragraph 20 below.

Audio and video recording of interviews

3 (1) The Secretary of State shall—

    (a) issue a code of practice about the audio recording of interviews to which this paragraph applies, and

    (b) make an order requiring the audio recording of interviews to which this paragraph applies in accordance with any relevant code of practice under paragraph (a).

 (2) The Secretary of State may make an order requiring the video recording of—

    (a) interviews to which this paragraph applies;

    (b) interviews to which this paragraph applies which take place in a particular Part of the United Kingdom.

 (3) An order under sub-paragraph (2) shall specify whether the video recording which it requires is to be silent or with sound.

 (4) Where an order is made under sub-paragraph (2)—

    (a) the Secretary of State shall issue a code of practice about the video recording of interviews to which the order applies, and

    (b) the order shall require the interviews to be video recorded in accordance with any relevant code of practice under paragraph (a).

 (5) Where the Secretary of State has made an order under sub-paragraph (2) requiring certain interviews to be video recorded with sound—

    (a) he need not make an order under sub-paragraph (1)(b) in relation to those interviews, but

    (b) he may do so.

 (6) This paragraph applies to any interview by a constable of a person detained under Schedule 7 or section 41 if the interview takes place in a police station.

 (7) A code of practice under this paragraph—

    (a) may make provision in relation to a particular Part of the United Kingdom;

    (b) may make different provision for different Parts of the United Kingdom.

4 (1) This paragraph applies to a code of practice under paragraph 3.

 (2) Where the Secretary of State proposes to issue a code of practice he shall—

    (a) publish a draft,

    (b) consider any representations made to him about the draft, and

    (c) if he thinks it appropriate, modify the draft in the light of any representations made to him.

(3) The Secretary of State shall lay a draft of the code before Parliament.

(4) When the Secretary of State has laid a draft code before Parliament he may bring it into operation by order.

(5) The Secretary of State may revise a code and issue the revised code; and sub-paragraphs (2) to (4) shall apply to a revised code as they apply to an original code.

(6) The failure by a constable to observe a provision of a code shall not of itself make him liable to criminal or civil proceedings.

(7) A code—

(a) shall be admissible in evidence in criminal and civil proceedings, and

(b) shall be taken into account by a court or tribunal in any case in which it appears to the court or tribunal to be relevant.

Status

5   A detained person shall be deemed to be in legal custody throughout the period of his detention.

Rights: England, Wales and Northern Ireland

6 (1) Subject to paragraph 8, a person detained under Schedule 7 or section 41 at a police station in England, Wales or Northern Ireland shall be entitled, if he so requests, to have one named person informed as soon as is reasonably practicable that he is being detained there.

(2) The person named must be—

(a) a friend of the detained person,

(b) a relative, or

(c) a person who is known to the detained person or who is likely to take an interest in his welfare.

(3) Where a detained person is transferred from one police station to another, he shall be entitled to exercise the right under this paragraph in respect of the police station to which he is transferred.

7 (1) Subject to paragraphs 8 and 9, a person detained under Schedule 7 or section 41 at a police station in England, Wales or Northern Ireland shall be entitled, if he so requests, to consult a solicitor as soon as is reasonably practicable, privately and at any time.

(2) Where a request is made under sub-paragraph (1), the request and the time at which it was made shall be recorded.

8 (1) Subject to sub-paragraph (2), an officer of at least the rank of superintendent may authorise a delay—

(a) in informing the person named by a detained person under paragraph 6;

(b) in permitting a detained person to consult a solicitor under paragraph 7.

(2) But where a person is detained under section 41 he must be permitted to exercise his rights under paragraphs 6 and 7 before the end of the period mentioned in subsection (3) of that section.

(3) Subject to sub-paragraph (5), an officer may give an authorisation under sub-paragraph (1) only if he has reasonable grounds for believing—

(a) in the case of an authorisation under sub-paragraph (1)(a), that informing the named person of the detained person's detention will have any of the consequences specified in sub-paragraph (4), or

(b) in the case of an authorisation under sub-paragraph (1)(b), that the exercise of the right under paragraph 7 at the time when the detained person desires to exercise it will have any of the consequences specified in sub-paragraph (4).

(4) Those consequences are—

   (a) interference with or harm to evidence of a serious offence,

   (b) interference with or physical injury to any person,

   (c) the alerting of persons who are suspected of having committed a serious offence but who have not been arrested for it,

   (d) the hindering of the recovery of property obtained as a result of a serious offence or in respect of which a forfeiture order could be made under section 23,

   (e) interference with the gathering of information about the commission, preparation or instigation of acts of terrorism,

   (f) the alerting of a person and thereby making it more difficult to prevent an act of terrorism, and

   (g) the alerting of a person and thereby making it more difficult to secure a person's apprehension, prosecution or conviction in connection with the commission, preparation or instigation of an act of terrorism.

(5) An officer may also give an authorisation under sub-paragraph (1) if he has reasonable grounds for believing that—

   (a) the detained person has benefited from his criminal conduct, and

   (b) the recovery of the value of the property constituting the benefit will be hindered by—

      (i) informing the named person of the detained person's detention (in the case of an authorisation under sub-paragraph (1)(a)), or

      (ii) the exercise of the right under paragraph 7 (in the case of an authorisation under sub-paragraph (1)(b)).

[(5A) For the purposes of sub-paragraph (5) the question whether a person has benefited from his criminal conduct is to be decided in accordance with Part 2 of the Proceeds of Crime Act 2002.][22]

(6) If an authorisation under sub-paragraph (1) is given orally, the person giving it shall confirm it in writing as soon as is reasonably practicable.

(7) Where an authorisation under sub-paragraph (1) is given—

   (a) the detained person shall be told the reason for the delay as soon as is reasonably practicable, and

   (b) the reason shall be recorded as soon as is reasonably practicable.

(8) Where the reason for authorising delay ceases to subsist there may be no further delay in permitting the exercise of the right in the absence of a further authorisation under sub-paragraph (1).

(9) In this paragraph, references to a "serious offence" are (in relation to England and Wales) to an indictable offence, and (in relation to Northern Ireland) to a serious arrestable offence within the meaning of Article 87 of the Police and Criminal Evidence (Northern Ireland) Order 1989; but also include—

   (a) an offence under any of the provisions mentioned in section 40(1)(a) of this Act, and

   (b) an attempt or conspiracy to commit an offence under any of the provisions mentioned in section 40(1)(a).

---

[22] As inserted by the Proceeds of Crime Act 2002.

131

9 (1) A direction under this paragraph may provide that a detained person who wishes to exercise the right under paragraph 7 may consult a solicitor only in the sight and hearing of a qualified officer.

(2) A direction under this paragraph may be given—

    (a) where the person is detained at a police station in England or Wales, by an officer of at least the rank of Commander or Assistant Chief Constable, or

    (b) where the person is detained at a police station in Northern Ireland, by an officer of at least the rank of Assistant Chief Constable.

(3) A direction under this paragraph may be given only if the officer giving it has reasonable grounds for believing that, unless the direction is given, the exercise of the right by the detained person will have any of the consequences specified in paragraph 8(4) or the consequence specified in paragraph 8(5)(c).

(4) In this paragraph "a qualified officer" means a police officer who—

    (a) is of at least the rank of inspector,

    (b) is of the uniformed branch of the force of which the officer giving the direction is a member, and

    (c) in the opinion of the officer giving the direction, has no connection with the detained person's case.

(5) A direction under this paragraph shall cease to have effect once the reason for giving it ceases to subsist.

10 (1) This paragraph applies where a person is detained in England, Wales or Northern Ireland under Schedule 7 or section 41.

(2) Fingerprints may be taken from the detained person only if they are taken by a constable—

    (a) with the appropriate consent given in writing, or

    (b) without that consent under sub-paragraph (4).

(3) A non-intimate sample may be taken from the detained person only if it is taken by a constable—

    (a) with the appropriate consent given in writing, or

    (b) without that consent under sub-paragraph (4).

(4) Fingerprints or a non-intimate sample may be taken from the detained person without the appropriate consent only if—

    (a) he is detained at a police station and a police officer of at least the rank of superintendent authorises the fingerprints or sample to be taken, or

    (b) he has been convicted of a recordable offence and, where a non-intimate sample is to be taken, he was convicted of the offence on or after 10th April 1995 (or 29th July 1996 where the non-intimate sample is to be taken in Northern Ireland).

(5) An intimate sample may be taken from the detained person only if—

    (a) he is detained at a police station,

    (b) the appropriate consent is given in writing,

    (c) a police officer of at least the rank of superintendent authorises the sample to be taken, and

    (d) subject to paragraph 13(2) and (3), the sample is taken by a constable.

(6) Subject to sub-paragraph (6A) an officer may give an authorisation under sub-paragraph (4)(a) or (5)(c) only if—

    (a) in the case of a person detained under section 41, the officer reasonably suspects that the person has been involved in an offence under any of the provisions mentioned in section 40(1)(a), and the officer reasonably believes that the fingerprints or sample will tend to confirm or disprove his involvement, or

   (b) in any case, the officer is satisfied that the taking of the fingerprints or sample from the person is necessary in order to assist in determining whether he falls within section 40(1)(b).

[(6A) An officer may also give an authorisation under sub-paragraph (4)(a) for the taking of fingerprints if—

   (a) he is satisfied that the fingerprints of the detained person will facilitate the ascertainment of that person's identity; and

   (b) that person has refused to identify himself or the officer has reasonable grounds for suspecting that that person is not who he claims to be.

(6B) In this paragraph references to ascertaining a person's identity include references to showing that he is not a particular person.][23]

(7) If an authorisation under sub-paragraph (4)(a) or (5)(c) is given orally, the person giving it shall confirm it in writing as soon as is reasonably practicable.

11 (1) Before fingerprints or a sample are taken from a person under paragraph 10, he shall be informed—

   (a) that the fingerprints or sample may be used for the purposes of paragraph 14(4), section 63A(1) of the Police and Criminal Evidence Act 1984 and Article 63A(1) of the Police and Criminal Evidence (Northern Ireland) Order 1989 (checking of fingerprints and samples), and

   (b) where the fingerprints or sample are to be taken under paragraph 10(2)(a), (3)(a) or (4)(b), of the reason for taking the fingerprints or sample.

(2) Before fingerprints or a sample are taken from a person upon an authorisation given under paragraph 10(4)(a) or (5)(c), he shall be informed—

   (a) that the authorisation has been given,

   (b) of the grounds upon which it has been given, and

   (c) where relevant, of the nature of the offence in which it is suspected that he has been involved.

(3) After fingerprints or a sample are taken under paragraph 10, there shall be recorded as soon as is reasonably practicable any of the following which apply—

   (a) the fact that the person has been informed in accordance with sub-paragraphs (1) and (2),

   (b) the reason referred to in sub-paragraph (1)(b),

   (c) the authorisation given under paragraph 10(4)(a) or (5)(c),

   (d) the grounds upon which that authorisation has been given, and

   (e) the fact that the appropriate consent has been given.

12 (1) This paragraph applies where—

   (a) two or more non-intimate samples suitable for the same means of analysis have been taken from a person under paragraph 10,

   (b) those samples have proved insufficient, and

   (c) the person has been released from detention.

(2) An intimate sample may be taken from the person if—

   (a) the appropriate consent is given in writing,

---

[23] Added by the 2001 Act, s.89(2).

     (b) a police officer of at least the rank of superintendent authorises the sample to be taken, and

     (c) subject to paragraph 13(2) and (3), the sample is taken by a constable.

  (3) Paragraphs 10(6) and (7) and 11 shall apply in relation to the taking of an intimate sample under this paragraph; and a reference to a person detained under section 41 shall be taken as a reference to a person who was detained under section 41 when the non-intimate samples mentioned in sub-paragraph (1)(a) were taken.

13 (1) Where appropriate written consent to the taking of an intimate sample from a person under paragraph 10 or 12 is refused without good cause, in any proceedings against that person for an offence—

     (a) the court, in determining whether to commit him for trial or whether there is a case to answer, may draw such inferences from the refusal as appear proper, and

     (b) the court or jury, in determining whether that person is guilty of the offence charged, may draw such inferences from the refusal as appear proper.

  (2) An intimate sample other than a sample of urine or a dental impression may be taken under paragraph 10 or 12 only by a registered medical practitioner acting on the authority of a constable.

  (3) An intimate sample which is a dental impression may be taken under paragraph 10 or 12 only by a registered dentist acting on the authority of a constable.

  (4) Where a sample of hair other than pubic hair is to be taken under paragraph 10 the sample may be taken either by cutting hairs or by plucking hairs with their roots so long as no more are plucked than the person taking the sample reasonably considers to be necessary for a sufficient sample.

14 (1) This paragraph applies to—

     (a) fingerprints or samples taken under paragraph 10 or 12, and

     (b) information derived from those samples.

  (2) The fingerprints and samples may be retained but shall not be used by any person except for the purposes of a terrorist investigation or for purposes related to the prevention or detection of crime, the investigation of an offence or the conduct of a prosecution.

  (3) In particular, a check may not be made against them under—

     (a) section 63A(1) of the Police and Criminal Evidence Act 1984 (checking of fingerprints and samples), or

     (b) Article 63A(1) of the Police and Criminal Evidence (Northern Ireland) Order 1989 (checking of fingerprints and samples),

except for the purpose of a terrorist investigation or for purposes related to the prevention or detection of crime, the investigation of an offence or the conduct of a prosecution.

  (4) The fingerprints, samples or information may be checked, subject to sub-paragraph (2), against—

     (a) other fingerprints or samples taken under paragraph 10 or 12 or information derived from those samples,

     (b) relevant physical data or samples taken by virtue of paragraph 20,

     (c) any of the fingerprints, samples and information mentioned in section 63A(1)(a) and (b) of the Police and Criminal Evidence Act 1984 (checking of fingerprints and samples),

(d) any of the fingerprints, samples and information mentioned in Article 63A(1)(a) and (b) of the Police and Criminal Evidence (Northern Ireland) Order 1989 (checking of fingerprints and samples), and

(e) fingerprints or samples taken under section 15(9) of, or paragraph 7(5) of Schedule 5 to, the Prevention of Terrorism (Temporary Provisions) Act 1989 or information derived from those samples.

[(4A) In this paragraph—

(a) a reference to crime includes a reference to any conduct which—

   (i) constitutes one or more criminal offences (whether under the law of a part of the United Kingdom or of a country or territory outside the United Kingdom); or

   (ii) is, or corresponds to, any conduct which, if it all took place in any one part of the United Kingdom, would constitute one or more criminal offences; and

(b) the references to an investigation and to a prosecution include references, respectively, to any investigation outside the United Kingdom of any crime or suspected crime and to a prosecution brought in respect of any crime in a country or territory outside the United Kingdom.][24]

(5) This paragraph (other than sub-paragraph (4)) shall apply to fingerprints or samples taken under section 15(9) of, or paragraph 7(5) of Schedule 5 to, the Prevention of Terrorism (Temporary Provisions) Act 1989 and information derived from those samples as it applies to fingerprints or samples taken under paragraph 10 or 12 and the information derived from those samples.

15 (1) In the application of paragraphs 10 to 14 in relation to a person detained in England or Wales the following expressions shall have the meaning given by section 65 of the Police and Criminal Evidence Act 1984 (Part V definitions)—

(a) "appropriate consent",

(b) "fingerprints",

(c) "insufficient",

(d) "intimate sample",

(e) "non-intimate sample",

(f) "registered dentist", and

(g) "sufficient".

(2) In the application of paragraphs 10 to 14 in relation to a person detained in Northern Ireland the expressions listed in sub-paragraph (1) shall have the meaning given by Article 53 of the Police and Criminal Evidence (Northern Ireland) Order 1989 (definitions).

(3) In paragraph 10 "recordable offence" shall have—

(a) in relation to a person detained in England or Wales, the meaning given by section 118(1) of the Police and Criminal Evidence Act 1984 (general interpretation), and

(b) in relation to a person detained in Northern Ireland, the meaning given by Article 2(2) of the Police and Criminal Evidence (Northern Ireland) Order 1989 (definitions).

[16 to 20 *Rights: Scotland . . .*]

---

[24] As inserted by the Criminal Justice and Police Act 2001, s.84(4).

PART II
REVIEW OF DETENTION UNDER SECTION 41

Requirement

21 (1) A person's detention shall be periodically reviewed by a review officer.

(2) The first review shall be carried out as soon as is reasonably practicable after the time of the person's arrest.

(3) Subsequent reviews shall, subject to paragraph 22, be carried out at intervals of not more than 12 hours.

(4) No review of a person's detention shall be carried out after a warrant extending his detention has been issued under Part III.

Postponement

22 (1) A review may be postponed if at the latest time at which it may be carried out in accordance with paragraph 21—

(a) the detained person is being questioned by a police officer and an officer is satisfied that an interruption of the questioning to carry out the review would prejudice the investigation in connection with which the person is being detained,

(b) no review officer is readily available, or

(c) it is not practicable for any other reason to carry out the review.

(2) Where a review is postponed it shall be carried out as soon as is reasonably practicable.

(3) For the purposes of ascertaining the time within which the next review is to be carried out, a postponed review shall be deemed to have been carried out at the latest time at which it could have been carried out in accordance with paragraph 21.

Grounds for continued detention

23 (1) A review officer may authorise a person's continued detention only if satisfied that it is necessary—

(a) to obtain relevant evidence whether by questioning him or otherwise,

(b) to preserve relevant evidence,

[(ba) pending the result of an examination or analysis of any relevant evidence or of anything the examination or analysis of which is to be or is being carried out with a view to obtaining relevant evidence],[25]

(c) pending a decision whether to apply to the Secretary of State for a deportation notice to be served on the detained person,

(d) pending the making of an application to the Secretary of State for a deportation notice to be served on the detained person,

(e) pending consideration by the Secretary of State whether to serve a deportation notice on the detained person, or

(f) pending a decision whether the detained person should be charged with an offence.

---

[25] As inserted by the 2006 Act, s.24(1).

(2) The review officer shall not authorise continued detention by virtue of sub-paragraph (1)(a) or (b) unless he is satisfied that the investigation in connection with which the person is detained is being conducted diligently and expeditiously.

(3) The review officer shall not authorise continued detention by virtue of sub-paragraph (1)(c) to (f) unless he is satisfied that the process pending the completion of which detention is necessary is being conducted diligently and expeditiously.

(4) In [this paragraph][26] "relevant evidence" means evidence which—

(a) relates to the commission by the detained person of an offence under any of the provisions mentioned in section 40(1)(a), or

(b) indicates that the detained person falls within section 40(1)(b).

(5) In sub-paragraph (1) "deportation notice" means notice of a decision to make a deportation order under the Immigration Act 1971.

Review officer

24 (1) The review officer shall be an officer who has not been directly involved in the investigation in connection with which the person is detained.

(2) In the case of a review carried out within the period of 24 hours beginning with the time of arrest, the review officer shall be an officer of at least the rank of inspector.

(3) In the case of any other review, the review officer shall be an officer of at least the rank of superintendent.

25 (1) This paragraph applies where—

(a) the review officer is of a rank lower than superintendent,

(b) an officer of higher rank than the review officer gives directions relating to the detained person, and

(c) those directions are at variance with the performance by the review officer of a duty imposed on him under this Schedule.

(2) The review officer shall refer the matter at once to an officer of at least the rank of superintendent.

Representations

26 (1) Before determining whether to authorise a person's continued detention, a review officer shall give either of the following persons an opportunity to make representations about the detention—

(a) the detained person, or

(b) a solicitor representing him who is available at the time of the review.

(2) Representations may be oral or written.

(3) A review officer may refuse to hear oral representations from the detained person if he considers that he is unfit to make representations because of his condition or behaviour.

Rights

27 (1) Where a review officer authorises continued detention he shall inform the detained person—

(a) of any of his rights under paragraphs 6 and 7 which he has not yet exercised, and

---

[26] As substituted by the 2006 Act, s.24(4).

    (b) if the exercise of any of his rights under either of those paragraphs is being delayed in accordance with the provisions of paragraph 8, of the fact that it is being so delayed.

  (2) Where a review of a person's detention is being carried out at a time when his exercise of a right under either of those paragraphs is being delayed—

    (a) the review officer shall consider whether the reason or reasons for which the delay was authorised continue to subsist, and

    (b) if in his opinion the reason or reasons have ceased to subsist, he shall inform the officer who authorised the delay of his opinion (unless he was that officer).

  (3) In the application of this paragraph to Scotland, for the references to paragraphs 6, 7 and 8 substitute references to paragraph 16.

  (4) The following provisions (requirement to bring an accused person before the court after his arrest) shall not apply to a person detained under section 41—

    (a) section 135(3) of the Criminal Procedure (Scotland) Act 1995, and

    (b) Article 8(1) of the Criminal Justice (Children) (Northern Ireland) Order 1998.

  (5) Section 22(1) of the Criminal Procedure (Scotland) Act 1995 (interim liberation by officer in charge of police station) shall not apply to a person detained under section 41.

Record

28 (1) A review officer carrying out a review shall make a written record of the outcome of the review and of any of the following which apply—

    (a) the grounds upon which continued detention is authorised,

    (b) the reason for postponement of the review,

    (c) the fact that the detained person has been informed as required under paragraph 27(1),

    (d) the officer's conclusion on the matter considered under paragraph 27(2)(a),

    (e) the fact that he has taken action under paragraph 27(2)(b), and

    (f) the fact that the detained person is being detained by virtue of section 41(5) or (6).

  (2) The review officer shall—

    (a) make the record in the presence of the detained person, and

    (b) inform him at that time whether the review officer is authorising continued detention, and if he is, of his grounds.

  (3) Sub-paragraph (2) shall not apply where, at the time when the record is made, the detained person is—

    (a) incapable of understanding what is said to him,

    (b) violent or likely to become violent, or

    (c) in urgent need of medical attention.

PART III
EXTENSION OF DETENTION UNDER SECTION 41

Warrants of further detention

29 (1) [Each of the following—

    (a) in England and Wales, a Crown Prosecutor,

    (b) in Scotland, the Lord Advocate or a procurator fiscal,

    (c) in Northern Ireland, the Director of Public Prosecutions for Northern Ireland,

(d) in any part of the United Kingdom, a police officer of at least the rank of superintendent,

may][27] apply to a judicial authority for the issue of a warrant of further detention under this Part.

(2) A warrant of further detention—
  (a) shall authorise the further detention under section 41 of a specified person for a specified period, and
  (b) shall state the time at which it is issued.

(3) [Subject to sub-paragraph (3A) and paragraph 36], the specified period in relation to a person shall be the period of seven days beginning—
  (a) with the time of his arrest under section 41, or
  (b) if he was being detained under Schedule 7 when he was arrested under section 41, with the time when his examination under that Schedule began.

[(3A) A judicial authority may issue a warrant of further detention in relation to a person which specifies a shorter period as the period for which that person's further detention is authorised if—
  (a) the application for the warrant is an application for a warrant specifying a shorter period; or
  (b) the judicial authority is satisfied that there are circumstances that would make it inappropriate for the specified period to be as long as the period of seven days mentioned in sub-paragraph (3).][28]

(4) In this Part "judicial authority" means—
  (a) in England and Wales, [. . .] a District Judge (Magistrates' Courts) who is designated for the purpose of this Part by the Lord Chief Justice of England and Wales after consulting the Lord Chancellor,
  (b) in Scotland, the sheriff, and
  (c) in Northern Ireland, a county court judge, or a resident magistrate who is designated for the purpose of this Part by the Lord Chief Justice of Northern Ireland after consulting the Lord Chancellor.

(5) The Lord Chief Justice may nominate a judicial office holder (as defined in section 109(4) of the Constitutional Reform Act 2005) to exercise his functions under sub-paragraph (4)(a).

(6) The Lord Chief Justice of Northern Ireland may nominate any of the following to exercise his functions under sub-paragraph (4)(c)—
  (a) the holder of one of the offices listed in Schedule 1 to the Justice (Northern Ireland) Act 2002;
  (b) a Lord Justice of Appeal (as defined in section 88 of that Act).

Time limit

30 (1) An application for a warrant shall be made—
  (a) during the period mentioned in section 41(3), or
  (b) within six hours of the end of that period.

(2) The judicial authority hearing an application made by virtue of sub-paragraph (1)(b) shall dismiss the application if he considers that it would have been reasonably practicable to make it during the period mentioned in section 41(3).

---

[27] As substituted by the 2006 Act, s.23(2).

[28] Words in square brackets as substituted or inserted by the 2006 Act, s.23(3).

(3) For the purposes of this Schedule, an application for a warrant is made when written or oral notice of an intention to make the application is given to a judicial authority.

Notice

31 An application for a warrant may not be heard unless the person to whom it relates has been given a notice stating—

(a) that the application has been made,

(b) the time at which the application was made,

(c) the time at which it is to be heard, and

(d) the grounds upon which further detention is sought.

Grounds for extension

32 (1) A judicial authority may issue a warrant of further detention only if satisfied that—

(a) there are reasonable grounds for believing that the further detention of the person to whom the application relates is as mentioned in sub-paragraph (1A), and

(b) the investigation in connection with which the person is detained is being conducted diligently and expeditiously.

[(1A) The further detention of a person is necessary as mentioned in this sub-paragraph if it is necessary—

(a) to obtain relevant evidence whether by questioning him or otherwise;

(b) to preserve relevant evidence; or

(c) pending the result of an examination or analysis of any relevant evidence or of anything the examination or analysis of which is to be or is being carried out with a view to obtaining relevant evidence.]

(2) [In this paragraph][29] "relevant evidence" means, in relation to the person to whom the application relates, evidence which—

(a) relates to his commission of an offence under any of the provisions mentioned in section 40(1)(a), or

(b) indicates that he is a person falling within section 40(1)(b).

Representation

33 (1) The person to whom an application relates shall—

(a) be given an opportunity to make oral or written representations to the judicial authority about the application, and

(b) subject to sub-paragraph (3), be entitled to be legally represented at the hearing.

(2) A judicial authority shall adjourn the hearing of an application to enable the person to whom the application relates to obtain legal representation where—

(a) he is not legally represented,

(b) he is entitled to be legally represented, and

(c) he wishes to be so represented.

(3) A judicial authority may exclude any of the following persons from any part of the hearing—

---

[29] Words as substituted by the 2006 Act, s.24(2); para 1A as inserted by s.24(3).

(a) the person to whom the application relates;

(b) anyone representing him.

(4) A judicial authority may, after giving an opportunity for representations to be made by or on behalf of the applicant and the person to whom the application relates, direct—

(a) that the hearing of the application must be conducted, and

(b) that all representations by or on behalf of a person for the purposes of the hearing must be made,

by such means (whether a live television link or other means) falling within sub-paragraph (5) as may be specified in the direction and not in the presence (apart from by those means) of the applicant, of the person to whom the application relates or of any legal representative of that person.

(5) A means of conducting the hearing and of making representations falls within this sub-paragraph if it allows the person to whom the application relates and any legal representative of his (without being present at the hearing and to the extent that they are not excluded from it under sub-paragraph (3))—

(a) to see and hear the judicial authority and the making of representations to it by other persons; and

(b) to be seen and heard by the judicial authority.

(6) If the person to whom the application relates wishes to make representations about whether a direction should be given under sub-paragraph (4), he must do so by using the facilities that will be used if the judicial authority decides to give a direction under that sub-paragraph.

(7) Sub-paragraph (2) applies to the hearing of representations about whether a direction should be given under sub-paragraph (4) in the case of any application as it applies to a hearing of the application.

(8) A judicial authority shall not give a direction under sub-paragraph (4) unless—

(a) it has been notified by the Secretary of State that facilities are available at the place where the person to whom the application relates is held for the judicial authority to conduct a hearing by means falling within sub-paragraph (5); and

(b) that notification has not been withdrawn.

(9) If in a case where it has power to do so a judicial authority decides not to give a direction under sub-paragraph (4), it shall state its reasons for not giving it.

Information

34 (1) The [person][30] who has made an application for a warrant may apply to the judicial authority for an order that specified information upon which he intends to rely be withheld from—

(a) the person to whom the application relates, and

(b) anyone representing him.

(2) Subject to sub-paragraph (3), a judicial authority may make an order under sub-paragraph (1) in relation to specified information only if satisfied that there are reasonable grounds for believing that if the information were disclosed—

(a) evidence of an offence under any of the provisions mentioned in section 40(1)(a) would be interfered with or harmed,

---

[30] As substituted by the 2006 Act, s.23(5).

141

    (b) the recovery of property obtained as a result of an offence under any of those provisions would be hindered,

    (c) the recovery of property in respect of which a forfeiture order could be made under section 23 would be hindered,

    (d) the apprehension, prosecution or conviction of a person who is suspected of falling within section 40(1)(a) or (b) would be made more difficult as a result of his being alerted,

    (e) the prevention of an act of terrorism would be made more difficult as a result of a person being alerted,

    (f) the gathering of information about the commission, preparation or instigation of an act of terrorism would be interfered with, or

    (g) a person would be interfered with or physically injured.

[(3) A judicial authority may also make an order under sub-paragraph (1) in relation to specified information if satisfied that there are reasonable grounds for believing that—

    (a) the detained person has benefited from his criminal conduct, and

    (b) the recovery of the value of the property constituting the benefit would be hindered if the information were disclosed.

(3A) For the purposes of sub-paragraph (3) the question whether a person has benefited from his criminal conduct is to be decided in accordance with Part 2 or 3 of the Proceeds of Crime Act 2002.][31]

(4) The judicial authority shall direct that the following be excluded from the hearing of the application under this paragraph—

    (a) the person to whom the application for a warrant relates, and

    (b) anyone representing him.

Adjournments

35 (1) A judicial authority may adjourn the hearing of an application for a warrant only if the hearing is adjourned to a date before the expiry of the period mentioned in section 41(3).

(2) This paragraph shall not apply to an adjournment under paragraph 33(2).

Extensions of warrants

36 (1) [Each of the following—

    (a) in England and Wales, a Crown Prosecutor,

    (b) in Scotland, the Lord Advocate or a procurator fiscal,

    (c) in Northern Ireland, the Director of Public Prosecutions for Northern Ireland,

    (d) in any part of the United Kingdom, a police officer of at least the rank of superintendent,

may][32] apply to a judicial authority for the extension or further extension of the period specified in a warrant of further detention.

[(1A) The person to whom an application under sub-paragraph (1) may be made is—

    (a) in the case of an application falling within sub-paragraph (1B), a judicial authority; and

    (b) in any other case, a senior judge.

---

[31] As substituted by the Proceeds of Crime Act 2002, Sch 11, para 39(5).

[32] As substituted by the 2006 Act, s.23(2).

(1B) An application for the extension or further extension of a period falls within this sub-paragraph if—

    (a) the grant of the application otherwise than in accordance with sub-paragraph (3AA)(b) would extend that period to a time that is no more than [fourteen days][33] after the relevant time; and

    (b) no application has previously been made to a senior judge in respect of that period.][34]

(2) Where the period specified is extended, the warrant shall be endorsed with a note stating the new specified period.

[(3) Subject to sub-paragraph (3A), the specified period shall end not later than the end of the period of seven days beginning with the relevant time.

(3A) Where the period specified in a warrant of further detention—

    (a) ends at the end of the period of seven days beginning with the relevant time, or

    (b) by virtue of a previous extension (or further extension) under this sub-paragraph, ends after the end of that period,

the specified period may, on an application under this paragraph, be extended or further extended to a period ending not later than the end of the period of fourteen days beginning with the relevant time.

(3) Subject to sub-paragraph (3AA), the period by which the specified period is extended or further extended shall be the period which—

    (a) begins with the time specified in sub-paragraph (3A); and

    (b) ends with whichever is the earlier of—

        (i) the end of the period of seven days beginning with that time; and

        (ii) the end of the period of 28 days beginning with the relevant time.

(3A) The time referred to in sub-paragraph (3)(a) is—

    (a) in the case of a warrant specifying a period which has not previously been extended under this paragraph, the end of the period specified in the warrant, and

    (b) in any other case, the end of the period for which the period specified in the warrant was last extended under this paragraph.

(3AA) A judicial authority or senior judge may extend or further extend the period specified in a warrant by a shorter period than is required by sub-paragraph (3) if—

    (a) the application for the extension is an application for an extension by a period that is shorter than is so required; or

    (b) the judicial authority or senior judge is satisfied that there are circumstances that would make it inappropriate for the period of the extension to be as long as the period so required.

(3B) In this paragraph "the relevant time", in relation to a person, means—

    (a) the time of his arrest under section 41, or

    (b) if he was being detained under Schedule 7 when he was arrested under section 41, the time when his examination under that Schedule began.][35]

(4) Paragraphs 30(3) and 31 to 34 shall apply to an application under this paragraph as they apply to an application for a warrant of further detention [but, in relation

---

[33] As substituted by the 2006 Act, s.25(3). The words "a judicial authority" as substituted by s.25(4).
[34] As inserted by the 2006 Act, s.23(6).
[35] As substituted by the 2006 Act, s.23(7).

to an application made by virtue of sub-paragraph (1A)(b) to a senior judge, as if—

    (a) references to a judicial authority were references to a senior judge; and

    (b) references to the judicial authority in question were references to the senior judge in question.][36]

(5) A judicial authority [or senior judge][37] may adjourn the hearing of an application under sub-paragraph (1) only if the hearing is adjourned to a date before the expiry of the period specified in the warrant.

(6) Sub-paragraph (5) shall not apply to an adjournment under paragraph 33(2).

[(7) In this paragraph and paragraph 37 'senior judge' means a judge of the High Court or of the High Court of Justiciary.][38]

Detention—conditions

[37 (1) This paragraph applies where—

    (a) a person ('the detained person') is detained by virtue of a warrant issued under this Part of this Schedule; and

    (b) his detention is not authorised by virtue of section 41(5) or (6) or otherwise apart from the warrant.

(2) If it at any time appears to the police officer or other person in charge of the detained person's case that any of the matters mentioned in paragraph 32(1)(a) and (b) on which the judicial authority or senior judge last authorised his further detention no longer apply, he must—

    (a) if he has custody of the detained person, release him immediately; and

    (b) if he does not, immediately inform the person who does have custody of the detained person that those matters no longer apply in the detained person's case.

(3) A person with custody of the detained person who is informed in accordance with this paragraph that those matters no longer apply in his case must release that person immediately.][39]

---

[36] As inserted by the 2006 Act, s.23(8).
[37] As inserted by the 2006 Act, s.23(9).
[38] As inserted by the 2006 Act, s.23(10).
[39] As substituted by the 2006 Act, s.23(11).

APPENDIX 2

The Terrorism Act 2006

CONTENTS

PART 1
OFFENCES

PART 2
MISCELLANEOUS PROVISIONS

PART 3
SUPPLEMENTAL PROVISIONS

TERRORISM ACT 2006
2006 CHAPTER 11

An Act to make provision for and about offences relating to conduct carried out, or capable of being carried out, for purposes connected with terrorism; to amend enactments relating to terrorism; to amend the Intelligence Services Act 1994 and the Regulation of Investigatory Powers Act 2000; and for connected purposes. [30th March 2006]

Be it enacted by the Queen's most Excellent Majesty, by and with the advice and consent of the Lords Spiritual and Temporal, and Commons, in this present Parliament assembled, and by the authority of the same, as follows:—

PART 1
OFFENCES

Encouragement etc. of terrorism

1 Encouragement of terrorism

(1) This section applies to a statement that is likely to be understood by some or all of the members of the public to whom it is published as a direct or indirect encouragement or other inducement to them to the commission, preparation or instigation of acts of terrorism or Convention offences.

(2) A person commits an offence if—

    (a) he publishes a statement to which this section applies or causes another to publish such a statement; and

    (b) at the time he publishes it or causes it to be published, he—

        (i) intends members of the public to be directly or indirectly encouraged or otherwise induced by the statement to commit, prepare or instigate acts of terrorism or Convention offences; or

        (ii) is reckless as to whether members of the public will be directly or indirectly encouraged or otherwise induced by the statement to commit, prepare or instigate such acts or offences.

(3) For the purposes of this section, the statements that are likely to be understood by members of the public as indirectly encouraging the commission or preparation of acts of terrorism or Convention offences include every statement which—

    (a) glorifies the commission or preparation (whether in the past, in the future or generally) of such acts or offences; and

    (b) is a statement from which those members of the public could reasonably be expected to infer that what is being glorified is being glorified as conduct that should be emulated by them in existing circumstances.

(4) For the purposes of this section the questions how a statement is likely to be understood and what members of the public could reasonably be expected to infer from it must be determined having regard both—

    (a) to the contents of the statement as a whole; and

    (b) to the circumstances and manner of its publication.

(5) It is irrelevant for the purposes of subsections (1) to (3)—

    (a) whether anything mentioned in those subsections relates to the commission, preparation or instigation of one or more particular acts of terrorism or

Convention offences, of acts of terrorism or Convention offences of a particular description or of acts of terrorism or Convention offences generally; and,

(b) whether any person is in fact encouraged or induced by the statement to commit, prepare or instigate any such act or offence.

(6) In proceedings for an offence under this section against a person in whose case it is not proved that he intended the statement directly or indirectly to encourage or otherwise induce the commission, preparation or instigation of acts of terrorism or Convention offences, it is a defence for him to show—

(a) that the statement neither expressed his views nor had his endorsement (whether by virtue of section 3 or otherwise); and

(b) that it was clear, in all the circumstances of the statement's publication, that it did not express his views and (apart from the possibility of his having been given and failed to comply with a notice under subsection (3) of that section) did not have his endorsement.

(7) A person guilty of an offence under this section shall be liable—

(a) on conviction on indictment, to imprisonment for a term not exceeding 7 years or to a fine, or to both;

(b) on summary conviction in England and Wales, to imprisonment for a term not exceeding 12 months or to a fine not exceeding the statutory maximum, or to both;

(c) on summary conviction in Scotland or Northern Ireland, to imprisonment for a term not exceeding 6 months or to a fine not exceeding the statutory maximum, or to both.

(8) In relation to an offence committed before the commencement of section 154(1) of the Criminal Justice Act 2003 (c. 44), the reference in subsection (7)(b) to 12 months is to be read as a reference to 6 months.

2 Dissemination of terrorist publications

(1) A person commits an offence if he engages in conduct falling within subsection (2) and, at the time he does so—

(a) he intends an effect of his conduct to be a direct or indirect encouragement or other inducement to the commission, preparation or instigation of acts of terrorism;

(b) he intends an effect of his conduct to be the provision of assistance in the commission or preparation of such acts; or (c) he is reckless as to whether his conduct has an effect mentioned in paragraph (a) or (b).

(2) For the purposes of this section a person engages in conduct falling within this subsection if he—

(a) distributes or circulates a terrorist publication;

(b) gives, sells or lends such a publication;

(c) offers such a publication for sale or loan;

(d) provides a service to others that enables them to obtain, read, listen to or look at such a publication, or to acquire it by means of a gift, sale or loan;

(e) transmits the contents of such a publication electronically; or

(f) has such a publication in his possession with a view to its becoming the subject of conduct falling within any of paragraphs (a) to (e).

(3) For the purposes of this section a publication is a terrorist publication, in relation to conduct falling within subsection (2), if matter contained in it is likely—

(a) to be understood, by some or all of the persons to whom it is or may become available as a consequence of that conduct, as a direct or indirect encouragement or other inducement to them to the commission, preparation or instigation of acts of terrorism; or

(b) to be useful in the commission or preparation of such acts and to be understood, by some or all of those persons, as contained in the publication, or made available to them, wholly or mainly for the purpose of being so useful to them.

(4) For the purposes of this section matter that is likely to be understood by a person as indirectly encouraging the commission or preparation of acts of terrorism includes any matter which—

(a) glorifies the commission or preparation (whether in the past, in the future or generally) of such acts; and

(b) is matter from which that person could reasonably be expected to infer that what is being glorified is being glorified as conduct that should be emulated by him in existing circumstances.

(5) For the purposes of this section the question whether a publication is a terrorist publication in relation to particular conduct must be determined—

(a) as at the time of that conduct; and

(b) having regard both to the contents of the publication as a whole and to the circumstances in which that conduct occurs.

(6) In subsection (1) references to the effect of a person's conduct in relation to a terrorist publication include references to an effect of the publication on one or more persons to whom it is or may become available as a consequence of that conduct.

(7) It is irrelevant for the purposes of this section whether anything mentioned in subsections (1) to (4) is in relation to the commission, preparation or instigation of one or more particular acts of terrorism, of acts of terrorism of a particular description or of acts of terrorism generally.

(8) For the purposes of this section it is also irrelevant, in relation to matter contained in any article whether any person—

(a) is in fact encouraged or induced by that matter to commit, prepare or instigate acts of terrorism; or

(b) in fact makes use of it in the commission or preparation of such acts.

(9) In proceedings for an offence under this section against a person in respect of conduct to which subsection (10) applies, it is a defence for him to show—

(a) that the matter by reference to which the publication in question was a terrorist publication neither expressed his views nor had his endorsement (whether by virtue of section 3 or otherwise); and

(b) that it was clear, in all the circumstances of the conduct, that that matter did not express his views and (apart from the possibility of his having been given and failed to comply with a notice under subsection (3) of that section) did not have his endorsement.

(10) This subsection applies to the conduct of a person to the extent that—

(a) the publication to which his conduct related contained matter by reference to which it was a terrorist publication by virtue of subsection (3)(a); and

(b) that person is not proved to have engaged in that conduct with the intention specified in subsection (1)(a).

(11) A person guilty of an offence under this section shall be liable—

(a) on conviction on indictment, to imprisonment for a term not exceeding 7 years or to a fine, or to both;

(b) on summary conviction in England and Wales, to imprisonment for a term not exceeding 12 months or to a fine not exceeding the statutory maximum, or to both;

(c) on summary conviction in Scotland or Northern Ireland, to imprisonment for a term not exceeding 6 months or to a fine not exceeding the statutory maximum, or to both.

(12) In relation to an offence committed before the commencement of section 154(1) of the Criminal Justice Act 2003 (c. 44), the reference in subsection (11)(b) to 12 months is to be read as a reference to 6 months.

(13) In this section—

"lend" includes let on hire, and "loan" is to be construed accordingly; "publication" means an article or record of any description that contains any of the following, or any combination of them—

(a) matter to be read;

(b) matter to be listened to;

(c) matter to be looked at or watched.

3 Application of ss. 1 and 2 to internet activity etc.

(1) This section applies for the purposes of sections 1 and 2 in relation to cases where—

(a) a statement is published or caused to be published in the course of, or in connection with, the provision or use of a service provided electronically; or

(b) conduct falling within section 2(2) was in the course of, or in connection with, the provision or use of such a service.

(2) The cases in which the statement, or the article or record to which the conduct relates, is to be regarded as having the endorsement of a person ("the relevant person") at any time include a case in which—

(a) a constable has given him a notice under subsection (3);

(b) that time falls more than 2 working days after the day on which the notice was given; and

(c) the relevant person has failed, without reasonable excuse, to comply with the notice.

(3) A notice under this subsection is a notice which—

(a) declares that, in the opinion of the constable giving it, the statement or the article or record is unlawfully terrorism-related;

(b) requires the relevant person to secure that the statement or the article or record, so far as it is so related, is not available to the public or is modified so as no longer to be so related;

(c) warns the relevant person that a failure to comply with the notice within 2 working days will result in the statement, or the article or record, being regarded as having his endorsement; and

(d) explains how, under subsection (4), he may become liable by virtue of the notice if the statement, or the article or record, becomes available to the public after he has complied with the notice.

(4) Where—

(a) a notice under subsection (3) has been given to the relevant person in respect of a statement, or an article or record, and he has complied with it, but

(b) he subsequently publishes or causes to be published a statement which is, or is for all practical purposes, the same or to the same effect as the statement to which the notice related, or to matter contained in the article or record to which it related, (a "repeat statement");

the requirements of subsection (2)(a) to (c) shall be regarded as satisfied in the case of the repeat statement in relation to the times of its subsequent publication by the relevant person.

(5) In proceedings against a person for an offence under section 1 or 2 the requirements of subsection (2)(a) to (c) are not, in his case, to be regarded as satisfied in relation to any time by virtue of subsection (4) if he shows that he—

(a) has, before that time, taken every step he reasonably could to prevent a repeat statement from becoming available to the public and to ascertain whether it does; and

(b) was, at that time, a person to whom subsection (6) applied.

(6) This subsection applies to a person at any time when he—

(a) is not aware of the publication of the repeat statement; or

(b) having become aware of its publication, has taken every step that he reasonably could to secure that it either ceased to be available to the public or was modified as mentioned in subsection (3)(b).

(7) For the purposes of this section a statement or an article or record is unlawfully terrorism-related if it constitutes, or if matter contained in the article or record constitutes—

(a) something that is likely to be understood, by any one or more of the persons to whom it has or may become available, as a direct or indirect encouragement or other inducement to the commission, preparation or instigation of acts of terrorism or Convention offences; or

(b) information which—

(i) is likely to be useful to any one or more of those persons in the commission or preparation of such acts; and

(ii) is in a form or context in which it is likely to be understood by any one or more of those persons as being wholly or mainly for the purpose of being so useful.

(8) The reference in subsection (7) to something that is likely to be understood as an indirect encouragement to the commission or preparation of acts of terrorism or Convention offences includes anything which is likely to be understood as—

(a) the glorification of the commission or preparation (whether in the past, in the future or generally) of such acts or such offences; and

(b) a suggestion that what is being glorified is being glorified as conduct that should be emulated in existing circumstances.

(9) In this section "working day" means any day other than—

(a) a Saturday or a Sunday;

(b) Christmas Day or Good Friday; or

(c) a day which is a bank holiday under the Banking and Financial Dealings Act 1971 (c. 80) in any part of the United Kingdom.

4 Giving of notices under s. 3

(1) Except in a case to which any of subsections (2) to (4) applies, a notice under section 3(3) may be given to a person only—

(a) by delivering it to him in person; or

    (b) by sending it to him, by means of a postal service providing for delivery to be recorded, at his last known address.

(2) Such a notice may be given to a body corporate only—

    (a) by delivering it to the secretary of that body in person; or

    (b) by sending it to the appropriate person, by means of a postal service providing for delivery to be recorded, at the address of the registered or principal office of the body.

(3) Such a notice may be given to a firm only—

    (a) by delivering it to a partner of the firm in person;

    (b) by so delivering it to a person having the control or management of the partnership business; or

    (c) by sending it to the appropriate person, by means of a postal service providing for delivery to be recorded, at the address of the principal office of the partnership.

(4) Such a notice may be given to an unincorporated body or association only—

    (a) by delivering it to a member of its governing body in person; or

    (b) by sending it to the appropriate person, by means of a postal service providing for delivery to be recorded, at the address of the principal office of the body or association.

(5) In the case of—

    (a) a company registered outside the United Kingdom,

    (b) a firm carrying on business outside the United Kingdom, or

    (c) an unincorporated body or association with offices outside the United Kingdom, the references in this section to its principal office include references to its principal office within the United Kingdom (if any).

(6) In this section "the appropriate person" means—

    (a) in the case of a body corporate, the body itself or its secretary;

    (b) in the case of a firm, the firm itself or a partner of the firm or a person having the control or management of the partnership business; and

    (c) in the case of an unincorporated body or association, the body or association itself or a member of its governing body.

(7) For the purposes of section 3 the time at which a notice under subsection (3) of that section is to be regarded as given is—

    (a) where it is delivered to a person, the time at which it is so delivered; and

    (b) where it is sent by a postal service providing for delivery to be recorded, the time recorded as the time of its delivery.

(8) In this section "secretary", in relation to a body corporate, means the secretary or other equivalent officer of the body.

Preparation of terrorist acts and terrorist training

5 Preparation of terrorist acts

(1) A person commits an offence if, with the intention of—

    (a) committing acts of terrorism, or

    (b) assisting another to commit such acts, he engages in any conduct in preparation for giving effect to his intention.

(2) It is irrelevant for the purposes of subsection (1) whether the intention and preparations relate to one or more particular acts of terrorism, acts of terrorism of a particular description or acts of terrorism generally.

(3) A person guilty of an offence under this section shall be liable, on conviction on indictment, to imprisonment for life.

6 Training for terrorism

(1) A person commits an offence if—

    (a) he provides instruction or training in any of the skills mentioned in subsection (3); and

    (b) at the time he provides the instruction or training, he knows that a person receiving it intends to use the skills in which he is being instructed or trained—

        (i) for or in connection with the commission or preparation of acts of terrorism or Convention offences; or

        (ii) for assisting the commission or preparation by others of such acts or offences.

(2) A person commits an offence if—

    (a) he receives instruction or training in any of the skills mentioned in subsection (3); and

    (b) at the time of the instruction or training, he intends to use the skills in which he is being instructed or trained—

        (i) for or in connection with the commission or preparation of acts of terrorism or Convention offences; or

        (ii) for assisting the commission or preparation by others of such acts or offences.

(3) The skills are—

    (a) the making, handling or use of a noxious substance, or of substances of a description of such substances;

    (b) the use of any method or technique for doing anything else that is capable of being done for the purposes of terrorism, in connection with the commission or preparation of an act of terrorism or Convention offence or in connection with assisting the commission or preparation by another of such an act or offence; and

    (c) the design or adaptation for the purposes of terrorism, or in connection with the commission or preparation of an act of terrorism or Convention offence, of any method or technique for doing anything.

(4) It is irrelevant for the purposes of subsections (1) and (2)—

    (a) whether any instruction or training that is provided is provided to one or more particular persons or generally;

    (b) whether the acts or offences in relation to which a person intends to use skills in which he is instructed or trained consist of one or more particular acts of terrorism or Convention offences, acts of terrorism or Convention offences of a particular description or acts of terrorism or Convention offences generally; and

    (c) whether assistance that a person intends to provide to others is intended to be provided to one or more particular persons or to one or more persons whose identities are not yet known.

(5) A person guilty of an offence under this section shall be liable—

    (a) on conviction on indictment, to imprisonment for a term not exceeding 10 years or to a fine, or to both;

    (b) on summary conviction in England and Wales, to imprisonment for a term not exceeding 12 months or to a fine not exceeding the statutory maximum, or to both;

    (c) on summary conviction in Scotland or Northern Ireland, to imprisonment for a term not exceeding 6 months or to a fine not exceeding the statutory maximum, or to both.

(6) In relation to an offence committed before the commencement of section 154(1) of the Criminal Justice Act 2003 (c. 44), the reference in subsection (5)(b) to 12 months is to be read as a reference to 6 months.

(7) In this section—

"noxious substance" means—

(a) a dangerous substance within the meaning of Part 7 of the Antiterrorism, Crime and Security Act 2001 (c. 24); or

(b) any other substance which is hazardous or noxious or which may be or become hazardous or noxious only in certain circumstances;

"substance" includes any natural or artificial substance (whatever its origin or method of production and whether in solid or liquid form or in the form of a gas or vapour) and any mixture of substances.

7 Powers of forfeiture in respect of offences under s. 6

(1) A court before which a person is convicted of an offence under section 6 may order the forfeiture of anything the court considers to have been in the person's possession for purposes connected with the offence.

(2) Before making an order under subsection (1) in relation to anything the court must give an opportunity of being heard to any person (in addition to the convicted person) who claims to be the owner of that thing or otherwise to have an interest in it.

(3) An order under subsection (1) may not be made so as to come into force at any time before there is no further possibility (disregarding any power to grant permission for the bringing of an appeal out of time) of the order's being varied or set aside on appeal.

(4) Where a court makes an order under subsection (1), it may also make such other provision as appears to it to be necessary for giving effect to the forfeiture.

(5) That provision may include, in particular, provision relating to the retention, handling, destruction or other disposal of what is forfeited.

(6) Provision made by virtue of this section may be varied at any time by the court that made it.

8 Attendance at a place used for terrorist training

(1) A person commits an offence if—

(a) he attends at any place, whether in the United Kingdom or elsewhere;

(b) while he is at that place, instruction or training of the type mentioned in section 6(1) of this Act or section 54(1) of the Terrorism Act 2000 (c. 11) (weapons training) is provided there;

(c) that instruction or training is provided there wholly or partly for purposes connected with the commission or preparation of acts of terrorism or Convention offences; and

(d) the requirements of subsection (2) are satisfied in relation to that person.

(2) The requirements of this subsection are satisfied in relation to a person if—

(a) he knows or believes that instruction or training is being provided there wholly or partly for purposes connected with the commission or preparation of acts of terrorism or Convention offences; or

(b) a person attending at that place throughout the period of that person's attendance could not reasonably have failed to understand that instruction or training was being provided there wholly or partly for such purposes.

(3) It is immaterial for the purposes of this section—

    (a) whether the person concerned receives the instruction or training himself; and

    (b) whether the instruction or training is provided for purposes connected with one or more particular acts of terrorism or Convention offences, acts of terrorism or Convention offences of a particular description or acts of terrorism or Convention offences generally.

(4) A person guilty of an offence under this section shall be liable—

    (a) on conviction on indictment, to imprisonment for a term not exceeding 10 years or to a fine, or to both;

    (b) on summary conviction in England and Wales, to imprisonment for a term not exceeding 12 months or to a fine not exceeding the statutory maximum, or to both;

    (c) on summary conviction in Scotland or Northern Ireland, to imprisonment for a term not exceeding 6 months or to a fine not exceeding the statutory maximum, or to both.

(5) In relation to an offence committed before the commencement of section 154(1) of the Criminal Justice Act 2003 (c. 44), the reference in subsection (4)(b) to 12 months is to be read as a reference to 6 months.

(6) References in this section to instruction or training being provided include references to its being made available.

Offences involving radioactive devices and materials and nuclear facilities and sites

9 Making and possession of devices or materials

(1) A person commits an offence if—

    (a) he makes or has in his possession a radioactive device, or

    (b) he has in his possession radioactive material, with the intention of using the device or material in the course of or in connection with the commission or preparation of an act of terrorism or for the purposes of terrorism, or of making it available to be so used.

(2) It is irrelevant for the purposes of subsection (1) whether the act of terrorism to which an intention relates is a particular act of terrorism, an act of terrorism of a particular description or an act of terrorism generally.

(3) A person guilty of an offence under this section shall be liable, on conviction on indictment, to imprisonment for life.

(4) In this section—

"radioactive device" means—

    (a) a nuclear weapon or other nuclear explosive device;

    (b) a radioactive material dispersal device;

    (c) a radiation-emitting device;

"radioactive material" means nuclear material or any other radioactive substance which—

    (a) contains nuclides that undergo spontaneous disintegration in a process accompanied by the emission of one or more types of ionising radiation, such as alpha radiation, beta radiation, neutron particles or gamma rays; and

    (b) is capable, owing to its radiological or fissile properties, of—

        (i) causing serious bodily injury to a person;

        (ii) causing serious damage to property;

  (iii) endangering a person's life; or

  (iv) creating a serious risk to the health or safety of the public.

(5) In subsection (4)—

"device" includes any of the following, whether or not fixed to land, namely, machinery, equipment, appliances, tanks, containers, pipes and conduits;

"nuclear material" has the same meaning as in the Nuclear Material (Offences) Act 1983 (c. 18) (see section 6 of that Act).

10 Misuse of devices or material and misuse and damage of facilities

(1) A person commits an offence if he uses—

 (a) a radioactive device, or

 (b) radioactive material,

in the course of or in connection with the commission of an act of terrorism or for the purposes of terrorism.

(2) A person commits an offence if, in the course of or in connection with the commission of an act of terrorism or for the purposes of terrorism, he uses or damages a nuclear facility in a manner which—

 (a) causes a release of radioactive material; or

 (b) creates or increases a risk that such material will be released.

(3) A person guilty of an offence under this section shall be liable, on conviction on indictment, to imprisonment for life.

(4) In this section—

"nuclear facility" means—

 (a) a nuclear reactor, including a reactor installed in or on any transportation device for use as an energy source in order to propel it or for any other purpose; or

 (b) a plant or conveyance being used for the production, storage, processing or transport of radioactive material;

"radioactive device" and "radioactive material" have the same meanings as in section 9.

(5) In subsection (4)—

"nuclear reactor" has the same meaning as in the Nuclear Installations Act 1965 (c. 57) (see section 26 of that Act);

"transportation device" means any vehicle or any space object (within the meaning of the Outer Space Act 1986 (c. 38)).

11 Terrorist threats relating to devices, materials or facilities

(1) A person commits an offence if, in the course of or in connection with the commission of an act of terrorism or for the purposes of terrorism—

 (a) he makes a demand—

  (i) for the supply to himself or to another of a radioactive device or of radioactive material;

  (ii) for a nuclear facility to be made available to himself or to another; or

  (iii) for access to such a facility to be given to himself or to another;

 (b) he supports the demand with a threat that he or another will take action if the demand is not met; and

 (c) the circumstances and manner of the threat are such that it is reasonable for the person to whom it is made to assume that there is real risk that the threat will be carried out if the demand is not met.

(2) A person also commits an offence if—

    (a) he makes a threat falling within subsection (3) in the course of or in connection with the commission of an act of terrorism or for the purposes of terrorism; and

    (b) the circumstances and manner of the threat are such that it is reasonable for the person to whom it is made to assume that there is real risk that the threat will be carried out, or would be carried out if demands made in association with the threat are not met.

(3) A threat falls within this subsection if it is—

    (a) a threat to use radioactive material;

    (b) a threat to use a radioactive device; or

    (c) a threat to use or damage a nuclear facility in a manner that releases radioactive material or creates or increases a risk that such material will be released.

(4) A person guilty of an offence under this section shall be liable, on conviction on indictment, to imprisonment for life.

(5) In this section—

"nuclear facility" has the same meaning as in section 10;

"radioactive device" and "radioactive material" have the same meanings as in section 9.

12 Trespassing etc. on nuclear sites

(1) The Serious Organised Crime and Police Act 2005 (c. 15) is amended as follows.

(2) In sections 128(1), (4) and (7) and 129(1), (4) and (6) (trespassing etc. on a designated site in England and Wales or Northern Ireland or in Scotland), for "designated", wherever occurring, substitute "protected".

(3) After section 128(1) (sites in England and Wales and Northern Ireland) insert—

    "(1A) In this section 'protected site' means—

        (a) a nuclear site; or

        (b) a designated site.

    (1B) In this section 'nuclear site' means—

        (a) so much of any premises in respect of which a nuclear site licence (within the meaning of the Nuclear Installations Act 1965) is for the time being in force as lies within the outer perimeter of the protection provided for those premises; and

        (b) so much of any other premises of which premises falling within paragraph (a) form a part as lies within that outer perimeter.

    (1C) For this purpose—

        (a) the outer perimeter of the protection provided for any premises is the line of the outermost fences, walls or other obstacles provided or relied on for protecting those premises from intruders; and

        (b) that line shall be determined on the assumption that every gate, door or other barrier across a way through a fence, wall or other obstacle is closed."

(4) After section 129(1) (sites in Scotland) insert—

    "(1A) In this section 'protected Scottish site' means—

        (a) a nuclear site in Scotland; or

        (b) a designated Scottish site.

    (1B) In this section 'nuclear site' means—

        (a) so much of any premises in respect of which a nuclear site licence (within the meaning of the Nuclear Installations Act 1965) is for the time being in force as lies within the outer perimeter of the protection provided for those premises; and

(b) so much of any other premises of which premises falling within paragraph (a) form a part as lies within that outer perimeter.

(1C) For this purpose—

(a) the outer perimeter of the protection provided for any premises is the line of the outermost fences, walls or other obstacles provided or relied on for protecting those premises from intruders; and

(b) that line shall be determined on the assumption that every gate, door or other barrier across a way through a fence, wall or other obstacle is closed."

Increases of penalties

13 Maximum penalty for possessing for terrorist purposes

(1) In section 57(4)(a) of the Terrorism Act 2000 (c. 11) (10 years maximum imprisonment for possession for terrorist purposes), for "10 years" substitute "15 years".

(2) Subsection (1) does not apply to offences committed before the commencement of this section.

14 Maximum penalty for certain offences relating to nuclear material

(1) In section 2 of the Nuclear Material (Offences) Act 1983 (c. 18) (offences involving preparatory acts and threats), for subsection (5) substitute—

"(5) A person guilty of an offence under this section shall be liable, on conviction on indictment, to imprisonment for life."

(2) Subsection (1) does not apply to offences committed before the commencement of this section.

15 Maximum penalty for contravening notice relating to encrypted information

(1) In section 53 of the Regulation of Investigatory Powers Act 2000 (c. 23) (offence of contravening disclosure requirement)—

(a) in paragraph (a) of subsection (5), for "two years" substitute "the appropriate maximum term"; and

(b) after that subsection insert the subsections set out in subsection (2).

(2) The inserted subsections are—

"(5A) In subsection (5) 'the appropriate maximum term' means—

(a) in a national security case, five years; and

(b) in any other case, two years.

(5B) In subsection (5A) 'a national security case' means a case in which the grounds specified in the notice to which the offence relates as the grounds for imposing a disclosure requirement were or included a belief that the imposition of the requirement was necessary in the interests of national security."

(3) This section does not apply to offences committed before the commencement of this section.

Incidental provisions about offences

16 Preparatory hearings in terrorism cases

(1) Section 29 of the Criminal Procedure and Investigations Act 1996 (c. 25) (power to order preparatory hearing) is amended as follows.

(2) Before subsection (2) insert—

"(1B) An order that a preparatory hearing shall be held must be made by a judge of the Crown Court in every case which (whether or not it falls within subsection (1) or (1A)) is a case in which at least one of the offences charged by the indictment against at least one of the persons charged is a terrorism offence.

(1C) An order that a preparatory hearing shall be held must also be made by a judge of the Crown court in every case which (whether or not it falls within subsection (1) or (1A)) is a case in which—

(a) at least one of the offences charged by the indictment against at least one of the persons charged is an offence carrying a maximum of at least 10 years' imprisonment; and

(b) it appears to the judge that evidence on the indictment reveals that conduct in respect of which that offence is charged had a terrorist connection."

(3) For subsection (3) (no order in serious and complex fraud cases) substitute—

"(3) In a case in which it appears to a judge of the Crown Court that evidence on an indictment reveals a case of fraud of such seriousness or complexity as is mentioned in section 7 of the Criminal Justice Act 1987 (preparatory hearings in cases of serious or complex fraud)—

(a) the judge may make an order for a preparatory hearing under this section only if he is required to do so by subsection (1B) or (1C);

(b) before making an order in pursuance of either of those subsections, he must determine whether to make an order for a preparatory hearing under that section; and

(c) he is not required by either of those subsections to make an order for a preparatory hearing under this section if he determines that an order should be made for a preparatory hearing under that section;

and, in a case in which an order is made for a preparatory hearing under that section, requirements imposed by those subsections apply only if that order ceases to have effect."

(4) In subsection (4) (orders to be capable of being made on application or on the judge's own motion), for the words before paragraph (a) substitute—

"(4) An order that a preparatory hearing shall be held may be made—"

(5) After sub-paragraph (5) insert—

"(6) In this section 'terrorism offence' means—

(a) an offence under section 11 or 12 of the Terrorism Act 2000 (c. 11) (offences relating to proscribed organisations);

(b) an offence under any of sections 15 to 18 of that Act (offences relating to terrorist property);

(c) an offence under section 38B of that Act (failure to disclose information about acts of terrorism);

(d) an offence under section 54 of that Act (weapons training);

(e) an offence under any of sections 56 to 59 of that Act (directing terrorism, possessing things and collecting information for the purposes of terrorism and inciting terrorism outside the United Kingdom);

(f) an offence in respect of which there is jurisdiction by virtue of section 62 of that Act (extra-territorial jurisdiction in respect of certain offences committed outside the United Kingdom for the purposes of terrorism etc.);

(g) an offence under Part 1 of the Terrorism Act 2006 (miscellaneous terrorist related offences);

(h) conspiring or attempting to commit a terrorism offence;

(i) incitement to commit a terrorism offence.

(7) For the purposes of this section an offence carries a maximum of at least 10 years' imprisonment if—

(a) it is punishable, on conviction on indictment, with imprisonment; and

(b) the maximum term of imprisonment that may be imposed on conviction on indictment of that offence is 10 years or more or is imprisonment for life.

(8) For the purposes of this section conduct has a terrorist connection if it is or takes place in the course of an act of terrorism or is for the purposes of terrorism.

(9) In subsection (8) 'terrorism' has the same meaning as in the Terrorism Act 2000 (see section 1 of that Act)."

17 Commission of offences abroad

(1) If—

(a) a person does anything outside the United Kingdom, and

(b) his action, if done in a part of the United Kingdom, would constitute an offence falling within subsection (2), he shall be guilty in that part of the United Kingdom of the offence.

(2) The offences falling within this subsection are—

(a) an offence under section 1 or 6 of this Act so far as it is committed in relation to any statement, instruction or training in relation to which that section has effect by reason of its relevance to the commission, preparation or instigation of one or more Convention offences;

(b) an offence under any of sections 8 to 11 of this Act;

(c) an offence under section 11(1) of the Terrorism Act 2000 (c. 11) (membership of proscribed organisations);

(d) an offence under section 54 of that Act (weapons training);

(e) conspiracy to commit an offence falling within this subsection;

(f) inciting a person to commit such an offence;

(g) attempting to commit such an offence;

(h) aiding, abetting, counselling or procuring the commission of such an offence.

(3) Subsection (1) applies irrespective of whether the person is a British citizen or, in the case of a company, a company incorporated in a part of the United Kingdom.

(4) In the case of an offence falling within subsection (2) which is committed wholly or partly outside the United Kingdom—

(a) proceedings for the offence may be taken at any place in the United Kingdom; and

(b) the offence may for all incidental purposes be treated as having been committed at any such place.

(5) In section 3(1)(a) and (b) of the Explosive Substances Act 1883 (c. 3) (offences committed in preparation for use of explosives with intent to endanger life or property in the United Kingdom or the Republic of Ireland), in each place, for "the Republic of Ireland" substitute "elsewhere".

(6) Subsection (5) does not extend to Scotland except in relation to—

(a) the doing of an act as an act of terrorism or for the purposes of terrorism; or

(b) the possession or control of a substance for the purposes of terrorism.

18 Liability of company directors etc.

(1) Where an offence under this Part is committed by a body corporate and is proved to have been committed with the consent or connivance of—
   (a) a director, manager, secretary or other similar officer of the body corporate, or
   (b) a person who was purporting to act in any such capacity, he (as well as the body corporate) is guilty of that offence and shall be liable to be proceeded against and punished accordingly.

(2) Where an offence under this Part—
   (a) is committed by a Scottish firm, and
   (b) is proved to have been committed with the consent or connivance of a partner of the firm, he (as well as the firm) is guilty of that offence and shall be liable to be proceeded against and punished accordingly.

(3) In this section "director", in relation to a body corporate whose affairs are managed by its members, means a member of the body corporate.

19 Consents to prosecutions

(1) Proceedings for an offence under this Part—
   (a) may be instituted in England and Wales only with the consent of the Director of Public Prosecutions; and
   (b) may be instituted in Northern Ireland only with the consent of the Director of Public Prosecutions for Northern Ireland.

(2) But if it appears to the Director of Public Prosecutions or the Director of Public Prosecutions for Northern Ireland that an offence under this Part has been committed for a purpose wholly or partly connected with the affairs of a country other than the United Kingdom, his consent for the purposes of this section may be given only with the permission—
   (a) in the case of the Director of Public Prosecutions, of the Attorney General; and
   (b) in the case of the Director of Public Prosecutions for Northern Ireland, of the Advocate General for Northern Ireland.

(3) In relation to any time before the coming into force of section 27(1) of the Justice (Northern Ireland) Act 2002 (c. 26), the reference in subsection (2)(b) to the Advocate General for Northern Ireland is to be read as a reference to the Attorney General for Northern Ireland.

Interpretation of Part 1

20 Interpretation of Part 1

(1) Expressions used in this Part and in the Terrorism Act 2000 (c. 11) have the same meanings in this Part as in that Act.

(2) In this Part—

"act of terrorism" includes anything constituting an action taken for the purposes of terrorism, within the meaning of the Terrorism Act 2000 (see section 1(5) of that Act);

"article" includes anything for storing data;

"Convention offence" means an offence listed in Schedule 1 or an equivalent offence under the law of a country or territory outside the United Kingdom;

"glorification" includes any form of praise or celebration, and cognate expressions are to be construed accordingly;

"public" is to be construed in accordance with subsection (3);

"publish" and cognate expressions are to be construed in accordance with subsection (4);

"record" means a record so far as not comprised in an article, including a temporary record created electronically and existing solely in the course of, and for the purposes of, the transmission of the whole or a part of its contents;

"statement" is to be construed in accordance with subsection (6).

(3) In this Part references to the public—

    (a) are references to the public of any part of the United Kingdom or of a country or territory outside the United Kingdom, or any section of the public; and

    (b) except in section 9(4), also include references to a meeting or other group of persons which is open to the public (whether unconditionally or on the making of a payment or the satisfaction of other conditions).

(4) In this Part references to a person's publishing a statement are references to—

    (a) his publishing it in any manner to the public;

    (b) his providing electronically any service by means of which the public have access to the statement; or

    (c) his using a service provided to him electronically by another so as to enable or to facilitate access by the public to the statement; but this subsection does not apply to the references to a publication in section 2.

(5) In this Part references to providing a service include references to making a facility available; and references to a service provided to a person are to be construed accordingly.

(6) In this Part references to a statement are references to a communication of any description, including a communication without words consisting of sounds or images or both.

(7) In this Part references to conduct that should be emulated in existing circumstances include references to conduct that is illustrative of a type of conduct that should be so emulated.

(8) In this Part references to what is contained in an article or record include references—

    (a) to anything that is embodied or stored in or on it; and

    (b) to anything that may be reproduced from it using apparatus designed or adapted for the purpose.

(9) The Secretary of State may by order made by statutory instrument—

    (a) modify Schedule 1 so as to add an offence to the offences listed in that Schedule;

    (b) modify that Schedule so as to remove an offence from the offences so listed;

    (c) make supplemental, incidental, consequential or transitional provision in connection with the addition or removal of an offence.

(10) An order under subsection (9) may add an offence in or as regards Scotland to the offences listed in Schedule 1 to the extent only that a provision creating the offence would be outside the legislative competence of the Scottish Parliament.

(11) The Secretary of State must not make an order containing (with or without other provision) any provision authorised by subsection (9) unless a draft of the order has been laid before Parliament and approved by a resolution of each House.

PART 2
MISCELLANEOUS PROVISIONS

Proscription of terrorist organisations

21 Grounds of proscription

In section 3 of the Terrorism Act 2000 (c. 11) (proscription of organisations), after subsection (5) insert—

"(5A) The cases in which an organisation promotes or encourages terrorism for the purposes of subsection (5)(c) include any case in which activities of the organisation—

(a) include the unlawful glorification of the commission or preparation (whether in the past, in the future or generally) of acts of terrorism; or

(b) are carried out in a manner that ensures that the organisation is associated with statements containing any such glorification.

(5B) The glorification of any conduct is unlawful for the purposes of subsection (5A) if there are persons who may become aware of it who could reasonably be expected to infer that what is being glorified, is being glorified as—

(a) conduct that should be emulated in existing circumstances, or

(b) conduct that is illustrative of a type of conduct that should be so emulated.

(5C) In this section—

'glorification' includes any form of praise or celebration, and cognate expressions are to be construed accordingly; 'statement' includes a communication without words consisting of sounds or images or both."

22 Name changes by proscribed organisations

(1) The Terrorism Act 2000 is amended as follows.

(2) In section 3 (proscription of organisations), at the end insert—

"(6) Where the Secretary of State believes—

(a) that an organisation listed in Schedule 2 is operating wholly or partly under a name that is not specified in that Schedule (whether as well as or instead of under the specified name), or

(b) that an organisation that is operating under a name that is not so specified is otherwise for all practical purposes the same as an organisation so listed, he may, by order, provide that the name that is not specified in that Schedule is to be treated as another name for the listed organisation.

(7) Where an order under subsection (6) provides for a name to be treated as another name for an organisation, this Act shall have effect in relation to acts occurring while—

(a) the order is in force, and

(b) the organisation continues to be listed in Schedule 2, as if the organisation were listed in that Schedule under the other name, as well as under the name specified in the Schedule.

(8) The Secretary of State may at any time by order revoke an order under subsection (6) or otherwise provide for a name specified in such an order to cease to be treated as a name for a particular organisation.

(9) Nothing in subsections (6) to (8) prevents any liability from being established in

163

any proceedings by proof that an organisation is the same as an organisation listed in Schedule 2, even though it is or was operating under a name specified neither in Schedule 2 nor in an order under subsection (6)."

(3) For subsection (1) of section 4 (applications for deproscription) substitute—

"(1) An application may be made to the Secretary of State for an order under section 3(3) or (8)—

(a) removing an organisation from Schedule 2, or

(b) providing for a name to cease to be treated as a name for an organisation listed in that Schedule."

(4) In subsection (2)(b) of that section (applications may be made by persons affected by the organisation's proscription), after "proscription" insert "or by the treatment of the name as a name for the organisation."

(5) In section 5 (appeals against refusals to deproscribe)—

(a) in subsection (3), after "an organisation" insert "or to provide for a name to cease to be treated as a name for an organisation";

(b) in subsection (4), omit "by or in respect of an organisation";

(c) in subsection (5), after "subsection (4)" insert "in respect of an appeal against a refusal to deproscribe an organisation,".

(6) After subsection (5) of that section insert—

"(5A) Where an order is made under subsection (4) in respect of an appeal against a refusal to provide for a name to cease to be treated as a name for an organisation, the Secretary of State shall, as soon as is reasonably practicable, make an order under section 3(8) providing that the name in question is to cease to be so treated in relation to that organisation."

(7) In section 7 (effect on conviction etc. of successful appeal), after subsection (1) insert—

"(1A) This section also applies where—

(a) an appeal under section 5 has been allowed in respect of a name treated as the name for an organisation,

(b) an order has been made under section 3(8) in respect of the name in accordance with an order of the Commission under section 5(4),

(c) a person has been convicted of an offence in respect of the organisation under any of sections 11 to 13, 15 to 19 and 56, and

(d) the activity to which the charge referred took place on or after the date of the refusal, against which the appeal under section 5 was brought, to provide for a name to cease to be treated as a name for the organisation."

(8) In that section—

(a) in subsection (2), after "(1)(c)" insert "or (1A)(c)";

(b) in subsection (4)(a), after "(1)(b)" insert "or (1A)(b)";

(c) in subsection (5), after "(1)(c)" insert "or (1A)(c)";

(d) in subsection (7)(a), after "(1)(b)" insert "or (1A)(b)".

(9) In section 9 (proceedings under the Human Rights Act 1998)—

(a) in subsection (2)(a), for "and (5)" substitute ", (5) and (5A)";

(b) in subsection (4), at the end insert ", and

(c) a reference to a refusal to provide for a name to cease to be treated as a name for an organisation shall be taken as a reference to the action of the Secretary of State which is found to be incompatible with a Convention right".

(10) In section 123(2) (orders and regulations subject to negative resolution procedure), before paragraph (a) insert—

"(za) section 3(6) or (8);".

(11) In paragraph 5(4) of Schedule 3 (the Proscribed Organisations Appeal Commission), after sub-paragraph (a) insert—

"(aa) provide for full particulars of the reasons for—
    (i) the making of an order under section 3(6), or
    (ii) a refusal to provide for a name to cease to be treated as a name for an organisation, to be withheld from the organisation or applicant concerned and from any person representing it or him;".

Detention of terrorist suspects

23 Extension of period of detention of terrorist suspects

(1) Schedule 8 to the Terrorism Act 2000 (c. 11) (detention of terrorist suspects) is amended as follows.

(2) In sub-paragraph (1) of each of paragraphs 29 and 36 (applications by a superintendent or above for a warrant extending detention or for the extension of the period of such a warrant), for the words from the beginning to "may" substitute—

"(1) Each of the following—
    (a) in England and Wales, a Crown Prosecutor,
    (b) in Scotland, the Lord Advocate or a procurator fiscal,
    (c) in Northern Ireland, the Director of Public Prosecutions for Northern Ireland,
    (d) in any part of the United Kingdom, a police officer of at least the rank of superintendent, may".

(3) In sub-paragraph (3) of paragraph 29 (period of extension to end no later than 7 days after arrest)—
    (a) for "Subject to paragraph 36(3A)" substitute "Subject to sub-paragraph (3A) and paragraph 36"; and (b) for "end not later than the end of" substitute "be".

(4) After that sub-paragraph insert—

"(3A) A judicial authority may issue a warrant of further detention in relation to a person which specifies a shorter period as the period for which that person's further detention is authorised if—
    (a) the application for the warrant is an application for a warrant specifying a shorter period; or
    (b) the judicial authority is satisfied that there are circumstances that would make it inappropriate for the specified period to be as long as the period of seven days mentioned in subparagraph (3)."

(5) In paragraph 34(1) (persons who can apply for information to be withheld from person to whom application for a warrant relates) for "officer" substitute "person".

(6) In paragraph 36 (applications for extension or further extension), omit the words "to a judicial authority" in sub-paragraph (1), and after that subparagraph insert—

"(1A) The person to whom an application under sub-paragraph (1) may be made is—
    (a) in the case of an application falling within sub-paragraph (1B), a judicial authority; and
    (b) in any other case, a senior judge.

(1B) An application for the extension or further extension of a period falls within this sub-paragraph if—
    (a) the grant of the application otherwise than in accordance with sub-paragraph (3AA)(b) would extend that period to a time that is no more than fourteen days after the relevant time; and

    (b) no application has previously been made to a senior judge in respect of that period."

(7) For sub-paragraphs (3) and (3A) of that paragraph (period for which warrants may be extended) substitute—

  "(3) Subject to sub-paragraph (3AA), the period by which the specified period is extended or further extended shall be the period which—

    (a) begins with the time specified in sub-paragraph (3A); and

    (b) ends with whichever is the earlier of—

        (i) the end of the period of seven days beginning with that time; and

        (ii) the end of the period of 28 days beginning with the relevant time.

  (3A) The time referred to in sub-paragraph (3)(a) is—

    (a) in the case of a warrant specifying a period which has not previously been extended under this paragraph, the end of the period specified in the warrant, and

    (b) in any other case, the end of the period for which the period specified in the warrant was last extended under this paragraph.

  (3AA) A judicial authority or senior judge may extend or further extend the period specified in a warrant by a shorter period than is required by sub-paragraph (3) if—

    (a) the application for the extension is an application for an extension by a period that is shorter than is so required; or

    (b) the judicial authority or senior judge is satisfied that there are circumstances that would make it inappropriate for the period of the extension to be as long as the period so required."

(8) In sub-paragraph (4) of that paragraph (application of paragraphs 30(3), and 31 to 34), at the end insert—

"but, in relation to an application made by virtue of subparagraph (1A)(b) to a senior judge, as if—

    (a) references to a judicial authority were references to a senior judge; and

    (b) references to the judicial authority in question were references to the senior judge in question."

(9) In sub-paragraph (5) of that paragraph, after "authority" insert "or senior judge".

(10) After sub-paragraph (6) of that paragraph insert—

  "(7) In this paragraph and paragraph 37 'senior judge' means a judge of the High Court or of the High Court of Justiciary."

(11) For paragraph 37 (release of detained person) substitute—

  "37(1) This paragraph applies where—

    (a) a person ('the detained person') is detained by virtue of a warrant issued under this Part of this Schedule; and

    (b) his detention is not authorised by virtue of section 41(5) or (6) or otherwise apart from the warrant.

  (2) If it at any time appears to the police officer or other person in charge of the detained person's case that any of the matters mentioned in paragraph 32(1)(a) and (b) on which the judicial authority or senior judge last authorised his further detention no longer apply, he must—

    (a) if he has custody of the detained person, release him immediately; and

    (b) if he does not, immediately inform the person who does have custody of the detained person that those matters no longer apply in the detained person's case.

(3) A person with custody of the detained person who is informed in accordance with this paragraph that those matters no longer apply in his case must release that person immediately."

(12) This section does not apply in a case in which—

(a) the arrest of the person detained under section 41 of the Terrorism Act 2000 (c. 11) took place before the commencement of this section; or

(b) his examination under Schedule 7 to that Act began before the commencement of this section.

24 Grounds for extending detention

(1) In Schedule 8 to the Terrorism Act 2000, in paragraph 23(1) (grounds on which a review officer may authorise continued detention), after paragraph (b) insert—

"(ba) pending the result of an examination or analysis of any relevant evidence or of anything the examination or analysis of which is to be or is being carried out with a view to obtaining relevant evidence;".

(2) In sub-paragraph (1) of paragraph 32 of that Schedule (grounds on which a judicial authority may authorise further detention), for the words from "to obtain" to "preserve relevant evidence" substitute "as mentioned in subparagraph (1A)".

(3) After that sub-paragraph insert—

"(1A) The further detention of a person is necessary as mentioned in this subparagraph if it is necessary—

(a) to obtain relevant evidence whether by questioning him or otherwise;

(b) to preserve relevant evidence; or

(c) pending the result of an examination or analysis of any relevant evidence or of anything the examination or analysis of which is to be or is being carried out with a view to obtaining relevant evidence."

(4) In paragraph 23(4) (meaning of "relevant evidence"), for "sub-paragraph (1)(a) and (b)" substitute "this paragraph".

(5) In paragraph 32(2) (meaning of "relevant evidence"), for "sub-paragraph (1)" substitute "this paragraph".

(6) This section does not apply in a case in which—

(a) the arrest of the person detained under section 41 of the Terrorism Act 2000 took place before the commencement of this section; or

(b) his examination under Schedule 7 to that Act began before the commencement of this section.

25 Expiry or renewal of extended maximum detention period

(1) This section applies to any time which—

(a) is more than one year after the commencement of section 23; and

(b) does not fall within a period in relation to which this section is disapplied by an order under subsection (2).

(2) The Secretary of State may by order made by statutory instrument disapply this section in relation to any period of not more than one year beginning with the coming into force of the order.

(3) Schedule 8 to the Terrorism Act 2000 (c. 11) has effect in relation to any further extension under paragraph 36 of that Schedule for a period beginning at a time to which this section applies—

(a) as if in sub-paragraph (3)(b) of that paragraph, for "28 days" there were substituted "14 days"; and

(b) as if that paragraph and paragraph 37 of that Schedule had effect with the further consequential modifications set out in subsection (4).

(4) The further consequential modifications are—

(a) the substitution of the words "a judicial authority" for paragraphs (a) and (b) of sub-paragraph (1A) of paragraph 36;

(b) the omission of sub-paragraphs (1B) and (7) of that paragraph;

(c) the omission of the words "or senior judge" wherever occurring in subparagraphs (3AA) and (5) of that paragraph and in paragraph 37(2); and

(d) the omission of the words from "but" onwards in paragraph 36(4).

(5) Where at a time to which this section applies—

(a) a person is being detained by virtue of a further extension under paragraph 36 of Schedule 8 to the Terrorism Act 2000,

(b) his further detention was authorised (at a time to which this section did not apply) for a period ending more than 14 days after the relevant time, and

(c) that 14 days has expired, the person with custody of that individual must release him immediately.

(6) The Secretary of State must not make an order containing (with or without other provision) any provision disapplying this section in relation to any period unless a draft of the order has been laid before Parliament and approved by a resolution of each House.

(7) In this section "the relevant time" has the same meaning as in paragraph 36 of Schedule 8 to the Terrorism Act 2000.

Searches etc.

26 All premises warrants: England and Wales and Northern Ireland

(1) Part 1 of Schedule 5 to the Terrorism Act 2000 (searches etc. for the purposes of terrorist investigations in England and Wales and Northern Ireland) is amended as follows.

(2) In paragraph 1 (search warrants authorising entry to specified premises), in sub-paragraph (2)(a), for "the premises specified in the warrant" substitute "premises mentioned in sub-paragraph (2A)".

(3) After sub-paragraph (2) of that paragraph insert—

"(2A) The premises referred to in sub-paragraph (2)(a) are—

(a) one or more sets of premises specified in the application (in which case the application is for a 'specific premises warrant'); or

(b) any premises occupied or controlled by a person specified in the application, including such sets of premises as are so specified (in which case the application is for an 'all premises warrant')."

(4) In sub-paragraph (5) of that paragraph—

(a) in paragraph (b), for "premises specified in the application" substitute "premises to which the application relates";

(b) in paragraph (c), at the end insert ", and"; and

(c) after that paragraph insert—

"(d) in the case of an application for an all premises warrant, that it is not reasonably practicable to specify in the application all the premises which the person so specified occupies or controls and which might need to be searched."

(5) In paragraph 2 (warrants as to which special conditions are satisfied), in subparagraph (1), after "an application" insert "for a specific premises warrant".

(6) After that paragraph insert—

"2A (1) This paragraph applies where an application for an all premises warrant is made under paragraph 1 and—

(a) the application is made by a police officer of at least the rank of superintendent, and

(b) the justice to whom the application is made is not satisfied of the matter referred to in paragraph 1(5)(c).

(2) The justice may grant the application if satisfied of the matters referred to in paragraph 1(5)(a), (b) and (d).

(3) Where a warrant under paragraph 1 is issued by virtue of this paragraph, the powers under paragraph 1(2)(a) and (b) are exercisable only—

(a) in respect of premises which are not residential premises, and (b) within the period of 24 hours beginning with the time when the warrant is issued.

(4) For the purpose of sub-paragraph (3) 'residential premises', in relation to a power under paragraph 1(2)(a) or (b), means any premises which the constable exercising the power has reasonable grounds for believing are used wholly or mainly as a dwelling."

(7) In paragraph 11 (applications for search warrants involving excluded or special procedure material), in sub-paragraph (2)(a), for "the premises specified in the warrant" substitute "premises mentioned in sub-paragraph (3A)".

(8) After sub-paragraph (3) of that paragraph insert—

"(3A) The premises referred to in sub-paragraph (2)(a) are—

(a) one or more sets of premises specified in the application (in which case the application is for a 'specific premises warrant'); or

(b) any premises occupied or controlled by a person specified in the application, including such sets of premises as are so specified (in which case the application is for an 'all premises warrant')."

(9) In paragraph 12 (grant of applications where excluded or special procedure material is involved), in each of sub-paragraphs (1) and (2), after "an application" insert "for a specific premises warrant".

(10) After sub-paragraph (2) of that paragraph insert—

"(2A) A Circuit judge or a District Judge (Magistrates' Courts) may grant an application for an all premises warrant under paragraph 11 if satisfied—

(a) that an order made under paragraph 5 has not been complied with, and

(b) that the person specified in the application is also specified in the order.

(2B) A Circuit judge or a District Judge (Magistrates' Courts) may also grant an application for an all premises warrant under paragraph 11 if satisfied that there are reasonable grounds for believing—

(a) that there is material on premises to which the application relates which consists of or includes excluded material or special procedure material but does not include items subject to legal privilege, and

(b) that the conditions in sub-paragraphs (3) and (4) are met."

(11) In sub-paragraph (4)(b) of that paragraph, for "the premises on which the material is situated" substitute "premises to which the application for the warrant relates".

27 All premises warrants: Scotland

(1) Part 2 of Schedule 5 to the Terrorism Act 2000 (c. 11) (searches etc. for the purposes of terrorist investigations in Scotland) is amended as follows.

(2) In paragraph 28 (search warrants authorising entry to specified premises in Scotland), in sub-paragraph (2)(a), for "the premises specified in the warrant" substitute "premises mentioned in sub-paragraph (2A)".

(3) After sub-paragraph (2) of that paragraph insert—
  "(2A) The premises referred to in sub-paragraph (2)(a) are—
      (a) one or more sets of premises specified in the application (in which case the application is for a 'specific premises warrant'); or
      (b) any premises occupied or controlled by a person specified in the application, including such sets of premises as are so specified (in which case the application is for an 'all premises warrant')."

(4) In sub-paragraph (4) of that paragraph—
      (a) in paragraph (b), for "premises specified in the application" substitute "premises to which the application relates";
      (b) in paragraph (c), at the end insert ", and"; and
      (c) after that paragraph insert—
          "(d) in the case of an application for an all premises warrant, that it is not reasonably practicable to specify in the application all the premises which the person so specified occupies or controls and which might need to be searched."

(5) In sub-paragraph (5) of that paragraph, for "a warrant" substitute "a specific premises warrant".

(6) After sub-paragraph (6) of that paragraph insert—
  "(6A) Where an all premises warrant is granted, entry and search in pursuance of the warrant of any premises which are non-residential premises must be within the period of 24 hours beginning with the time when the warrant is granted.
  (6B) For the purpose of sub-paragraph (6A) 'non-residential premises' means any premises other than those which the constable executing the warrant has reasonable grounds for believing are used wholly or mainly as a dwelling."

(7) In paragraph 29 (conditions for grant of warrant under paragraph 28)—
      (a) in sub-paragraph (1)(a), after "with" insert "and, in the case of an application for an all premises warrant, the person specified in the order in pursuance of paragraph 22(3) is also specified in the application"; and
      (b) in sub-paragraph (2)(b), for "on which the material is situated" substitute "to which the application for the warrant relates".

(8) In paragraph 33(2) (power to open lockfast places)—
      (a) for "premises specified in" substitute "premises which he is entitled to enter in pursuance of"; and
      (b) for "a notice under paragraph 32" substitute "an order under paragraph 31".

28 Search, seizure and forfeiture of terrorist publications

(1) If a justice of the peace is satisfied that there are reasonable grounds for suspecting that articles to which this section applies are likely to be found on any premises, he may issue a warrant authorising a constable—
      (a) to enter and search the premises; and
      (b) to seize anything found there which the constable has reason to believe is such an article.

(2) This section applies to an article if—
  (a) it is likely to be the subject of conduct falling within subsection (2)(a) to (e) of section 2; and
  (b) it would fall for the purposes of that section to be treated, in the context of the conduct to which it is likely to be subject, as a terrorist publication.
(3) A person exercising a power conferred by a warrant under this section may use such force as is reasonable in the circumstances for exercising that power.
(4) An article seized under the authority of a warrant issued under this section—
  (a) may be removed by a constable to such place as he thinks fit; and
  (b) must be retained there in the custody of a constable until returned or otherwise disposed of in accordance with this Act.
(5) An article to which this section applies which is seized under the authority of a warrant issued under this section on an information laid by or on behalf of the Director of Public Prosecutions or the Director of Public Prosecutions for Northern Ireland—
  (a) shall be liable to forfeiture; and
  (b) if forfeited, may be destroyed or otherwise disposed of by a constable in whatever manner he thinks fit.
(6) In Schedule 1 to the Criminal Justice and Police Act 2001 (c. 16) (powers which relate to the seizure of property in bulk)—
  (a) in Part 1, at the end insert—
    "73H The power of seizure conferred by section 28 of the Terrorism Act 2006."
  (b) in Part 3, at the end insert—
    "113 The power of seizure conferred by section 28 of the Terrorism Act 2006."
(7) Nothing in—
  (a) the Police (Property) Act 1897 (c. 30) (property seized in the investigation of an offence), or
  (b) section 31 of the Police (Northern Ireland) Act 1998 (c. 32) (which makes similar provision in Northern Ireland), applies to an article seized under the authority of a warrant under this section.
(8) Schedule 2 (which makes provision about the forfeiture of articles to which this section applies) has effect.
(9) In this section—
  "article" has the same meaning as in Part 1 of this Act;
  "forfeited" means treated or condemned as forfeited under Schedule 2, and "forfeiture" is to be construed accordingly;
  "premises" has the same meaning as in the Police and Criminal Evidence Act 1984 (c. 60) (see section 23 of that Act).
(10) In the application of this section to Scotland—
  (a) in subsection (1), for the words from the beginning to "satisfied" substitute "If a sheriff, on the application of a procurator fiscal, is satisfied";
  (b) in subsection (5) omit "on an information laid by or on behalf of the Director of Public Prosecutions or the Director of Public Prosecutions for Northern Ireland";
  (c) in subsection (9), for the definition of ' "premises" substitute—
    " 'premises' has the same meaning as in the Terrorism Act 2000 (c. 11) (see section 121 of that Act)."

29 Power to search vehicles under Schedule 7 to the Terrorism Act 2000

In paragraph 8 of Schedule 7 to the Terrorism Act 2000 (c. 11) (search of a person at a port or in the border area to ascertain if he is involved in terrorism), after sub-paragraph (1)(d) insert—

> "(e) search a vehicle which is on a ship or aircraft; (f) search a vehicle which the examining officer reasonably believes has been, or is about to be, on a ship or aircraft."

30 Extension to internal waters of authorisations to stop and search

(1) The Terrorism Act 2000 is amended as follows.

(2) In section 44 (authorisations for stop and search), after subsection (4) insert—

> "(4ZA) The power of a person mentioned in subsection (4) to give an authorisation specifying an area or place so mentioned includes power to give such an authorisation specifying such an area or place together with—
>
> (a) the internal waters adjacent to that area or place; or
>
> (b) such area of those internal waters as is specified in the authorisation."

(3) After subsection (5) of that section insert—

> "(5A) In this section—
>
> 'driver', in relation to an aircraft, hovercraft or vessel, means the captain, pilot or other person with control of the aircraft, hovercraft or vessel or any member of its crew and, in relation to a train, includes any member of its crew; 'internal waters' means waters in the United Kingdom that are not comprised in any police area."

(4) In section 45 (exercise of powers), after subsection (6) insert—

> "(7) In this section 'driver' has the same meaning as in section 44."

Other investigatory powers

31 Amendment of the Intelligence Services Act 1994

(1) The Intelligence Services Act 1994 (c. 13) is amended as follows.

(2) In subsection (1) of section 6 (persons under whose hand a warrant to act within the British Islands may be issued), after paragraph (c) insert "or (d) in an urgent case where the Secretary of State has expressly authorised the issue of warrants in accordance with this paragraph by specified senior officials and a statement of that fact is endorsed on the warrant, under the hand of any of the specified officials."

(3) After that subsection insert—

> "(1A) But a warrant issued in accordance with subsection (1)(d) may authorise the taking of an action only if the action is an action in relation to property which, immediately before the issue of the warrant, would, if done outside the British Islands, have been authorised by virtue of an authorisation under section 7 that was in force at that time."
>
> (1B) A senior official who issues a warrant in accordance with subsection (1)(d) must inform the Secretary of State about the issue of the warrant as soon as practicable after issuing it."

(4) In subsection (2)(b) of that section (duration of warrants issued by senior officials), for "second" substitute "fifth".

(5) In subsection (6)(b) of section 7 (duration of authorisations to act outside the British Islands that are issued by senior officials), for "second" substitute "fifth".

(6) After subsection (9) of that section insert—

"(10) Where—

(a) a person is authorised by virtue of this section to do an act outside the British Islands in relation to property,

(b) the act is one which, in relation to property within the British Islands, is capable of being authorised by a warrant under section 5,

(c) a person authorised by virtue of this section to do that act outside the British Islands, does the act in relation to that property while it is within the British Islands, and

(d) the act is done in circumstances falling within subsection (11) or (12), this section shall have effect as if the act were done outside the British Islands in relation to that property.

(11) An act is done in circumstances falling within this subsection if it is done in relation to the property at a time when it is believed to be outside the British Islands.

(12) An act is done in circumstances falling within this subsection if it—

(a) is done in relation to property which was mistakenly believed to be outside the British Islands either when the authorisation under this section was given or at a subsequent time or which has been brought within the British Islands since the giving of the authorisation; but

(b) is done before the end of the fifth working day after the day on which the presence of the property in the British Islands first becomes known.

(13) In subsection (12) the reference to the day on which the presence of the property in the British Islands first becomes known is a reference to the day on which it first appears to a member of the Intelligence Service or of GCHQ, after the relevant time—

(a) that the belief that the property was outside the British Islands was mistaken; or

(b) that the property is within those Islands.

(14) In subsection (13) 'the relevant time' means, as the case may be—

(a) the time of the mistaken belief mentioned in subsection (12)(a); or

(b) the time at which the property was, or was most recently, brought within the British Islands."

32 Interception warrants

(1) The Regulation of Investigatory Powers Act 2000 (c. 23) is amended as follows.

(2) In section 9(6) (period for which interception warrants can be issued or renewed), after paragraph (a) insert—

"(ab) in relation to an unrenewed warrant which is endorsed under the hand of the Secretary of State with a statement that the issue of the warrant is believed to be necessary on grounds falling within section 5(3)(a) or (c), means the period of six months beginning with the day of the warrant's issue;".

(3) For subsection (6) of section 10 (prohibition on modification of scheduled parts of warrant by the person to whom the warrant is addressed or his subordinates) substitute—

"(6) Subsection (4) authorises the modification of the scheduled parts of an interception warrant under the hand of a senior official who is either—

(a) the person to whom the warrant is addressed, or

    (b) a person holding a position subordinate to that person, only if the applicable condition specified in subsection (6A) is satisfied and a statement that the condition is satisfied is endorsed on the modifying instrument.

  (6A) The applicable condition is—

    (a) in the case of an unrenewed warrant, that the warrant is endorsed with a statement that the issue of the warrant is believed to be necessary in the interests of national security; and

    (b) in the case of a renewed warrant, that the instrument by which it was last renewed is endorsed with a statement that the renewal is believed to be necessary in the interests of national security."

(4) In subsection (9)(b) (modifications made otherwise than by Secretary of State ceasing to have effect after five days), after "(5A)(b)" insert ", (6)".

(5) In section 16 (extra safeguards in the case of certificated warrants)—

    (a) in subsection (3)(b) (exception for communications sent during a specified three month period), for "a period of not more than three months specified in the certificate" substitute "a period specified in the certificate that is no longer than the permitted maximum"; and

    (b) in subsection (5)(c) (exception for material selected before the end of the first working day after a relevant change of circumstances), for the words from "the first working day" onwards substitute "the permitted period".

(6) After subsection (3) of that section insert—

  "(3A) In subsection (3)(b) 'the permitted maximum' means—

    (a) in the case of material the examination of which is certified for the purposes of section 8(4) as necessary in the interests of national security, six months; and

    (b) in any other case, three months."

(7) After subsection (5) of that section insert—

  "(5A) In subsection (5)(c) 'the permitted period' means—

    (a) in the case of material the examination of which is certified for the purposes of section 8(4) as necessary in the interests of national security, the period ending with the end of the fifth working day after it first appeared as mentioned in subsection (5)(a) to the person to whom the warrant is addressed; and

    (b) in any other case, the period ending with the end of the first working day after it first so appeared to that person."

33 Disclosure notices for the purposes of terrorist investigations

(1) In section 60 of the Serious Organised Crime and Police Act 2005 (c. 15) (investigatory powers of DPP etc.), in subsection (1), after "applies" insert "or in connection with a terrorist investigation".

(2) After subsection (6) of that section insert—

  "(7) In this Chapter 'terrorist investigation' means an investigation of—

    (a) the commission, preparation or instigation of acts of terrorism,

    (b) any act or omission which appears to have been for the purposes of terrorism and which consists in or involves the commission, preparation or instigation of an offence, or

    (c) the commission, preparation or instigation of an offence under the Terrorism Act 2000 (c. 11) or under Part 1 of the Terrorism Act 2006 other than an offence under section 1 or 2 of that Act."

(3) In section 62 of that Act (disclosure notices), insert—

  "(1A) If it appears to the Investigating Authority—

(a) that any person has information (whether or not contained in a document) which relates to a matter relevant to a terrorist investigation, and

(b) that there are reasonable grounds for believing that information which may be provided by that person in compliance with a disclosure notice is likely to be of substantial value (whether or not by itself) to that investigation, he may give, or authorise an appropriate person to give, a disclosure notice to that person."

(4) In section 70(1) of that Act (interpretation of Chapter 1)—

(a) before the definition of "appropriate person" insert—

" 'act of terrorism' includes anything constituting an action taken for the purposes of terrorism, within the meaning of the Terrorism Act 2000 (see section 1(5) of that Act);"

(b) after the definition of "document" insert—

" 'terrorism' has the same meaning as in the Terrorism Act 2000 (see section 1(1) to (4) of that Act); 'terrorist investigation' has the meaning given by section 60(7)."

Definition of terrorism etc.

34 Amendment of the definition of "terrorism" etc.

In each of—

(a) section 1(1)(b) of the Terrorism Act 2000 (c. 11) (under which actions and threats designed to influence a government may be terrorism), and

(b) section 113(1)(c) of the Anti-terrorism, Crime and Security Act 2001 (c. 24) (offence of using noxious substances or things to influence a government or to intimidate), after "government" insert "or an international governmental organisation".

Other amendments

35 Applications for extended detention of seized cash

(1) In paragraph 3 of Schedule 1 to the Anti-terrorism, Crime and Security Act 2001 (application relating to period of detention of seized terrorist cash), after sub-paragraph (3) insert—

"(3A) An application to a justice of the peace or the sheriff for an order under sub-paragraph (2) making the first extension of the period—

(a) may be made and heard without notice of the application or hearing having been given to any of the persons affected by the application or to the legal representative of such a person, and

(b) may be heard and determined in private in the absence of persons so affected and of their legal representatives."

(2) This section applies to applications made after the commencement of this section.

PART 3
SUPPLEMENTAL PROVISIONS

36 Review of terrorism legislation

(1) The Secretary of State must appoint a person to review the operation of the provisions of the Terrorism Act 2000 and of Part 1 of this Act.

(2) That person may, from time to time, carry out a review of those provisions and, where he does so, must send a report on the outcome of his review to the Secretary of State as soon as reasonably practicable after completing the review.

(3) That person must carry out and report on his first review under this section before the end of the period of 12 months after the laying before Parliament of the last report to be so laid under section 126 of the Terrorism Act 2000 before the commencement of this section.

(4) That person must carry out and report on a review under this section at least once in every twelve month period ending with an anniversary of the end of the twelve month period mentioned in subsection (3).

(5) On receiving a report under this section, the Secretary of State must lay a copy of it before Parliament.

(6) The Secretary of State may, out of money provided by Parliament, pay a person appointed to carry out a review under this section, both his expenses and also such allowances as the Secretary of State determines.

37 Consequential amendments and repeals

(1) In section 32(e) of the Terrorism Act 2000 (c. 11) (meaning of "terrorist investigation"), after "offence under this Act" insert "or under Part 1 of the Terrorism Act 2006 other than an offence under section 1 or 2 of that Act".

(2) In section 117 of that Act (consents to prosecutions), for subsection (3) substitute—

"(2A) But if it appears to the Director of Public Prosecutions or the Director of Public Prosecutions for Northern Ireland that an offence to which this section applies has been committed for a purpose wholly or partly connected with the affairs of a country other than the United Kingdom, his consent for the purposes of this section may be given only with the permission—

(a) in the case of the Director of Public Prosecutions, of the Attorney General; and

(b) in the case of the Director of Public Prosecutions for Northern Ireland, of the Advocate General for Northern Ireland.

(2B) In relation to any time before the coming into force of section 27(1) of the Justice (Northern Ireland) Act 2002, the reference in subsection (2A) to the Advocate General for Northern Ireland is to be read as a reference to the Attorney General for Northern Ireland."

(3) After section 120 of that Act insert—

"120A Supplemental powers of court in respect of forfeiture orders

(1) Where court makes an order under section 54, 58 or 103 for the forfeiture of anything, it may also make such other provision as appears to it to be necessary for giving effect to the forfeiture.

(2) That provision may include, in particular, provision relating to the retention, handling, disposal or destruction of what is forfeited.

(3) Provision made by virtue of this section may be varied at any time by the court that made it."

(4) In Part 1 of Schedule 9 to that Act (scheduled offences), at the end insert—

"Terrorism Act 2006

22C Offences under Part 1 of the Terrorism Act 2006 (terrorism-related offences)."

(5) The enactments listed in column 1 of Schedule 3 are repealed to the extent set out in column 2 of that Schedule.

38 Expenses

There shall be paid out of money provided by Parliament any increase attributable to this Act in the sums payable out of such money under any other Act.

39 Short title, commencement and extent

(1) This Act may be cited as the Terrorism Act 2006.
(2) This Act (apart from this section) shall come into force on such day as the Secretary of State may by order made by statutory instrument appoint.
(3) An order made under subsection (2) may make different provision for different purposes.
(4) Subject to section 17(6), an amendment or repeal by this Act of another enactment has the same extent as the enactment amended or repealed.
(5) Subject to section 17(6) and to subsection (4) of this section, this Act extends to the whole of the United Kingdom.
(6) Her Majesty may by Order in Council direct that any provisions of this Act shall extend, with such modifications as appear to Her Majesty to be appropriate, to any of the Channel Islands or the Isle of Man.
(7) In subsection (6) "modification" includes omissions, additions and alterations.

SCHEDULES

SCHEDULE 1
CONVENTION OFFENCES

Section 20

Explosives offences

1 (1) Subject to sub-paragraph (3), an offence under any of sections 28 to 30 of the Offences against the Person Act 1861 (c. 100) (causing injury by explosions, causing explosions and handling or placing explosives).
　(2) Subject to sub-paragraph (3), an offence under any of the following provisions of the Explosive Substances Act 1883 (c. 3)—
　　(a) section 2 (causing an explosion likely to endanger life);
　　(b) section 3 (preparation of explosions);
　　(c) section 5 (ancillary offences).
　(3) An offence in or as regards Scotland is a Convention offence by virtue of this paragraph only if it consists in—
　　(a) the doing of an act as an act of terrorism; or
　　(b) an action for the purposes of terrorism.

Biological weapons

2 An offence under section 1 of the Biological Weapons Act 1974 (c. 6) development etc. of biological weapons).

Offences against internationally protected persons

3 (1) Subject to sub-paragraph (4), an offence mentioned in section 1(1)(a) of the Internationally Protected Persons Act 1978 (c. 17) (attacks against protected persons committed outside the United Kingdom) which is committed (whether in the United Kingdom or elsewhere) in relation to a protected person.

(2) Subject to sub-paragraph (4), an offence mentioned in section 1(1)(b) of that Act (attacks on relevant premises etc.) which is committed (whether in the United Kingdom or elsewhere) in connection with an attack—

    (a) on relevant premises or on a vehicle ordinarily used by a protected person, and

    (b) at a time when a protected person is in or on the premises or vehicle.

(3) Subject to sub-paragraph (4), an offence under section 1(3) of that Act (threats etc. in relation to protected persons).

(4) An offence in or as regards Scotland is a Convention offence by virtue of this paragraph only if it consists in—

    (a) the doing of an act as an act of terrorism; or

    (b) an action for the purposes of terrorism.

(5) Expressions used in this paragraph and section 1 of that Act have the same meanings in this paragraph as in that section.

Hostage-taking

4   An offence under section 1 of the Taking of Hostages Act 1982 (c. 28) (hostage-taking).

Hijacking and other offences against aircraft

5   Offences under any of the following provisions of the Aviation Security Act 1982 (c. 36)—

    (a) section 1 (hijacking);

    (b) section 2 (destroying, damaging or endangering safety of aircraft);

    (c) section 3 (other acts endangering or likely to endanger safety of aircraft);

    (d) section 6(2) (ancillary offences).

Offences involving nuclear material

6 (1) An offence mentioned in section 1(1) of the Nuclear Material (Offences) Act 1983 (c. 18) (offences in relation to nuclear material committed outside the United Kingdom) which is committed (whether in the United Kingdom or elsewhere) in relation to or by means of nuclear material.

(2) An offence under section 2 of that Act (offence involving preparatory acts and threats in relation to nuclear material).

(3) In this paragraph "nuclear material" has the same meaning as in that Act.

Offences under the Aviation and Maritime Security Act 1990 (c. 31)

7   Offences under any of the following provisions of the Aviation and Maritime Security Act 1990—

    (a) section 1 (endangering safety at aerodromes);

    (b) section 9 (hijacking of ships);

    (c) section 10 (seizing or exercising control of fixed platforms);

    (d) section 11 (destroying ships or fixed platforms or endangering their safety);

    (e) section 12 (other acts endangering or likely to endanger safe navigation);

    (f) section 13 (offences involving threats relating to ships or fixed platforms);

    (g) section 14 (ancillary offences).

Offences involving chemical weapons

8   An offence under section 2 of the Chemical Weapons Act 1996 (c. 6) (use, development etc. of chemical weapons).

Terrorist funds

9   An offence under any of the following provisions of the Terrorism Act 2000 (c. 11)—
   (a) section 15 (terrorist fund-raising);
   (b) section 16 (use or possession of terrorist funds);
   (c) section 17 (funding arrangements for terrorism);
   (d) section 18 (money laundering of terrorist funds).

Directing terrorist organisations

10   An offence under section 56 of the Terrorism Act 2000 (directing a terrorist organisation).

Offences involving nuclear weapons

11   An offence under section 47 of the Anti-terrorism, Crime and Security Act 2001 (c. 24) (use, development etc. of nuclear weapons).

Conspiracy etc.

12   Any of the following offences—
   (a) conspiracy to commit a Convention offence;
   (b) inciting the commission of a Convention offence;
   (c) attempting to commit a Convention offence;
   (d) aiding, abetting, counselling or procuring the commission of a Convention offence.

SCHEDULE 2
SEIZURE AND FORFEITURE OF TERRORIST PUBLICATIONS

Section 28

Application of Schedule

1   This Schedule applies where an article—
   (a) has been seized under the authority of a warrant under section 28; and
   (b) is being retained in the custody of a constable ("the relevant constable").

Notice of seizure

2 (1) The relevant constable must give notice of the article's seizure to—
   (a) every person whom he believes to have been the owner of the article, or one of its owners, at the time of the seizure; and
   (b) if there is no such person or it is not reasonably practicable to give him notice, every person whom the relevant constable believes to have been an occupier at that time of the premises where the article was seized.
   (2) The notice must set out what has been seized and the grounds for the seizure.
   (3) The notice may be given to a person only by—
   (a) delivering it to him personally;
   (b) addressing it to him and leaving it for him at the appropriate address; or
   (c) addressing it to him and sending it to him at that address by post.
   (4) But where it is not practicable to give a notice in accordance with subparagraph (3), a notice given by virtue of sub-paragraph (1)(b) to the occupier of the premises where the article was seized may be given by—
   (a) addressing it to "the occupier" of those premises, without naming him; and

179

(b) leaving it for him at those premises or sending it to him at those premises by post.

(5) An article may be treated or condemned as forfeited under this Schedule only if—

    (a) the requirements of this paragraph have been complied with in the case of that article; or

    (b) it was not reasonably practicable for them to be complied with.

(6) In this paragraph "the appropriate address", in relation to a person, means—

    (a) in the case of a body corporate, its registered or principal office in the United Kingdom;

    (b) in the case of a firm, the principal office of the partnership;

    (c) in the case of an unincorporated body or association, the principal office of the body or association; and

    (d) in any other case, his usual or last known place of residence in the United Kingdom or his last known place of business in the United Kingdom.

(7) In the case of—

    (a) a company registered outside the United Kingdom,

    (b) a firm carrying on business outside the United Kingdom, or

    (c) an unincorporated body or association with offices outside the United Kingdom, the references in this paragraph to its principal office include references to its principal office within the United Kingdom (if any).

Notice of claim

3 (1) A person claiming that the seized article is not liable to forfeiture may give notice of his claim to a constable at any police station in the police area in which the premises where the seizure took place are located.

(2) Oral notice is not sufficient for these purposes.

4 (1) A notice of claim may not be given more than one month after—

    (a) the day of the giving of the notice of seizure; or

    (b) if no such notice has been given, the day of the seizure.

(2) A notice of claim must specify—

    (a) the name and address of the claimant; and

    (b) in the case of a claimant who is outside the United Kingdom, the name and address of a solicitor in the United Kingdom who is authorised to accept service, and to act, on behalf of the claimant.

(3) Service upon a solicitor so specified is to be taken to be service on the claimant for the purposes of any proceedings by virtue of this Schedule.

(4) In a case in which notice of the seizure was given to different persons on different days, the reference in this paragraph to the day on which that notice was given is a reference—

    (a) in relation to a person to whom notice of the seizure was given, to the day on which that notice was given to that person; and

    (b) in relation to any other person, to the day on which notice of the seizure was given to the last person to be given such a notice.

Automatic forfeiture in a case where no claim is made

5 The article is to be treated as forfeited if, by the end of the period for the giving of a notice of claim in respect of it—

    (a) no such notice has been given; or

(b) the requirements of paragraphs 3 and 4 have not been complied with in relation to the only notice or notices of claim that have been given.

Forfeiture by the court in other cases

6 (1) Where a notice of claim in respect of an article is duly given in accordance with paragraphs 3 and 4, the relevant constable must decide whether to take proceedings to ask the court to condemn the article as forfeited.

(2) The decision whether to take such proceedings must be made as soon as reasonably practicable after the giving of the notice of claim.

(3) If the relevant constable takes such proceedings and the court—
(a) finds that the article was liable to forfeiture at the time of its seizure, and
(b) is not satisfied that its forfeiture would be inappropriate, the court must condemn the article as forfeited.

(4) If that constable takes such proceedings and the court—
(a) finds that the article was not liable to forfeiture at the time of its seizure, or
(b) is satisfied that its forfeiture would be inappropriate, the court must order the return of the article to the person who appears to the court to be entitled to it.

(5) If the relevant constable decides not to take proceedings for condemnation in a case in which a notice of claim has been given, he must return the article to the person who appears to him to be the owner of the article, or to one of the persons who appear to him to be owners of it.

(6) An article required to be returned in accordance with sub-paragraph (5) must be returned as soon as reasonably practicable after the decision not to take proceedings for condemnation.

Forfeiture proceedings

7 Proceedings by virtue of this Schedule are civil proceedings and may be instituted—
(a) in England or Wales, either in the High Court or in a magistrates' court;
(b) in Scotland, either in the Court of Session or in the sheriff court; and
(c) in Northern Ireland, either in the High Court or in a court of summary jurisdiction.

8 Proceedings by virtue of this Schedule in—
(a) a magistrates' court in England or Wales,
(b) the sheriff court in Scotland, or
(c) a court of summary jurisdiction in Northern Ireland, may be instituted in that court only if it has jurisdiction in relation to the place where the article to which they relate was seized.

9 (1) In proceedings by virtue of this Schedule that are instituted in England and Wales or Northern Ireland, the claimant or his solicitor must make his oath that, at the time of the seizure, the seized article was, or was to the best of his knowledge and belief, the property of the claimant.

(2) In any such proceedings instituted in the High Court—
(a) the court may require the claimant to give such security for the costs of the proceedings as may be determined by the court; and
(b) the claimant must comply with any such requirement.

(3) If a requirement of this paragraph is not complied with, the court must find against the claimant.

10 (1) In the case of proceedings by virtue of this Schedule that are instituted in a magistrates' court in England or Wales, either party may appeal against the decision of that court to the Crown Court.

(2) In the case of such proceedings that are instituted in a court of summary jurisdiction in Northern Ireland, either party may appeal against the decision of that court to the county court.

(3) This paragraph does not affect any right to require the statement of a case for the opinion of the High Court.

11 Where an appeal has been made (whether by case stated or otherwise) against the decision of the court in proceedings by virtue of this Schedule in relation to an article, the article is to be left in the custody of a constable pending the final determination of the matter.

Effect of forfeiture

12 Where an article is treated or condemned as forfeited under this Schedule, the forfeiture is to be treated as having taken effect as from the time of the seizure.

Disposal of unclaimed property

13 (1) This paragraph applies where the article seized under the authority of a warrant under section 28 is required to be returned to a person.

(2) If—

(a) the article is (without having been returned) still in the custody of a constable after the end of the period of 12 months beginning with the day after the requirement to return it arose, and

(b) it is not practicable to dispose of the article by returning it immediately to the person to whom it is required to be returned, the constable may dispose of it in any manner he thinks fit.

Provisions as to proof

14 In proceedings arising out of the seizure of an article, the fact, form and manner of the seizure is to be taken, without further evidence and unless the contrary is shown, to have been as set forth in the process.

15 In proceedings, the condemnation by a court of an article as forfeited under this Schedule may be proved by the production of either—

(a) the order of condemnation; or

(b) a certified copy of the order purporting to be signed by an officer of the court by which the order was made.

Special provisions as to certain claimants

16 (1) This paragraph applies where, at the time of the seizure of the article, it was—

(a) the property of a body corporate;

(b) the property of two or more partners; or

(c) the property of more than five persons.

(2) The oath required by paragraph 9, and any other thing required by this chedule or by rules of court to be done by an owner of the article, may be sworn or done by—

(a) a person falling within sub-paragraph (3); or

(b) a person authorised to act on behalf of a person so falling.

(3) The persons falling within this sub-paragraph are—

(a) where the owner is a body corporate, the secretary or some duly authorised officer of that body;

(b) where the owners are in partnership, any one or more of the owners;

(c) where there are more than five owners and they are not in partnership, any two or more of the owners acting on behalf of themselves and any of their co-owners who are not acting on their own behalf.

Saving for owner's rights

17 Neither the imposition of a requirement by virtue of this Schedule to return an article to a person nor the return of an article to a person in accordance with such a requirement affects—

(a) the rights in relation to that article of any other person; or

(b) the right of any other person to enforce his rights against the person to whom it is returned.

Interpretation of Schedule

18 In this Schedule—

"article" has the same meaning as in Part 1 of this Act;

"the court" is to be construed in accordance with paragraph 7.

SCHEDULE 3
REPEALS

Section 37

Short title and chapter	Extent of repeal
Terrorism Act 2000 (c. 11)	In section 5(4), the words "by or in respect of an organisation".
	In section 9(4), the word "and" at the end of paragraph (b).
	In section 63A(1)(b), the words "section 54 or".
	Section 126.
	In Schedule 5, in each of paragraphs 1(5) and 28(4), the "and" at the end of paragraph (b).
	In Schedule 8, in paragraph 36(1), the words "to a judicial authority".
Justice (Northern Ireland) Act 2002 (c. 26)	In Schedule 7, paragraph 35.
	Section 45(8).
Criminal Justice Act 2003 (c. 44)	Section 306(2) and (3).

Council of Europe Convention on the Prevention of Terrorism

Warsaw, 16. V. 2005

The member States of the Council of Europe and the other Signatories hereto,

Considering that the aim of the Council of Europe is to achieve greater unity between its members;

Recognising the value of reinforcing co-operation with the other Parties to this Convention;

Wishing to take effective measures to prevent terrorism and to counter, in particular, public provocation to commit terrorist offences and recruitment and training for terrorism;

Aware of the grave concern caused by the increase in terrorist offences and the growing terrorist threat;

Aware of the precarious situation faced by those who suffer from terrorism, and in this connection reaffirming their profound solidarity with the victims of terrorism and their families;

Recognising that terrorist offences and the offences set forth in this Convention, by whoever perpetrated, are under no circumstances justifiable by considerations of a political, philosophical, ideological, racial, ethnic, religious or other similar nature, and recalling the obligation of all Parties to prevent such offences and, if not prevented, to prosecute and ensure that they are punishable by penalties which take into account their grave nature;

Recalling the need to strengthen the fight against terrorism and reaffirming that all measures taken to prevent or suppress terrorist offences have to respect the rule of law and democratic values, human rights and fundamental freedoms as well as other provisions of international law, including, where applicable, international humanitarian law;

Recognising that this Convention is not intended to affect established principles relating to freedom of expression and freedom of association;

Recalling that acts of terrorism have the purpose by their nature or context to seriously intimidate a population or unduly compel a government or an international organisation to perform or abstain from performing any act or seriously destabilise or destroy the fundamental political, constitutional, economic or social structures of a country or an international organisation;

Have agreed as follows:

Article 1—Terminology

1 For the purposes of this Convention, "terrorist offence" means any of the offences within the scope of and as defined in one of the treaties listed in the Appendix.

2 On depositing its instrument of ratification, acceptance, approval or accession, a State or the European Community which is not a party to a treaty listed in the Appendix may declare that, in the application of this Convention to the Party concerned, that treaty shall be deemed not to be included in the Appendix. This declaration shall cease to have effect as soon as the treaty enters into force for the Party having made such a declaration, which shall notify the Secretary General of the Council of Europe of this entry into force.

Article 2—Purpose

The purpose of the present Convention is to enhance the efforts of Parties in preventing terrorism and its negative effects on the full enjoyment of human rights, in particular the right to life, both by measures to be taken at national level and through international co-operation, with due regard to the existing applicable multilateral or bilateral treaties or agreements between the Parties.

Article 3—National prevention policies

1 Each Party shall take appropriate measures, particularly in the field of training of law enforcement authorities and other bodies, and in the fields of education, culture, information, media and public awareness raising, with a view to preventing terrorist offences and their negative effects while respecting human rights obligations as set forth in, where applicable to that Party, the Convention for the Protection of Human Rights and Fundamental Freedoms, the International Covenant on Civil and Political Rights, and other obligations under international law.

2 Each Party shall take such measures as may be necessary to improve and develop the co-operation among national authorities with a view to preventing terrorist offences and their negative effects by, *inter alia*:
   a exchanging information;
   b improving the physical protection of persons and facilities;
   c enhancing training and coordination plans for civil emergencies.

3 Each Party shall promote tolerance by encouraging inter-religious and cross-cultural dialogue involving, where appropriate, non-governmental organisations and other elements of civil society with a view to preventing tensions that might contribute to the commission of terrorist offences.

4 Each Party shall endeavour to promote public awareness regarding the existence, causes and gravity of and the threat posed by terrorist offences and the offences set forth in this Convention and consider encouraging the public to provide factual, specific help to its competent authorities that may contribute to preventing terrorist offences and offences set forth in this Convention.

Article 4—International co-operation on prevention

Parties shall, as appropriate and with due regard to their capabilities, assist and support each other with a view to enhancing their capacity to prevent the commission of terrorist offences, including through exchange of information and best practices, as well as through training and other joint efforts of a preventive character.

Article 5—Public provocation to commit a terrorist offence

1   For the purposes of this Convention, "public provocation to commit a terrorist offence" means the distribution, or otherwise making available, of a message to the public, with the intent to incite the commission of a terrorist offence, where such conduct, whether or not directly advocating terrorist offences, causes a danger that one or more such offences may be committed.

2   Each Party shall adopt such measures as may be necessary to establish public provocation to commit a terrorist offence, as defined in paragraph 1, when committed unlawfully and intentionally, as a criminal offence under its domestic law.

Article 6—Recruitment for terrorism

1   For the purposes of this Convention, "recruitment for terrorism" means to solicit another person to commit or participate in the commission of a terrorist offence, or to join an association or group, for the purpose of contributing to the commission of one or more terrorist offences by the association or the group.

2   Each Party shall adopt such measures as may be necessary to establish recruitment for terrorism, as defined in paragraph 1, when committed unlawfully and intentionally, as a criminal offence under its domestic law.

Article 7—Training for terrorism

1   For the purposes of this Convention, "training for terrorism" means to provide instruction in the making or use of explosives, firearms or other weapons or noxious or hazardous substances, or in other specific methods or techniques, for the purpose of carrying out or contributing to the commission of a terrorist offence, knowing that the skills provided are intended to be used for this purpose.

2   Each Party shall adopt such measures as may be necessary to establish training for terrorism, as defined in paragraph 1, when committed unlawfully and intentionally, as a criminal offence under its domestic law.

Article 8—Irrelevance of the commission of a terrorist offence

For an act to constitute an offence as set forth in Articles 5 to 7 of this Convention, it shall not be necessary that a terrorist offence be actually committed.

Article 9—Ancillary offences

1   Each Party shall adopt such measures as may be necessary to establish as a criminal offence under its domestic law:

  a   Participating as an accomplice in an offence as set forth in Articles 5 to 7 of this Convention;

  b   Organising or directing others to commit an offence as set forth in Articles 5 to 7 of this Convention;

  c   Contributing to the commission of one or more offences as set forth in Articles 5 to 7 of this Convention by a group of persons acting with a common purpose. Such contribution shall be intentional and shall either:

    i   be made with the aim of furthering the criminal activity or criminal purpose of the group, where such activity or purpose involves the commission of an offence as set forth in Articles 5 to 7 of this Convention; or

    ii   be made in the knowledge of the intention of the group to commit an offence as set forth in Articles 5 to 7 of this Convention.

2 Each Party shall also adopt such measures as may be necessary to establish as a criminal offence under, and in accordance with, its domestic law the attempt to commit an offence as set forth in Articles 6 and 7 of this Convention.

Article 10—Liability of legal entities

1 Each Party shall adopt such measures as may be necessary, in accordance with its legal principles, to establish the liability of legal entities for participation in the offences set forth in Articles 5 to 7 and 9 of this Convention.
2 Subject to the legal principles of the Party, the liability of legal entities may be criminal, civil or administrative.
3 Such liability shall be without prejudice to the criminal liability of the natural persons who have committed the offences.

Article 11—Sanctions and measures

1 Each Party shall adopt such measures as may be necessary to make the offences set forth in Articles 5 to 7 and 9 of this Convention punishable by effective, proportionate and dissuasive penalties.
2 Previous final convictions pronounced in foreign States for offences set forth in the present Convention may, to the extent permitted by domestic law, be taken into account for the purpose of determining the sentence in accordance with domestic law.
3 Each Party shall ensure that legal entities held liable in accordance with Article 10 are subject to effective, proportionate and dissuasive criminal or non-criminal sanctions, including monetary sanctions.

Article 12—Conditions and safeguards

1 Each Party shall ensure that the establishment, implementation and application of the criminalisation under Articles 5 to 7 and 9 of this Convention are carried out while respecting human rights obligations, in particular the right to freedom of expression, freedom of association and freedom of religion, as set forth in, where applicable to that Party, the Convention for the Protection of Human Rights and Fundamental Freedoms, the International Covenant on Civil and Political Rights, and other obligations under international law.
2 The establishment, implementation and application of the criminalisation under Articles 5 to 7 and 9 of this Convention should furthermore be subject to the principle of proportionality, with respect to the legitimate aims pursued and to their necessity in a democratic society, and should exclude any form of arbitrariness or discriminatory or racist treatment.

Article 13—Protection, compensation and support for victims of terrorism

Each Party shall adopt such measures as may be necessary to protect and support the victims of terrorism that has been committed within its own territory. These measures may include, through the appropriate national schemes and subject to domestic legislation, *inter alia*, financial assistance and compensation for victims of terrorism and their close family members.

Article 14—Jurisdiction

1 Each Party shall take such measures as may be necessary to establish its jurisdiction over the offences set forth in this Convention:
   a when the offence is committed in the territory of that Party;

b   when the offence is committed on board a ship flying the flag of that Party, or on board an aircraft registered under the laws of that Party;

c   when the offence is committed by a national of that Party.

2   Each Party may also establish its jurisdiction over the offences set forth in this Convention:

    a   when the offence was directed towards or resulted in the carrying out of an offence referred to in Article 1 of this Convention, in the territory of or against a national of that Party;

    b   when the offence was directed towards or resulted in the carrying out of an offence referred to in Article 1 of this Convention, against a State or government facility of that Party abroad, including diplomatic or consular premises of that Party;

    c   when the offence was directed towards or resulted in an offence referred to in Article 1 of this Convention, committed in an attempt to compel that Party to do or abstain from doing any act;

    d   when the offence is committed by a stateless person who has his or her habitual residence in the territory of that Party;

    e   when the offence is committed on board an aircraft which is operated by the Government of that Party.

3   Each Party shall take such measures as may be necessary to establish its jurisdiction over the offences set forth in this Convention in the case where the alleged offender is present in its territory and it does not extradite him or her to a Party whose jurisdiction is based on a rule of jurisdiction existing equally in the law of the requested Party.

4   This Convention does not exclude any criminal jurisdiction exercised in accordance with national law.

5   When more than one Party claims jurisdiction over an alleged offence set forth in this Convention, the Parties involved shall, where appropriate, consult with a view to determining the most appropriate jurisdiction for prosecution.

Article 15—Duty to investigate

1   Upon receiving information that a person who has committed or who is alleged to have committed an offence set forth in this Convention may be present in its territory, the Party concerned shall take such measures as may be necessary under its domestic law to investigate the facts contained in the information.

2   Upon being satisfied that the circumstances so warrant, the Party in whose territory the offender or alleged offender is present shall take the appropriate measures under its domestic law so as to ensure that person's presence for the purpose of prosecution or extradition.

3   Any person in respect of whom the measures referred to in paragraph 2 are being taken shall be entitled to:

    a   communicate without delay with the nearest appropriate representative of the State of which that person is a national or which is otherwise entitled to protect that person's rights or, if that person is a stateless person, the State in the territory of which that person habitually resides;

    b   be visited by a representative of that State;

    c   be informed of that person's rights under subparagraphs a and b.

4   The rights referred to in paragraph 3 shall be exercised in conformity with the laws and regulations of the Party in the territory of which the offender or alleged offender

is present, subject to the provision that the said laws and regulations must enable full effect to be given to the purposes for which the rights accorded under paragraph 3 are intended.

5   The provisions of paragraphs 3 and 4 shall be without prejudice to the right of any Party having a claim of jurisdiction in accordance with Article 14, paragraphs 1.c and 2.d to invite the International Committee of the Red Cross to communicate with and visit the alleged offender.

Article 16—Non application of the Convention

This Convention shall not apply where any of the offences established in accordance with Articles 5 to 7 and 9 is committed within a single State, the alleged offender is a national of that State and is present in the territory of that State, and no other State has a basis under Article 14, paragraph 1 or 2 of this Convention, to exercise jurisdiction, it being understood that the provisions of Articles 17 and 20 to 22 of this Convention shall, as appropriate, apply in those cases.

Article 17—International co-operation in criminal matters

1   Parties shall afford one another the greatest measure of assistance in connection with criminal investigations or criminal or extradition proceedings in respect of the offences set forth in Articles 5 to 7 and 9 of this Convention, including assistance in obtaining evidence in their possession necessary for the proceedings.

2   Parties shall carry out their obligations under paragraph 1 in conformity with any treaties or other agreements on mutual legal assistance that may exist between them. In the absence of such treaties or agreements, Parties shall afford one another assistance in accordance with their domestic law.

3   Parties shall co-operate with each other to the fullest extent possible under relevant law, treaties, agreements and arrangements of the requested Party with respect to criminal investigations or proceedings in relation to the offences for which a legal entity may be held liable in accordance with Article 10 of this Convention in the requesting Party.

4   Each Party may give consideration to establishing additional mechanisms to share with other Parties information or evidence needed to establish criminal, civil or administrative liability pursuant to Article 10.

Article 18—Extradite or prosecute

1   The Party in the territory of which the alleged offender is present shall, when it has jurisdiction in accordance with Article 14, if it does not extradite that person, be obliged, without exception whatsoever and whether or not the offence was committed in its territory, to submit the case without undue delay to its competent authorities for the purpose of prosecution, through proceedings in accordance with the laws of that Party. Those authorities shall take their decision in the same manner as in the case of any other offence of a serious nature under the law of that Party.

2   Whenever a Party is permitted under its domestic law to extradite or otherwise surrender one of its nationals only upon the condition that the person will be returned to that Party to serve the sentence imposed as a result of the trial or proceeding for which the extradition or surrender of the person was sought, and this Party and the Party seeking the extradition of the person agree with this option and other terms

they may deem appropriate, such a conditional extradition or surrender shall be sufficient to discharge the obligation set forth in paragraph 1.

Article 19—Extradition

1   The offences set forth in Articles 5 to 7 and 9 of this Convention shall be deemed to be included as extraditable offences in any extradition treaty existing between any of the Parties before the entry into force of this Convention. Parties undertake to include such offences as extraditable offences in every extradition treaty to be subsequently concluded between them.

2   When a Party which makes extradition conditional on the existence of a treaty receives a request for extradition from another Party with which it has no extradition treaty, the requested Party may, if it so decides, consider this Convention as a legal basis for extradition in respect of the offences set forth in Articles 5 to 7 and 9 of this Convention. Extradition shall be subject to the other conditions provided by the law of the requested Party.

3   Parties which do not make extradition conditional on the existence of a treaty shall recognise the offences set forth in Articles 5 to 7 and 9 of this Convention as extraditable offences between themselves, subject to the conditions provided by the law of the requested Party.

4   Where necessary, the offences set forth in Articles 5 to 7 and 9 of this Convention shall be treated, for the purposes of extradition between Parties, as if they had been committed not only in the place in which they occurred but also in the territory of the Parties that have established jurisdiction in accordance with Article 14.

5   The provisions of all extradition treaties and agreements concluded between Parties in respect of offences set forth in Articles 5 to 7 and 9 of this Convention shall be deemed to be modified as between Parties to the extent that they are incompatible with this Convention.

Article 20—Exclusion of the political exception clause

1   None of the offences referred to in Articles 5 to 7 and 9 of this Convention, shall be regarded, for the purposes of extradition or mutual legal assistance, as a political offence, an offence connected with a political offence, or as an offence inspired by political motives. Accordingly, a request for extradition or for mutual legal assistance based on such an offence may not be refused on the sole ground that it concerns a political offence or an offence connected with a political offence or an offence inspired by political motives.

2   Without prejudice to the application of Articles 19 to 23 of the Vienna Convention on the Law of Treaties of 23 May 1969 to the other Articles of this Convention, any State or the European Community may, at the time of signature or when depositing its instrument of ratification, acceptance, approval or accession of the Convention, declare that it reserves the right to not apply paragraph 1 of this Article as far as extradition in respect of an offence set forth in this Convention is concerned. The Party undertakes to apply this reservation on a case-by-case basis, through a duly reasoned decision.

3   Any Party may wholly or partly withdraw a reservation it has made in accordance with paragraph 2 by means of a declaration addressed to the Secretary General of the Council of Europe which shall become effective as from the date of its receipt.

4   A Party which has made a reservation in accordance with paragraph 2 of this Article may not claim the application of paragraph 1 of this Article by any other Party; it may, however, if its reservation is partial or conditional, claim the application of this article in so far as it has itself accepted it.

5   The reservation shall be valid for a period of three years from the day of the entry into force of this Convention in respect of the Party concerned. However, such reservation may be renewed for periods of the same duration.

6   Twelve months before the date of expiry of the reservation, the Secretary General of the Council of Europe shall give notice of that expiry to the Party concerned. No later than three months before expiry, the Party shall notify the Secretary General of the Council of Europe that it is upholding, amending or withdrawing its reservation. Where a Party notifies the Secretary General of the Council of Europe that it is upholding its reservation, it shall provide an explanation of the grounds justifying its continuance. In the absence of notification by the Party concerned, the Secretary General of the Council of Europe shall inform that Party that its reservation is considered to have been extended automatically for a period of six months. Failure by the Party concerned to notify its intention to uphold or modify its reservation before the expiry of that period shall cause the reservation to lapse.

7   Where a Party does not extradite a person in application of this reservation, after receiving an extradition request from another Party, it shall submit the case, without exception whatsoever and without undue delay, to its competent authorities for the purpose of prosecution, unless the requesting Party and the requested Party agree otherwise. The competent authorities, for the purpose of prosecution in the requested Party, shall take their decision in the same manner as in the case of any offence of a grave nature under the law of that Party. The requested Party shall communicate, without undue delay, the final outcome of the proceedings to the requesting Party and to the Secretary General of the Council of Europe, who shall forward it to the Consultation of the Parties provided for in Article 30.

8   The decision to refuse the extradition request on the basis of this reservation shall be forwarded promptly to the requesting Party. If within a reasonable time no judicial decision on the merits has been taken in the requested Party according to paragraph 7, the requesting Party may communicate this fact to the Secretary General of the Council of Europe, who shall submit the matter to the Consultation of the Parties provided for in Article 30. This Consultation shall consider the matter and issue an opinion on the conformity of the refusal with the Convention and shall submit it to the Committee of Ministers for the purpose of issuing a declaration thereon. When performing its functions under this paragraph, the Committee of Ministers shall meet in its composition restricted to the States Parties.

Article 21—Discrimination clause

1   Nothing in this Convention shall be interpreted as imposing an obligation to extradite or to afford mutual legal assistance, if the requested Party has substantial grounds for believing that the request for extradition for offences set forth in Articles 5 to 7 and 9 or for mutual legal assistance with respect to such offences has been made for the purpose of prosecuting or punishing a person on account of that person's race, religion, nationality, ethnic origin or political opinion or that compliance with the request would cause prejudice to that person's position for any of these reasons.

2 Nothing in this Convention shall be interpreted as imposing an obligation to extradite if the person who is the subject of the extradition request risks being exposed to torture or to inhuman or degrading treatment or punishment.

3 Nothing in this Convention shall be interpreted either as imposing an obligation to extradite if the person who is the subject of the extradition request risks being exposed to the death penalty or, where the law of the requested Party does not allow for life imprisonment, to life imprisonment without the possibility of parole, unless under applicable extradition treaties the requested Party is under the obligation to extradite if the requesting Party gives such assurance as the requested Party considers sufficient that the death penalty will not be imposed or, where imposed, will not be carried out, or that the person concerned will not be subject to life imprisonment without the possibility of parole.

Article 22—Spontaneous information

1 Without prejudice to their own investigations or proceedings, the competent authorities of a Party may, without prior request, forward to the competent authorities of another Party information obtained within the framework of their own investigations, when they consider that the disclosure of such information might assist the Party receiving the information in initiating or carrying out investigations or proceedings, or might lead to a request by that Party under this Convention.

2 The Party providing the information may, pursuant to its national law, impose conditions on the use of such information by the Party receiving the information.

3 The Party receiving the information shall be bound by those conditions.

4 However, any Party may, at any time, by means of a declaration addressed to the Secretary General of the Council of Europe, declare that it reserves the right not to be bound by the conditions imposed by the Party providing the information under paragraph 2 above, unless it receives prior notice of the nature of the information to be provided and agrees to its transmission.

Article 23—Signature and entry into force

1 This Convention shall be open for signature by the member States of the Council of Europe, the European Community and by non-member States which have participated in its elaboration.

2 This Convention is subject to ratification, acceptance or approval. Instruments of ratification, acceptance or approval shall be deposited with the Secretary General of the Council of Europe.

3 This Convention shall enter into force on the first day of the month following the expiration of a period of three months after the date on which six Signatories, including at least four member States of the Council of Europe, have expressed their consent to be bound by the Convention in accordance with the provisions of paragraph 2.

4 In respect of any Signatory which subsequently expresses its consent to be bound by it, the Convention shall enter into force on the first day of the month following the expiration of a period of three months after the date of the expression of its consent to be bound by the Convention in accordance with the provisions of paragraph 2.

Article 24—Accession to the Convention

1 After the entry into force of this Convention, the Committee of Ministers of the Council of Europe, after consulting with and obtaining the unanimous consent of

the Parties to the Convention, may invite any State which is not a member of the Council of Europe and which has not participated in its elaboration to accede to this convention. The decision shall be taken by the majority provided for in Article 20.d of the Statute of the Council of Europe and by the unanimous vote of the representatives of the Parties entitled to sit on the Committee of Ministers.

2 In respect of any State acceding to the convention under paragraph 1 above, the Convention shall enter into force on the first day of the month following the expiration of a period of three months after the date of deposit of the instrument of accession with the Secretary General of the Council of Europe.

Article 25—Territorial application

1 Any State or the European Community may, at the time of signature or when depositing its instrument of ratification, acceptance, approval or accession, specify the territory or territories to which this Convention shall apply.

2 Any Party may, at any later date, by a declaration addressed to the Secretary General of the Council of Europe, extend the application of this Convention to any other territory specified in the declaration. In respect of such territory the Convention shall enter into force on the first day of the month following the expiration of a period of three months after the date of receipt of the declaration by the Secretary General.

3 Any declaration made under the two preceding paragraphs may, in respect of any territory specified in such declaration, be withdrawn by a notification addressed to the Secretary General of the Council of Europe. The withdrawal shall become effective on the first day of the month following the expiration of a period of three months after the date of receipt of such notification by the Secretary General.

Article 26—Effects of the Convention

1 The present Convention supplements applicable multilateral or bilateral treaties or agreements between the Parties, including the provisions of the following Council of Europe treaties:

— European Convention on Extradition, opened for signature, in Paris, on 13 December 1957 (ETS No. 24);

— European Convention on Mutual Assistance in Criminal Matters, opened for signature, in Strasbourg, on 20 April 1959 (ETS No. 30);

— European Convention on the Suppression of Terrorism, opened for signature, in Strasbourg, on 27 January 1977 (ETS No. 90);

— Additional Protocol to the European Convention on Mutual Assistance in Criminal Matters, opened for signature in Strasbourg on 17 March 1978 (ETS No. 99);

— Second Additional Protocol to the European Convention on Mutual Assistance in Criminal Matters, opened for signature in Strasbourg on 8 November 2001 (ETS No. 182);

— Protocol amending the European Convention on the Suppression of Terrorism, opened for signature in Strasbourg on 15 May 2003 (ETS No. 190).

2 If two or more Parties have already concluded an agreement or treaty on the matters dealt with in this Convention or have otherwise established their relations on such matters, or should they in future do so, they shall also be entitled to apply that agreement or treaty or to regulate those relations accordingly. However, where Parties establish their relations in respect of the matters dealt with in the present Convention

193

other than as regulated therein, they shall do so in a manner that is not inconsistent with the Convention's objectives and principles.

3   Parties which are members of the European Union shall, in their mutual relations, apply Community and European Union rules in so far as there are Community or European Union rules governing the particular subject concerned and applicable to the specific case, without prejudice to the object and purpose of the present Convention and without prejudice to its full application with other Parties. (1)

4   Nothing in this Convention shall affect other rights, obligations and responsibilities of a Party and individuals under international law, including international humanitarian law.

5   The activities of armed forces during an armed conflict, as those terms are understood under international humanitarian law, which are governed by that law, are not governed by this Convention, and the activities undertaken by military forces of a Party in the exercise of their official duties, inasmuch as they are governed by other rules of international law, are not governed by this Convention.

Article 27—Amendments to the Convention

1   Amendments to this Convention may be proposed by any Party, the Committee of Ministers of the Council of Europe or the Consultation of the Parties.

2   Any proposal for amendment shall be communicated by the Secretary General of the Council of Europe to the Parties.

3   Moreover, any amendment proposed by a Party or the Committee of Ministers shall be communicated to the Consultation of the Parties, which shall submit to the Committee of Ministers its opinion on the proposed amendment.

4   The Committee of Ministers shall consider the proposed amendment and any opinion submitted by the Consultation of the Parties and may approve the amendment.

5   The text of any amendment approved by the Committee of Ministers in accordance with paragraph 4 shall be forwarded to the Parties for acceptance.

6   Any amendment approved in accordance with paragraph 4 shall come into force on the thirtieth day after all Parties have informed the Secretary General of their acceptance thereof.

Article 28—Revision of the Appendix

1   In order to update the list of treaties in the Appendix, amendments may be proposed by any Party or by the Committee of Ministers. These proposals for amendment shall only concern universal treaties concluded within the United Nations system dealing specifically with international terrorism and having entered into force. They shall be communicated by the Secretary General of the Council of Europe to the Parties.

2   After having consulted the non-member Parties, the Committee of Ministers may adopt a proposed amendment by the majority provided for in Article 20.d of the Statute of the Council of Europe. The amendment shall enter into force following the expiry of a period of one year after the date on which it has been forwarded to the Parties. During this period, any Party may notify the Secretary General of the Council of Europe of any objection to the entry into force of the amendment in respect of that Party.

3   If one third of the Parties notifies the Secretary General of the Council of Europe of an objection to the entry into force of the amendment, the amendment shall not enter into force.

4   If less than one third of the Parties notifies an objection, the amendment shall enter into force for those Parties which have not notified an objection.

5   Once an amendment has entered into force in accordance with paragraph 2 and a Party has notified an objection to it, this amendment shall come into force in respect of the Party concerned on the first day of the month following the date on which it notifies the Secretary General of the Council of Europe of its acceptance.

Article 29—Settlement of disputes

In the event of a dispute between Parties as to the interpretation or application of this Convention, they shall seek a settlement of the dispute through negotiation or any other peaceful means of their choice, including submission of the dispute to an arbitral tribunal whose decisions shall be binding upon the Parties to the dispute, or to the International Court of Justice, as agreed upon by the Parties concerned.

Article 30—Consultation of the Parties

1   The Parties shall consult periodically with a view to:
  a   making proposals to facilitate or improve the effective use and implementation of this Convention, including the identification of any problems and the effects of any declaration made under this Convention;
  b   formulating its opinion on the conformity of a refusal to extradite which is referred to them in accordance with Article 20, paragraph 8;
  c   making proposals for the amendment of this Convention in accordance with Article 27;
  d   formulating their opinion on any proposal for the amendment of this Convention which is referred to them in accordance with Article 27, paragraph 3;
  e   expressing an opinion on any question concerning the application of this Convention and facilitating the exchange of information on significant legal, policy or technological developments.

2   The Consultation of the Parties shall be convened by the Secretary General of the Council of Europe whenever he finds it necessary and in any case when a majority of the Parties or the Committee of Ministers request its convocation.

3   The Parties shall be assisted by the Secretariat of the Council of Europe in carrying out their functions pursuant to this article.

Article 31—Denunciation

1   Any Party may, at any time, denounce this Convention by means of a notification addressed to the Secretary General of the Council of Europe.

2   Such denunciation shall become effective on the first day of the month following the expiration of a period of three months after the date of receipt of the notification by the Secretary General.

Article 32—Notification

The Secretary General of the Council of Europe shall notify the member States of the Council of Europe, the European Community, the non-member States which have participated in the elaboration of this Convention as well as any State which has acceded to, or has been invited to accede to, this Convention of:

a   any signature;
b   the deposit of any instrument of ratification, acceptance, approval or accession;
c   any date of entry into force of this Convention in accordance with Article 23;

d   any declaration made under Article 1, paragraph 2, 22, paragraph 4, and 25 ;

e   any other act, notification or communication relating to this Convention.

In witness whereof the undersigned, being duly authorised thereto, have signed this Convention.

Done at Warsaw, this 16th day of May 2005, in English and in French, both texts being equally authentic, in a single copy which shall be deposited in the archives of the Council of Europe. The Secretary General of the Council of Europe shall transmit certified copies to each member State of the Council of Europe, to the European Community, to the non-member States which have participated in the elaboration of this Convention, and to any State invited to accede to it.

Note by the Secretariat: See the Declaration formulated by the European Community and the Member States of the European Union upon the adoption of the Convention by the Committee of Ministers of the Council of Europe, on 3 May 2005:

"The European Community/European Union and its Member States reaffirm that their objective in requesting the inclusion of a 'disconnection clause' is to take account of the institutional structure of the Union when acceding to international conventions, in particular in case of transfer of sovereign powers from the Member States to the Community.

This clause is not aimed at reducing the rights or increasing the obligations of a non-European Union Party vis-à-vis the European Community/European Union and its Member States, inasmuch as the latter are also parties to this Convention.

The disconnection clause is necessary for those parts of the Convention which fall within the competence of the Community/Union, in order to indicate that European Union Member States cannot invoke and apply the rights and obligations deriving from the Convention directly among themselves (or between themselves and the European Community/Union). This does not detract from the fact that the Convention applies fully between the European Community/European Union and its Member States on the one hand, and the other Parties to the Convention, on the other; the Community and the European Union Members States will be bound by the Convention and will apply it like any Party to the Convention, if necessary, through Community/Union legislation. They will thus guarantee the full respect of the Convention's provisions vis-à-vis non-European Union Parties."

Appendix

1   Convention for the Suppression of Unlawful Seizure of Aircraft, signed at The Hague on 16 December 1970;

2   Convention for the Suppression of Unlawful Acts Against the Safety of Civil Aviation, concluded at Montreal on 23 September 1971;

3   Convention on the Prevention and Punishment of Crimes Against Internationally Protected Persons, Including Diplomatic Agents, adopted in New York on 14 December 1973;

4   International Convention Against the Taking of Hostages, adopted in New York on 17 December 1979;

5   Convention on the Physical Protection of Nuclear Material, adopted in Vienna on 3 March 1980;

6   Protocol for the Suppression of Unlawful Acts of Violence at Airports Serving International Civil Aviation, done at Montreal on 24 February 1988;

7   Convention for the Suppression of Unlawful Acts Against the Safety of Maritime Navigation, done at Rome on 10 March 1988;

8   Protocol for the Suppression of Unlawful Acts Against the Safety of Fixed Platforms Located on the Continental Shelf, done at Rome on 10 March 1988;

9   International Convention for the Suppression of Terrorist Bombings, adopted in New York on 15 December 1997;

10 International Convention for the Suppression of the Financing of Terrorism, adopted in New York on 9 December 1999.

Prevention and Suppression of Terrorism

The Terrorism Act 2006 (Commencement No. 1) Order 2006

(SI 2006/1013)

Made 30th March 2006

The Secretary of State makes the following Order in exercise of the powers conferred on him by section 39(2) of the Terrorism Act 2006.

1. This Order may be cited as the Terrorism Act 2006 (Commencement No. 1) Order 2006.

2.—(1) The following provisions of the Terrorism Act 2006 shall come into force on 13th April 2006.

(2) Those provisions are—

(a) sections 1 to 22, together with Schedule 1;

(b) sections 26 to 36, together with Schedule 2;

(c) sections 37(1) to (4) and 38;

(d) section 37(5) in so far as it relates to the entries in Schedule 3 brought into force by sub-paragraph (e) below; and

(e) all of the entries in Schedule 3 except those relating to paragraph 36(1) of Schedule 8 to the Terrorism Act 2000 and section 306(2) and (3) of the Criminal Justice Act 2003.

EXPLANATORY NOTE

(This note is not part of the Order)

Article 2(1) of this Order brings the provisions of the Terrorism Act 2006 which are listed in article 2(2) into force on 13th April 2006.

Index

References are to paragraph numbers.

Lightning Source UK Ltd.
Milton Keynes UK
01 May 2010

153654UK00001B/1/P